• THE •

Walt Disney® World Trivia Book

Secrets, History and Fun Facts Behind the Magic

Louis A. Mongello

The Walt Disney World® Trivia Book:
Secrets, History and Fun Facts Behind the Magic

Published by The Intrepid Traveler, P.O. Box 531, Branford, CT 06405
http://www.intrepidtraveler.com

Copyright ©2004 by Louis A. Mongello
First Edition, Third Printing Revised
ISBN: 1-887140-49-2
Library of Congress Control Number: 2003114403

Book Jacket: George Foster, Foster & Foster, Inc.
Interior Design: Ellen Lytle and Ivan Trujillo, City Design

Printed in the United States of America
10 9 8 7 6 5 4

Copyrights, Trademarks, Etc.

Photo Credits

About the Author

Louis A. Mongello has been fascinated by Walt Disney World (WDW) since the age of three, when he first visited with his family. At the time, WDW and the Magic Kingdom were just a month old. He's visited dozens of times since and devoted a considerable amount of energy to learning everything he can about the "Vacation Kingdom of the World," amassing an extensive — and still growing — collection of Walt Disney World memorabilia in the process. It includes rare documents outlining Walt Disney's original plans for his Florida project, books and articles about the parks and resorts, and materials available only to WDW Cast Members. He's also spent countless hours pouring over old property maps, information about bygone attractions, and video and still images of the "World" from its initial construction to the present day.

A few years ago, Mongello decided he should "do something" with all the "useless knowledge" he had accumulated in order to share more of WDW's history, secrets, and inner workings with its millions of fans. Thus this book. He hopes it will add extra magic to your visits to Walt Disney World. Mongello has practiced law since 1994. He holds a bachelor's degree in Sociology from Villanova University and a Juris Doctor from Seton Hall University School of Law. Before forming his own computer consulting and web development company, Imagine Enterprises, in 1995, he served as law clerk to the Presiding Judge of the largest civil court division in the state of New Jersey. His other interests include computers, travel, martial arts training, poker, and running the DisneyWorldTrivia.com web site. Mongello lives in Edison, New Jersey, with his wife Deanna and daughter Marion Rose, who coincidentally was born on Mickey Mouse's 75th birthday.

Dedication

I dedicate this book to my family: my parents, Marianne and Nick, my brother Fred, my wife, Deanna, and our new baby, Marion Rose.

• *To my mom and dad,* thanks are hardly enough. You brought me to Walt Disney World more times than I can remember, put up with my repeated requests to go on every ride—often more than once, held me on your shoulders after walking for hours, and treated me to more souvenirs than I can count. Thank you for making me understand and appreciate that it is family and the memories we've created and shared together that made, and continue to make, our vacations so special. Without your love and guidance behind my every endeavor, including this book, I wouldn't be the man I am today. I hope I have made you proud.

• *Fred,* thanks for being not just an incredible brother, but such a great friend, and for always being there when I needed you. You mean more to me than you'll ever know. You're the best.

• *To my wife and best friend Deanna,* thank you for all you have given me. You are my biggest fan and loudest cheerleader. Together we have shared great laughs and created wonderful memories at what has always been our favorite vacation spot. I look forward to creating even more memorable moments with you and our new daughter, Marion Rose. Even though I may not know how many dots there are on Minnie's dress, I can't thank you enough for your selfless love and encouragement. You always stand behind me when I need support and beside me when I need guidance and strength.

• *To my daughter Marion,* you'll never know how much joy you've brought into our lives. God has blessed us with you, and words simply cannot express the love I will always have for you. And yes, we're going to WDW — *again.*

Louis A. Mongello

Acknowledgements

I could not have created this book without the many individuals who helped along the way. (My apologies if I leave anyone out.) First, I thank Kelly Monaghan and Sally Scanlon, my publisher and editor at The Intrepid Traveler, for giving me the chance to write this book. I can't thank you enough for being so supportive and helpful in making this concept a reality. It's been a long journey, and I've really enjoyed the ride (even when I was writing at 4:30 a.m.!). I'd also like to thank everyone in my family, you always made our trips "magical gatherings" even before there was such a thing; "MickeyBabe" (Val); Susan and Greg H. (current and former Cast Members); all of the people around me who supported and encouraged me during the writing of the book; and the "founding members" of our online community at DisneyWorldTrivia.com.

I would also like to thank all of the Cast Members who have taken Walt's vision and philosophy and made it their own, from security guards, to hosts and hostesses, ride operators, cashiers, entertainers, and restaurant staffs. You see that each and every Guest is treated like a VIP and always enjoys nothing less than a special visit. Each of you does your own special part to add a special bit of "magic." Without you, WDW would be just another theme park complex.

Table of Contents

INTRODUCTION

"Walt Disney World." Those three words evoke a range of emotions and images in almost anyone who hears them — and in most cases, a smile as well. Its magic draws tens of millions of adults and children on recurring pilgrimages, my family and I among them. Although I don't remember my first visit (because I was only about three years old), I know now how fortunate I was to have been there. And I'm not alone. Since then, I have been to Walt Disney World dozens of times, and I'm always looking forward to my next visit. And I'm not alone. Walt Disney World is the number one vacation destination in the world, with more than 40 million visitors every year, and more newlyweds spend their honeymoons there than anywhere else on the planet.

It's somewhat difficult to describe the unique feeling I get when I'm at the Walt Disney World® Resort (WDW). If you've been there and enjoy it as much as my family and I do, then you know what I'm talking about. From the moment we arrive, the "real" world seems wonderfully far off, just as Walt would have wanted it. We're in a place that elicits the best in people, where families feel safe, perfect strangers are friendly to one another, and nearly everyone is smiling. This "happy place," as the Magic Kingdom's dedication plaque reads, is one of fantasy, adventure, and make-believe, where adults find an escape from reality and children live out their dreams. It is a completely immersive experience that brings out the inner, wide-eyed child in all of us.

The best thing about visiting WDW is the happiness you get from sharing the experience with family and friends. I came to love Walt Disney World for many reasons, but mainly because of the incredible memories I have of being there with my family. I think I know now how my dad managed to carry my brother and me on his shoulders through the heat and crowds. He could do it because of the great times we were having together; seeing his children smile made it worth it. I look forward to sharing that happiness with my own children.

Of course, there's a lot more to WDW than you see at first glance. The unparalleled attention to detail, which people tend to take for granted, requires a "backstage" infrastructure that is truly awesome. Few guests ever think about (and even fewer get to see) the behind-the-scenes facilities and operations that keep WDW running 24 hours a day, 7 days a week, 365 days a year. Nor do a lot of visitors notice the incredible details and small touches scattered throughout the parks and resorts that are there simply to delight guests who happen to notice them — like the brushes on *Tom Sawyer Island*, the talking trash cans, janitors who sing and dance, subtle changes in the background music and pavement between lands in the Magic Kingdom, hidden Mickeys, the paw prints at the entrance to the Wilderness Lodge, the sounds of singing coming from the Main Street, U.S.A. window advertising singing lessons, and so much more. Most visitors don't know that almost everything they see at WDW has a purpose and a story behind it that gives it meaning.

The book and how it is organized

This book will help you discover Walt Disney World's secrets, history, hidden treasures, and the little details that make everything so wonderful. It is divided into six chapters. Chapter One covers the "World" in general; the next four chapters cover each of the theme parks; and the sixth and last focuses on the areas "Beyond the Parks" — the resort hotels, the monorail, Downtown Disney, and the water parks. Each chapter begins with multiple-choice questions, followed by the correct answers and additional fun facts about the subject. Chapter Two: The Magic Kingdom opens with general questions about the park and then is subdivided by land (Adventureland, Frontierland, etc.), while Chapter Three: Epcot, starts with general questions and then is subdivided by its two "Worlds." Thus, a question about *Space Mountain*, for example, would be found in the Tomorrowland section of Chapter Two.

The questions in Chapter One challenge you to remember WDW history and to identify where in WDW you might find a particular character, prop, attraction, etc. or hear a particular line of dialogue (taken from an attraction script or theme song). It also includes questions related to any and all parts of WDW. Chapter Six, in contrast, quizzes you specifically on your knowledge of the non-theme park parts of WDW.

Walt Disney World has gone through many changes in its 30-plus years. So some questions let readers take a step back in time to revisit original concepts and attractions that no longer exist. Fans who miss *Mr. Toad's Wild Ride* or were never able to experience

Horizons firsthand, for example, can stay in touch or get better acquainted with them here. To add to the fun, you'll find fascinating tidbits of information highlighted throughout the book.

Looking for all the information you can get about a particular ride, resort, or whatever? Check the Index and look for your subject by name. And try not to be too disappointed if you don't find it. While this book contains hundreds of questions about Walt Disney World, WDW has thousands of nooks and crannies. One book simply can't cover them all.

About Names

Over time, many park and attraction names and naming styles have changed. For example, when Epcot opened it was called "EPCOT Center." Its name was later changed to "EPCOT," and then to "Epcot." Unless the question relates specifically to an earlier stage or version of the park or attraction, I have used the current name. Also, in the interests of space, many names are spelled out in full only the first time they are mentioned in a chapter. After that, they may be shortened. For example, Walt Disney World® Resort may be abbreviated WDW, *Rock 'n' Roller Coaster Starring Aerosmith* may become *Rock 'n' Roller Coaster.*

"If we can dream it. . ."

I sincerely hope that you have as much fun reading this book as I did researching and writing it. I hope

not only to enhance your love for WDW, but to spark your interest in what makes the magic really happen. Strangely enough, I find the more I learn about how Disney creates its wonderful effects and the extraordinary efforts Imagineers and Cast Members go through to make WDW so special, the more magical it becomes for me. I am still amazed at how things work, how my emotions are tapped, and how I always leave WDW with a smile on my face.

To continue enjoying the magic at home, be sure to come by my free message forums and photo galleries at www.DisneyWorldTrivia.com. It's a great place to meet other WDW fans, find news and rumors about WDW, learn even more secrets and fun facts, play trivia games with other members, ask questions, post and view photos, get tips, and buy, sell and trade Disneyana. It's fun and free, so I'd love to have you to stop by!

Accuracy and Other Impossible Dreams

All facts and statistics are accurate as of the time this book goes to press. But WDW is constantly changing. So you may want to check my web site, www.DisneyWorldTrivia.com, for updates. And if you have any questions, comments, or suggestions — or notice that I may have missed something, you can let me know by emailing me personally at lou@disneyworldtrivia.com.

Did You Know?

WALT DISNEY BUILT A MINIATURE RAILROAD IN HIS BACKYARD IN CALIFORNIA CALLED THE CAROLWOOD PACIFIC. IT WAS PART OF HIS INSPIRATION TO BUILD DISNEYLAND AND EVENTUALLY WDW — AND WHY EACH PARK CONTAINS A RAILROAD AND NUMEROUS TRIBUTES TO ANTIQUE TRAINS.

CHAPTER ONE

ALL AROUND THE 'WORLD'

1. In what year did Walt Disney World open?
- a.) 1965
- b.) 1969
- c.) 1970
- d.) 1971

2. About how many acres of the more than 30,000 that make up Walt Disney World® Resort (WDW) are actually developed?
- a.) 4,500
- b.) 7,100
- c.) 11,000
- d.) 21,000

3. How much did it cost to develop WDW, from initial planning to opening day?
- a.) $10 million
- b.) $50 million
- c.) $200 million
- d.) $400 million

4. WDW was the first to do what in Florida?
- a.) Use nuclear power
- b.) Use the 911 emergency system
- c.) Establish its own police force
- d.) Make its own lake

5. What name was originally planned for Walt Disney World?
- a.) Florida Disney
- b.) Disney America
- c.) Disney World
- d.) Discoveryland

6. Which of these attractions was present on WDW's Opening Day?
- a.) *Big Thunder Mountain Railroad*
- b.) *it's a small world*
- c.) *Pirates of the Caribbean*
- d.) *Space Mountain*

7. About how many miles of paved roads are there in WDW?
- a.) 39
- b.) 77
- c.) 167
- d.) 253

8. In what town is WDW actually located?
- a.) Orlando
- b.) Kissimmee
- c.) Celebration
- d.) Lake Buena Vista

9. What was the approximate total price the Disney companies paid for the land used for WDW?
- a.) $3 million
- b.) $5 million
- c.) $11 million
- d.) $23 million

10. Which Disney family member dedicated Walt Disney World in October 1971?
- a.) Walt Disney's wife, Lillian Disney
- b.) Walt Disney's brother, Roy O. Disney
- c.) Walt Disney's nephew, Roy E. Disney
- d.) Walt Disney himself

11. In what year was the plan for "Disney World" revealed to the public?
- a.) 1963
- b.) 1965
- c.) 1969
- d.) 1970

12. When did construction begin on WDW?
- a.) 1967
- b.) 1969
- c.) 1955
- d.) 1971

13. What term did Walt Disney use to describe the focal points of each theme park "land"?
- a.) Weenies
- b.) Anchors
- c.) Mouse-ears
- d.) Illusion-ations

14. Approximately what percentage of WDW visitors come from outside the United States?
- a.) 5%
- b.) 1%
- c.) 25%
- d.) 35%

15. How does WDW compare in size to Disneyland in California?
- a.) Approximately the same size
- b.) WDW is about 20 times the size of Disneyland

Did You Know?

THERE ARE ENOUGH "MOUSE EAR" HATS SOLD EACH YEAR IN WDW TO COVER THE HEAD OF EVERY MAN, WOMAN AND CHILD IN PITTSBURGH.

c.) Disneyland is twice as big as WDW

d.) WDW is more than 100 times the size of Disneyland

16. Epcot opened how long after the Magic Kingdom?
a.) 5 years
b.) 9 years
c.) 11 years
d.) 15 years

17. Since its opening in 1971, what is the longest stretch of time that WDW has gone without the addition of a major attraction to one of its theme parks?
a.) 6 months
b.) 1 year
c.) 3 years
d.) 5 years

18. WDW offers about how many different places to eat?
a.) 110
b.) 250
c.) 300
d.) 400

19. A Cast Member just said "Takk" to you? Where are you?
a.) Disney's Animal Kingdom
b.) Disney's Polynesian Resort
c.) Norway in World Showcase
d.) *Kilimanjaro Safaris*

20. At the end of what ride do you find yourself in the VIP parking lot?
a.) *Test Track*
b.) *The Great Movie Ride*
c.) *Rock 'n' Roller Coaster Starring Aerosmith*
d.) *Ellen's Energy Adventure*

21. What was Discovery Island in Bay Lake originally called?
a.) Raz Island
b.) Bay Lake Isle
c.) Blackbeard's Island
d.) Treasure Island

22. "Explore", "Amaze," and "Journey" are the names of what?
a.) Characters you can find in Epcot
b.) Parking lot areas in Epcot
c.) "Zones" in DisneyQuest
d.) Monorail trains

23. Where have you heard, "A long time ago, I made me a rule. Let people do what they want"?
a.) *The American Adventure*
b.) *Jungle Cruise*
c.) *The Great Movie Ride*
d.) *Captain EO*

24. About how many couples take the plunge and get married each year at WDW?
a.) About 150
b.) About 900
c.) About 1,600
d.) About 2,300

25. Before Walt Disney World opened in 1971, a "Preview Center" was built on property to give guests a tour of the upcoming theme park and resorts. Which of these signature attractions had its own Preview Center?
a.) *Space Mountain*
b.) *Test Track*
c.) *Expedition: Everest*
d.) *Mission: SPACE*

26. What is the fastest ride in WDW?
a.) *Big Thunder Mountain Railroad*
b.) *Test Track*
c.) *Rock 'n' Roller Coaster Starring Aerosmith*
d.) *The Twilight Zone™ Tower of Terror*

27. Where will you find "General Knowledge"?
a.) Innoventions
b.) *The Timekeeper*
c.) *Cranium Command*
d.) *The Living Seas*

28. In what attraction do guests travel in space cruisers to the Gamma Quadrant?
a.) *Space Mountain*
b.) *Stich's Great Escape*
c.) *Buzz Lightyear's Space Ranger Spin*
d.) *Astro Orbiter*

29. What is "Ear Force One"?
a.) Walt Disney's private jet
b.) A hot air balloon
c.) One of the coaster cars at *Space Mountain*
d.) The nickname of the giant water tower in Disney-MGM Studios

30. About how many pounds of laundry are done each day at WDW?
a.) 20,000
b.) 50,000
c.) 120,000
d.) 220,000

31. Where was the first wave-making technology used in WDW?
a.) *The Living Seas* in Epcot
b.) *Typhoon Lagoon*
c.) Disney's Polynesian Resort
d.) *Blizzard Beach*

32. Which of these opened first?
a.) *Maelstrom*
b.) *Jim Henson's MuppetVision 3D*
c.) Disney's Fairy Tale Weddings pavilion
d.) BoardWalk Inn & Villas

33. Both *Spaceship Earth* and *The Timekeeper* feature the talents of which of these actors?
a.) Walter Cronkite
b.) Jeremy Irons
c.) Robin Williams
d.) Thurl Ravenscroft

34. "Chief Nammie" can be found in what Disney attraction?
a.) *Big Thunder Mountain Railroad*
b.) *Cranium Command*
c.) *El Rio del Tiempo*
d.) *Jungle Cruise*

35. Where can you find a pool, a geyser, an earthquake, and an avalanche?
a.) *Disney-MGM Studios Backlot Tour*
b.) Disney's Wilderness Lodge
c.) *Dinosaur*
d.) *Big Thunder Mountain Railroad*

36. Where is Parrot Cay Island?
a.) Bay Lake
b.) Disney's Animal Kingdom
c.) Disney-MGM Studios
d.) Disney's Caribbean Beach Resort

37. Alcohol is served in all of these locations except:
a.) Disney's Animal Kingdom
b.) Magic Kingdom
c.) Disney's All-Star Resorts
d.) Epcot

38. About how many miles a year do the WDW buses travel?
a.) 90,000
b.) 200,000
c.) 2 million
d.) 12 million

39. How deep is Bay Lake?
a.) 3 feet
b.) 12 feet
c.) 19 feet
d.) 29 feet

40. Magician Doug Henning was a consultant for the creation of which WDW property?
a.) *The Haunted Mansion*
b.) Adventurers Club
c.) Main Street Magic Shop
d.) Cirque du Soleil

41. What is the busiest day of the year at WDW?
a.) The day after Thanksgiving
b.) Christmas Day
c.) New Year's Eve
d.) July 4

Did You Know?

WDW IS THE NUMBER ONE HONEYMOON DESTINATION IN THE WORLD.

Did You Know?

WDW IS HOST TO 2,500 DIFFERENT SPECIES OF PLANTS, REPRESENTING FLORA GATHERED FROM THE USA AND 50 OTHER COUNTRIES.

42. How many attractions in the WDW theme parks involve guests boarding boats?
- a.) 7
- b.) 10
- c.) 11
- d.) 14

43. In the 1980s, the Walt Disney Imagineers developed the next generation of Audio-Animatronics figure, the "A-100," featuring greatly enhanced technology. Where was the first A-100 figure used in WDW?
- a.) Bill Clinton in *The Hall of Presidents*
- b.) Hopper in *It's Tough to be a Bug!*
- c.) 9-Eye in *The Timekeeper*
- d.) The Wicked Witch in *The Great Movie Ride*

44. In what hotel is the "Tip Top Club" located?
- a.) Disney's Grand Floridian Resort & Spa
- b.) Disney's Contemporary Resort
- c.) The Walt Disney World Swan
- d.) Hollywood Tower Hotel

45. Downtown Disney Marketplace was known by all of these names except:
  a.) Lake Buena Vista Village
  b.) Walt Disney World Marketplace
  c.) Disney Village Marketplace
  d.) Walt Disney World Village

46. What movie had it's world premiere in WDW in 1990?
  a.) *A Bug's Life!*
  b.) *Toy Story*
  c.) *Dick Tracy*
  d.) *Aladdin*

47. Who was the first sports personality to say "I'm going to Disney World" after winning an NFL championship and MVP honors?
  a.) Phil Simms
  b.) John Elway
  c.) Otis Anderson
  d.) Troy Aikman

48. In what parade can you find *Star Wars* characters?
  a.) *Share a Dream Come True*
  b.) *SpectroMagic*
  c.) *Star Wars Weekends Character Festival*
  d.) *Disney Stars & Motorcars Parade*

49. What WDW attraction has Disney's longest ride track, 5,246 feet?
  a.) *Space Mountain*
  b.) *Test Track*
  c.) *it's a small world*
  d.) *Rock 'n' Roller Coaster*

50. Where can you see the "back side of water?"
  a.) *Splash Mountain*
  b.) *Jungle Cruise*
  c.) Imagination! pavilion
  d.) Canada pavilion

51. When did *Magic Journeys* move from Epcot to the Magic Kingdom?
  a.) 1983
  b.) 1987
  c.) 1993
  d.) *Magic Journeys* was never in Epcot

52. Which popular attraction opened exactly seven years after Walt Disney's death?
  a.) *Space Mountain*
  b.) *Pirates of the Caribbean*
  c.) *it's a small world*
  d.) *The Haunted Mansion*

Did You Know?

SINCE 1971, MORE THAN 100,000 TREES AND 2,000,000 SHRUBS HAVE BEEN PLANTED AT WDW. FOR A BURST OF COLOR, ANOTHER 3,000,000 BEDDING PLANTS ARE ADDED EVERY YEAR.

53. What is a Cast Member referring to if he reports a "Code 101?"
a.) A lost child
b.) A broken down attraction
c.) A VIP in line
d.) A guest needing medical attention

54. In what year did WDW welcome its 500 millionth visitor?
a.) 1989
b.) 1995
c.) 1997
d.) 2000

55. Where was the *Radio Disney River Cruise* located?
a.) Magic Kingdom
b.) Epcot
c.) Disney-MGM Studios
d.) Disney's Animal Kingdom

56. What did Walt Disney consider the most important part of his "Florida Project"?
a.) EPCOT
b.) Magic Kingdom
c.) The quality of the resort hotels
d.) The establishment of a self-governing municipality

57. About how many people does WDW currently employ?
a.) 19,000
b.) 25,000
c.) 55,000
d.) 73,000

58. Finish this Walt Disney quote: "It was all started. . ."
a.) By my love of children
b.) By a mouse
c.) Way back at the World's Fair
d.) With a suggestion from my wife

59. How many outfits does Mickey Mouse have to wear at WDW?
a.) 33
b.) 89
c.) 175
d.) 312

60. What attraction closed in the 1990s and had some of its figures sent to Disneyland's *Pirates of the Caribbean* attraction?
a.) Horizons
b.) World of Motion
c.) Journey Into Imagination
d.) Kitchen Kabaret

61. Prior to 1999, the year *Test Track* opened, what was the fastest ride you could take at WDW?
a.) The Walt Disney World buses
b.) *Primeval Whirl*
c.) *Big Thunder Mountain Railroad*
d.) The monorail

Did You Know?

THERE ARE MORE THAN 20,000 DIFFERENT COLORS OF PAINT USED IN WDW.

62. Where have you heard, ". . .a world of laughter, a world of tears . . ."?
- a.) *Spaceship Earth*
- b.) *it's a small world*
- c.) *The Many Adventures of Winnie the Pooh*
- d.) *Peter Pan's Flight*

63. Many attractions in WDW have two separate entry lines, usually a left and a right. Which of these has only one?
- a.) *Space Mountain*
- b.) *The Twilight Zone Tower of Terror*
- c.) *Pirates of the Caribbean*
- d.) *The Haunted Mansion*

64. Where can kids take a pirate cruise?
- a.) Adventureland
- b.) Disney's Wilderness Lodge
- c.) Downtown Disney
- d.) Disney's Grand Floridian Resort & Spa

65. What attraction was "flight-tested" by U.S. astronauts and Russian cosmonauts?
- a.) *Test Track*
- b.) *Mission: SPACE*
- c.) *Space Mountain*
- d.) *Spaceship Earth*

66. Where have you heard, "Hi, could you find us a stranger please?"
- a.) *Indiana Jones Epic Stunt Spectacular*
- b.) *Fantasmic!*

69. Where is the Animation Academy?
- a.) Celebration
- b.) DisneyQuest
- c.) Disney-M
- d.) The Di

70. H

- c.) *Sounds Dangerous-Starring Drew Carey*
- d.) *Who Wants to be a Millionaire — Play It!*

67. On what attraction can you find "Flik"?
- a.) *Snow White's Scary Adventures*
- b.) *It's Tough to be a Bug!*
- c.) *Dinosaur*
- d.) Innoventions

68. The largest moving sets in the world are found at which location?
- a.) *The Great Movie Ride*
- b.) *Universe of Energy*
- c.) *Indiana Jones Epic Stunt Spectacular*
- d.) *Fantasmic!*

GM Studios
sney Institute

w many kennels are there in
W?
a.) 2
b.) 5
c.) 7
d.) None; WDW doesn't allow
pets.

71. The Transportation and Ticket Center is closest to which of the following?

a.) Disney's Polynesian Resort
b.) Epcot
c.) Disney's Contemporary Resort
d.) Downtown Disney

72. In what year were the A through E ticket books discontinued?

a.) 1975
b.) 1979
c.) 1980
d.) 1983

73. Where have you heard, "Folks, ahead of us lies the future"?

Did You Know?

IT WOULD TAKE ONE PERSON, EATING TWO HAMBURGERS AT EVERY MEAL, 4,109 YEARS AND 215 DAYS TO EAT THE NUMBER OF BURGERS SERVED AT WDW EACH YEAR.

a.) *Space Mountain*
b.) *Spaceship Earth*
c.) *The Timekeeper*
d.) *Walt Disney World Railroad*

74. What date marked the first time in WDW history that the theme parks were entirely closed down?
   a.) September 11, 2001
   b.) September 14, 1999
   c.) November 22, 1963, the day JFK was assassinated
   d.) WDW has never closed its parks for any reason

75. Where would you find a gurgling suitcase?
   a.) *Country Bear Jamboree*
   b.) Disney's Old Key West Resort
   c.) *Journey Into Imagination With Figment*
   d.) *Disney-MGM Studios Backlot Tour*

76. What remark did President Nixon make during a 1973 press conference at the Contemporary Hotel at WDW?
   a.) "Walt Disney World is a shining example what you can achieve in America if you have a dream and the will to pursue it."
   b.) "I am not a crook."
   c.) "That Mr. Toad is quite a funny guy."
   d.) "You won't have Nixon to kick around anymore."

77. Where will you find "Tike's Peak"?
   a.) Magic Kingdom
   b.) *Typhoon Lagoon*
   c.) *Blizzard Beach*
   d.) Disney's Animal Kingdom

78. What attraction's outer surface is largely covered with a material called "alucobond"?
   a.) Spaceship Earth
   b.) Universe of Energy
   c.) The Tree of Life
   d.) Cinderella Castle

79. How many 3D films have played at WDW?
   a.) 2
   b.) 3
   c.) 5
   d.) 7

80. Where have you heard, "Ah, no. Ain't nothin' gonna ruin this birthday"?
   a.) *Minnie's Country House*
   b.) *The American Adventure*
   c.) *The Timekeeper*
   d.) *Honey, I Shrunk the Audience*

81. What attraction was moved from Disneyland to WDW?
   a.) *Country Bear Jamboree*
   b.) *Dumbo the Flying Elephant*
   c.) *Carousel of Progress*
   d.) *The Timekeeper*

82. Which of the following opened first?
a.) *Space Mountain*
b.) *Treasure Island*
c.) *Big Thunder Mountain Railroad*
d.) *Spaceship Earth*

83. What theme park has the largest merchandise shop?
a.) Magic Kingdom
b.) Epcot
c.) Disney-MGM Studios
d.) Disney's Animal Kingdom

84. Where is the largest fountain in WDW?
a.) Epcot's Future World
b.) Disney's Polynesian Resort
c.) *Jim Henson's MuppetVision 3D*
d.) Disney's Grand Floridian Resort & Spa

85. How many passengers can each of the WDW ferryboats hold?
a.) 150
b.) 300
c.) 600
d.) 999

86. Where have you heard, "But enough of this chit chat, yick yack, and flim flam"?
a.) *Jim Henson's MuppetVision 3D*
b.) *Food Rocks*
c.) *Country Bear Jamboree*
d.) *The Enchanted Tiki Room - Under New Management*

87. What WDW theme park site was moved in the early stages of its development because a bird's nest was found on the job site?
a.) Magic Kingdom
b.) Epcot
c.) Disney-MGM Studios
d.) Disney's Animal Kingdom

88. Where can you buy a Beaver Tail?
a.) DinoLand, U.S.A.
b.) Camp Minnie-Mickey
c.) Canada pavilion
d.) *Tom Sawyer Island*

89. What is the biggest theme park at WDW?
a.) Magic Kingdom
b.) Epcot
c.) Disney-MGM Studios
d.) Disney's Animal Kingdom

90. In what attraction can you find a dog named Nana?
a.) *Carousel of Progress*
b.) *Honey, I Shrunk the Audience*
c.) *Peter Pan's Flight*
d.) *If You Had Wings*

91. Where have you heard, "Ah, take whatever you need. I don't wanna miss any of the game"?
a.) *Ellen's Energy Adventure*
b.) *Spaceship Earth*
c.) *Playhouse Disney — Live on Stage!*
d.) *The Great Movie Ride*

Did You Know?

WDW PAYS MORE THAN $500 MILLION A YEAR IN TAXES AND ALSO CONTRIBUTES ABOUT $3 BILLION PER YEAR TO THE LOCAL ECONOMY.

92. Which of the following rides has the fastest 0 to 60 mph acceleration?
a.) *Test Track*
b.) *Rock 'n' Roller Coaster*
c.) *Space Mountain*
d.) *Mission: SPACE*

93. What is the tallest attraction at WDW?
a.) *The Twilight Zone Tower of Terror*
b.) Cinderella Castle
c.) *Spaceship Earth*
d.) *The Tree of Life*

94. In the pre-show of which of these attractions will you find a little girl holding a Mickey Mouse doll?
a.) *Star Tours*
b.) *The Great Movie Ride*
c.) *The American Adventure*
d.) *The Twilight Zone Tower of Terror*

95. Where is the world's tallest and fastest free-fall water slide?
a.) *River Country*
b.) *Typhoon Lagoon*
c.) *Blizzard Beach*
d.) *Splash Mountain*

96. On what attraction do you ride in a "Time Rover"?
a.) *Ellen's Energy Adventure*
b.) *The Timekeeper*
c.) *Dinosaur*
d.) *Spaceship Earth*

97. How many screens are in a Circle-Vision movie theater?
a.) 360
b.) 12
c.) 9
d.) 6

98. What does "DACS" stand for?
a.) Disney Always Causes Smiles
b.) Digital Animation Control System
c.) Disney Automatic Communications System
d.) Digital Audio Command Stations

99. Where can you find "Niue"?
a.) Adventureland
b.) Disney's Polynesian Resort
c.) World Showcase
d.) Downtown Disney

100. What happens to all the change collected in the fountains at WDW?
- a.) It is collected and shared among Cast Members as "tips"
- b.) It is used for park rehabilitation
- c.) It is awarded to needy families in the Orlando area
- d.) It is given to Disney executives as a bonus

101. Which one of these "geological features" can NOT be found at WDW?

- a.) Catastrophe Canyon
- b.) Chickapin Hill
- c.) Ketchakiddie Creek
- d.) Rainbow Falls

102. Where can you find an unattended, parked armored car bearing the company name "Lacks Security"?
- a.) Mickey's Toontown Fair
- b.) Main Street, U.S.A.
- c.) New York Street in Disney-MGM Studios
- d.) Planet Hollywood in Downtown Disney

Did You Know?

CERTAIN AUDIO-ANIMATRONICS FIGURES CONTROLLED BY THE DACS SYSTEM ARE KNOWN AS "101" FIGURES, WHICH MEANS THAT IF THAT CHARACTER WERE TO STOP WORKING IN AN ATTRACTION, THE ENTIRE RIDE COULD BE CLOSED FOR WHAT IS KNOWN AS "BAD SHOW." AN EXAMPLE IS THE AUCTIONEER IN THE *PIRATES OF THE CARIBBEAN* ATTRACTION.

103. What was the name of the first attraction at WDW where guests could choose how the ride was going to end?
- a.) *Flight to the Moon*
- b.) *World of Motion*
- c.) *Horizons*
- d.) *If You Had Wings*

104. In which of these attractions does your ride car NOT travel backwards at some point?
- a.) *The Haunted Mansion*
- b.) *Maelstrom*
- c.) *Spaceship Earth*
- d.) *Peter Pan's Flight*

105. What was the first roller coaster in WDW?
- a.) *Big Thunder Mountain Railroad*
- b.) *Space Mountain*
- c.) *Rock 'n' Roller Coaster*
- d.) *Primeval Whirl*

106. Where can you order a "Chocolate Wave"?
- a.) *Typhoon Lagoon's* snack bar, Typhoon Tilly's
- b.) Flying Fish Café on the BoardWalk
- c.) Casey's Corner in the Magic Kingdom
- d.) The Coral Reef restaurant in Epcot's *The Living Seas*

107. What ride uses a 1/8-inch thick wire to guide your vehicle?
- a.) *it's a small world*

- b.) *The Haunted Mansion*
- c.) *Ellen's Energy Adventure*
- d.) *Tomorrowland Transit Authority*

108. Where have you heard, "Donating libraries Andy. . . now, there's a grand idea. . ."?
- a.) *The American Adventure*
- b.) *The Hall of Presidents*
- c.) *Journey Into Imagination*
- d.) *Spaceship Earth*

109. What is/was the "Movie Pavilion"?
- a.) A proposed ride through the movies in Epcot
- b.) The nickname of the restrooms behind *The Great Movie Ride*
- c.) A gift shop in Disney-MGM Studios
- d.) The building on Main Street, U.S.A. where guests can see old Mickey Mouse movies

110. How many holes of golf does WDW offer?
- a.) 200
- b.) 99
- c.) 118
- d.) 58

111. In what year was Walt Disney born? (You'll find the answer in a number of places in WDW.)
a.) 1900
b.) 1901
c.) 1911
d.) 1922

112. Where will you find the "Hall of Brains"?
a.) *Jim Henson's MuppetVision 3D*
b.) *Cranium Command*
c.) Innoventions East
d.) *Journey Into Imagination*

113. What is the most popular attraction in the WDW theme parks?
a.) *Pirates of the Caribbean*
b.) *it's a small world*
c.) *Spaceship Earth*
d.) *Space Mountain*

114. Which of these attractions opened first?
a.) *Splash Mountain*
b.) *The Twilight Zone Tower of Terror*
c.) *The Haunted Mansion*
d.) *Space Mountain*

115. Where will you find Hourglass Lake?
a.) Disney's Animal Kingdom
b.) Disney's Pop Century Resort
c.) Downtown Disney
d.) *Typhoon Lagoon*

116. What topiary figure can be found along the banks of the river surrounding Cinderella Castle?
a.) Pete's Dragon, Elliot
b.) A dancing hippo
c.) A sea serpent
d.) Pluto

117. Which of these can NOT be found on the original, pre-construction, wall-size "Master Plan" of Disney World?
a.) Magic Kingdom
b.) An Ice Rink
c.) A Roller Dome
d.) Downtown Disney

118. What is the only major attraction to be featured at every Disney theme park but in different lands?
a.) *The Haunted Mansion*
b.) *Splash Mountain*
c.) *Pirates of the Caribbean*
d.) *it's a small world*

119. What is the name of the location on WDW property where all of the props, signs, buildings, and anything else that needs to be fabricated are made?
a.) Imagineering Central
b.) Central Shops
c.) Design Depot
d.) Concepts and Creation

120. What is the largest Disney theme park in the world?
a.) Disneyland

b.) Disney's Animal Kingdom
c.) Epcot
d.) Tokyo Disneyland

121. At which of these locations will you NOT find a pyramid?
a.) Mexico pavilion
b.) Imagination! pavilion
c.) Disney's Coronado Springs Resort
d.) *Kali River Rapids*

122. Where have you heard, "Don't. . . move. . . a. . . muscle"?
a.) *Dinosaur*
b.) *Mission: SPACE*
c.) *It's Tough to be a Bug!*
d.) *Honey, I Shrunk the Audience*

123. In what attraction can characters "Buy A Bride"?
a.) *Jungle Cruise*
b.) *Pirates of the Caribbean*
c.) *The Great Movie Ride*
d.) *Jim Henson's MuppetVision 3D*

124. Harper's Mill is located in?
a.) *Splash Mountain*
b.) *The American Adventure*
c.) *Tom Sawyer Island*
d.) Discovery Island

125. Where could you hear the line "And you guys will all have me to thank when they're linin' up at the door"?
a.) *The ExtraTERRORestrial Alien Encounter*
b.) *The Enchanted Tiki Room – Under New Management*
c.) *It's Tough to be a Bug!*
d.) *The Timekeeper*

126. How long did the refurbishment take when *If You Had Wings* became *If You Could Fly?*
a.) 5 days
b.) 5 weeks
c.) 5 months
d.) 15 months

127. In which attraction's pre-show can you hear the song "True Colors"?
a.) *The American Adventure*
b.) *Journey Into Imagination with Figment*
c.) *Spaceship Earth*
d.) *Honey, I Shrunk the Audience*

128. What is Scuttle's Landing?
a.) A restaurant in Fantasyland
b.) A dock at the Yacht and Beach Clubs

Did You Know?

THE NAMES OF TWO OF THE APPROACH PROCEDURES THAT AIRCRAFT FOLLOW WHEN ARRIVING AT ORLANDO INTERNATIONAL AIRPORT ARE "GOOFY TWO" AND "MINNIE TWO."

Did You Know?

SOME WDW BUSES HAVE
OVER A MILLION MILES
ON THEM.

c.) The restroom facilities on
Tom Sawyer's Island

d.) A water slide in Typhoon
Lagoon

129. Where can you find an attraction that flipped off its tracks during its initial testing phase?

a.) Magic Kingdom

b.) Epcot

c.) Disney-MGM Studios

d.) Disney's Animal Kingdom

130. Which attraction has 109 Audio-Animatronics figures?

a.) *Splash Mountain*

b.) *it's a small world*

c.) *The Great Movie Ride*

d.) *The Haunted Mansion*

131. The remains of what technology lie abandoned at the bottom of the Seven Seas Lagoon?

a.) The first linear induction
riverboats

b.) A sunken submarine intended to transport guests to the Magic Kingdom

c.) A failed wave-making machine

d.) The first production models for the *Electrical Water Pageant*

132. Where have you heard, "Little Red is okay!"?

a.) *The ExtraTERRORestrial Alien Encounter*

b.) *The Living Seas*

c.) *Kilimanjaro Safaris*

d.) *Voyage of the Little Mermaid*

133. Which of WDW's theme parks has more than one entrance?

a.) Magic Kingdom

b.) Epcot

c.) Disney-MGM Studios

d.) Disney's Animal Kingdom

134. What is "Kids Nite Out"?

a.) A guided nighttime tour of the Magic Kingdom for kids under 16

b.) Private in-room baby-sitting

c.) A supervised dance club in Disney's Contemporary Resort

d.) An interactive game show at Disney-MGM Studios

135. Where have you heard, "Did you remember to turn off those robots"?

a.) *Test Track*

b.) *Body Wars*

c.) *Journey Into Imagination*

d.) *Innoventions*

136. On what ride can/could you see a "Corkscrew Ahead" sign?

a.) *Mr. Toad's Wild Ride*

b.) *Jim Henson's MuppetVision 3D*

c.) *Rock 'n' Roller Coaster Starring Aerosmith*
d.) *Journey Into Imagination with Figment*

137. In what former attraction was the song "One Little Spark" heard?
a.) *Horizons*
b.) The original *Carousel of Progress*
c.) *Journey Into Imagination*
d.) The original *Spaceship Earth*

138. Where can you find a classic Greek play being performed?
a.) *The Great Movie Ride*
b.) World Showcase
c.) Main Street Cinema
d.) *Spaceship Earth*

139. In which theme park can you find "Ice Cream of Extinction"?
a.) Magic Kingdom
b.) Epcot
c.) Disney-MGM Studios
d.) Disney's Animal Kingdom

140. Ride cars travel around a center spindle in each of these attractions. Which one travels clockwise?
a.) *Astro Orbiter*
b.) *Triceratops Spin*
c.) *Dumbo the Flying Elephant*
d.) *The Magic Carpets of Aladdin*

141. Where can you still find a car used in *Mr. Toad's Wild Ride?*

a.) *Disney-MGM Studios Backlot Tour*
b.) Downtown Disney
c.) The Walt Disney World Speedway
d.) Town Square Exposition Hall on Main Street, U.S.A.

142. What's the only WDW 3D attraction that actually calls its 3D glasses "3D Glasses"?

Did You Know?

WDW GUESTS EAT MORE THAN 9 MILLION BURGERS, 7 MILLION HOT DOGS, AND 9 MILLION POUNDS OF FRENCH FRIES EVERY YEAR.

a.) *Mickey's PhilharMagic*
b.) *Jim Henson's MuppetVision 3D*
c.) *Honey, I Shrunk the Audience*
d.) *It's Tough to be a Bug!*

143. Where have you heard, "... you will disappear, disappear!"?
a.) *Pirates of the Caribbean*
b.) *The Haunted Mansion*
c.) *Maelstrom*
d.) *Tower of Terror*

144. Where will you find the "Torre del Cielo"?
a.) Mexico pavilion
b.) Pecos Bill Cafe
c.) El Pirata Y El Perico
d.) *Pirates of the Caribbean*

145. What "Street" disappeared in 2001?
a.) West Center Street
b.) Tomorrowland Turnpike
c.) Main Street, U.S.A.
d.) Sunshine Street

146. Where have you heard, "It's land ho, me hearties, at last we've arrived. . ."?
a.) *Pirates of the Caribbean*
b.) *20,000 Leagues Under the Sea*
c.) *The American Adventure*
d.) *Liberty Square Riverboat*

147. What area of WDW is accessible to guests only by train?
a.) Mickey's Toontown Fair
b.) Rafiki's Planet Watch
c.) Fort Wilderness Resort and Campground
d.) *Kilimanjaro Safaris*

148. From what attraction is/was the song "Heffalumps and Woozles"?
a.) *Peter Pan's Flight*
b.) *Mr. Toad's Wild Ride*
c.) *Mickey's Toontown Fair*
d.) *The Many Adventures of Winnie the Pooh*

THE ANSWERS
TO CHAPTER ONE

1. d.) 1971
October 1, 1971, was the official opening day of Walt Disney World and the Magic Kingdom, the Resort's original and most popular theme park. However, it was not officially dedicated until October 25. NBC broadcast the dedication on October 29.

2. b.) 7,100
WDW comprises 47 square miles of land. With less than one quarter of it developed and another quarter set aside as a permanent conservation area, there's quite a lot of room for expansion. Walt Disney himself set aside the 7,500-acre (11.7-square-mile) tract that will never be developed. It's called the Wildlife Management Conservation Area.

3. d.) $400 million
Phase One of WDW opened to the public in 1971. Built by 9,000 workers at an estimated cost of over 400 million dollars, it was the largest private construction project in the world up to that time.

4. b.) Use the 911 emergency system
Since there were no telephone lines on the desolate property that became Walt Disney World, the Disney company formed a partnership with Florida Telephone Company to create a completely new, state-of-the-art phone system. The result was the first totally electronic phone system using underground cable instead of standard overhead lines. It was the first in Florida to use the 911 emergency system.

5. c.) Disney World
When Walt Disney passed away on December 15, 1966, there was great concern within the Disney organization that Disney World would never be built without his leadership and guidance. But his brother, Roy O. Disney, postponed his planned retirement to helm the organization, and the first item on his to-do list was to complete "Disney World." As it neared completion, Roy officially changed the name to Walt Disney World so, "People will always know that this was Walt's dream."

6. b.) *it's a small world*
WDW was a very different place back in 1971. There were only three hotels, two golf courses, and the Magic Kingdom (MK) theme park. There were no thrill rides, such as

roller coasters or log flumes, and one of the MK's current lands didn't yet exist. *it's a small world*, however, was there from day one. *Space Mountain* opened January 15, 1973; *Pirates of the Caribbean*, December 15, 1973; and *Big Thunder Mountain Railroad*, September 23, 1980.

7. c.) 167
There are about 167 lane-miles of paved roads on WDW property.

8. d.) Lake Buena Vista
Lake Buena Vista, a Disney-governed municipality, is about 20 miles southwest of Orlando.

9. b.) $5 million
Using a number of dummy corporations so as not to tip off landowners that it was Disney purchasing the property, the organization was able to purchase more than 27,000 acres for a total sum of $5,018,770, which works out to less than $200 per acre.

10. b.) Walt Disney's brother Roy O. Disney
Walt Disney passed away in December 1966, long before Walt Disney World was complete. His brother and partner, Roy O. Disney, continued his work and dedicated the resort on October 25, 1971 – more than three weeks after the Magic Kingdom opened to the public. During his dedication speech at Main Street, U.S.A.'s Town Square,

Roy said, "Walt Disney World is a tribute to the philosophy and life of Walter Elias Disney – and to the talents, the dedication, and the loyalty of the entire Disney organization that made Walt Disney's dream come true. May Walt Disney World bring Joy and Inspiration and New Knowledge to all who come to this happy place. . . a Magic Kingdom where the young at heart of all ages can laugh and play and learn. . . together."

11. b.) 1965
Walt Disney, seeking to open a second theme park without the space restrictions he suffered in Disneyland, began a super-secret project in the early 1960s to find and acquire land for a second theme park. He wanted to locate his new park near a major population center, with good weather, good highways, and (most importantly) cheap land. The property that would become Walt Disney World Resort was exactly right. Beginning in early 1965, companies with odd-sounding names such as the Latin-American Development and Managers Corporation, Bay Lake Properties, Inc., and the Reedy Creek Ranch Corporation began buying up properties just south of Orlando in Osceola County. On May 4 of that year, the *Orlando Sentinel*, which at the time was a local paper for a small farming community, ran an article about the recent

purchases of two large tracts of land for a total of $1.5 million, plus numerous smaller tracts of flatlands and cattle pastures, all in the same area. Speculation about the buyer began to surface. Walt Disney was one of the rumored purchasers, along with such aerospace firms as McDonnell Douglas and Lockheed (because Orlando is fairly close to Cape Canaveral) and major auto manufacturers such as Ford, Chrysler, and Volkswagen. All denied involvement. On October 17, 1965, after more than 27,000 acres had been purchased, reporter Emily Bavar ran a story in the *Sentinel* claiming for the first time that she was convinced the purchaser was indeed Walt Disney. The news was confirmed eight days later by Governor Haydon Burns. Finally, on November 15, 1965, Walt Disney, with his brother Roy and the governor at his side, introduced the public to his plans for Disney World.

12. b.) 1969

Since most of Central Florida basically "floats" on a body of fresh water, the first task for Disney engineers was to deal with issues regarding the area's water supply and the poten-tial environmental consequences of development. Therefore, in October 1965, 300 acres were cleared on the northwest corner of the 27,000-acre property to conduct water control and drainage studies. These were completed in 1967, and groundbreaking and site preparation started on May 30, 1967. However, actual construction did not begin until April 1969. At the time, it was the largest private construction project on the planet.

13. a.) Weenies

When Walt Disney was designing Disneyland in Anaheim, California, he wanted each of his themed lands to have an obvious landmark that would act as a "visual magnet" to pull guests from one land to another. He called these icons 'weenies'. The Castle that would stand in the center of the park would be the largest weenie, visible from every "land." It would draw guests further down Main Street. Once they reached the central hub (i.e., the Castle), weenies such as Space Mountain to the right or Big Thunder Mountain to the left would draw them into Tomorowland or Frontierland. The use of weenies

Did You Know?

WALT DISNEY, THE VISIONARY BEHIND THE ENTIRE DISNEY EMPIRE, ATTENDED ONLY ONE YEAR OF HIGH SCHOOL.

continued in WDW. Magic Kingdom has Cinderella Castle, Epcot has *Spaceship Earth*, Disney-MGM Studios has the Sorcerer Mickey Hat, and Disney's Animal Kingdom has *The Tree of Life*.

14. c.) 25%
WDW welcomes millions of international visitors and offers numerous amenities to cater to them, including telephone information in many languages, guidebooks to the four major parks in Spanish, French, German, Portuguese, and Japanese, and currency exchanges. Cast Members who speak a foreign language identify themselves to guests by wearing a badge with the flag of the appropriate country on their name tags.

15. d.) WDW is more than 100 times the size of Disneyland
Walt Disney once said, "Here in Florida, we have something special that we never enjoyed at Disneyland . . . the blessing of size. There's enough land here to hold all the ideas and plans we can possibly imagine." Disneyland encompasses fewer than 300 acres, including Disney's California Adventure theme park and additional hotel properties. The limited size (all of Disneyland could fit inside of Epcot) prevented Disney from creating a buffer zone around Disneyland that would let it control the park's surroundings and ensure that everything in them complemented the theme-park experience.

16. c.) 11 years
Epcot opened on October 1, 1982, exactly 11 years to the day after the Magic Kingdom.

17. d.) 5 years
WDW is always in a state of change, with attractions being added, "refurbished for your future enjoyment," or replaced by new rides. However, early on, there were often long stretches of time when no new attractions opened. The longest, almost five years, passed between the openings of such Tomorrowland stalwarts as *Space Mountain* and *Walt Disney's Carousel of Progress* in

Did You Know?

MORE THAN 100 PAIRS OF SUNGLASSES ARE TURNED INTO WDW's LOST & FOUND EVERY DAY — ENOUGH EACH YEAR TO COVER THE EYES OF EVERY SINGLE RESIDENT OF SUN CITY, CALIFORNIA AND SUN CITY, FLORIDA!

1975 and the opening of *Big Thunder Mountain Railroad* in 1980.

18. c.) 300
There are more than 300 places to dine in WDW - NOT counting the portable food carts. In all, more than 6,000 different food items are available throughout the Resort.

19. c.) Norway in World Showcase
"Takk" (pronounced "TOCK") means "Thank You" and will likely be heard in and around the Norway pavilion in Epcot's World Showcase.

20. c.) *Rock 'n' Roller Coaster Starring Aerosmith*
Your "stretch limo" takes you through Hollywood at night on your way to the Aerosmith concert. Once you get there, you are dropped off in the "VIP Parking Lot."

21. a.) Raz Island
Discovery Island, located in the center of Bay Lake, has had many names, among them Blackbeard's Island and Treasure Island. Disney legend has it that as Walt Disney was flying over the land he was interested in purchasing for his Florida theme park, Raz Island caught his eye and he decided that the property was the ideal place to build. The name Raz Island goes back to the early 1900s, when the Raz family owned and lived on the remote island. By the time Disney purchased it, it was called "Riles Island."

22. b.) Parking lot areas in Epcot
While the names of the lots in Epcot's parking lot are meant to reflect concepts that deal with your imagination (such as "Creative"), the Magic Kingdom lots have character names (such as Mickey, Minnie, and Goofy) with associated images for easy recognition.

23. c.) *The Great Movie Ride*
As you head into the "Old West" scenes, you see Clint Eastwood and John Wayne on your right and left, respectively. Wayne repeats this line from his 1956 film *The Searchers*, and then warns, "Well, that's a mighty tough territory you're headin' into, pilgrim. I'd think about turnin' back if I were you."

24. d.) About 2,300
Since September 1991, WDW has hosted nearly 15,000 weddings, and now hosts over 2,300 a year. Disney's Fairy Tale Weddings provides couples with a Disney Wedding Planning Team to help them shape a ceremony and reception limited only by their imagination (and budget).

Originally, though, Disney frowned on nuptials at the parks, and guests dressed in wedding attire were not admitted. Desperate lovers would sometimes enter the Magic Kingdom with their bridal attire hidden underneath their street clothes! Then they would casually walk up to Cinderella Castle with the person performing the ceremony, quickly remove their disguises, and exchange their vows in gown and tux.

25. b.) *Test Track*
After World of Motion closed early in 1996, the GM *Test Track* Preview Center opened. Scale models, concept art, layout diagrams, one of the *Test Track* ride vehicles, and a video were on display, along with a large mural painted by French artist Catherine Feff. The very first Preview Center, for WDW itself, was built in 1970 and located on what was then known as Preview Boulevard (now Hotel Plaza Boulevard). Inside were artists' renderings and an aerial view of the park, as well as a motion-picture presentation. Visitors could even make reservations with hostesses for the as-yet-unbuilt Contemporary and Polynesian Village hotels.

26. b.) *Test Track*
With a top speed of 65 mph, *Test Track* in Epcot is the longest and fastest ride at WDW. This attraction, which opened March 17, 1999, takes guests on a nearly five-minute

ride through a 150,000-square-foot pavilion with hairpin turns, spirals, and spins. In contrast, the Studios' *Rock 'n' Roller Coaster* takes you from 0 to 60 mph in 2.8 seconds, while its *Twilight Zone Tower of Terror* reaches only about 39 mph — and then only because it is pulled downward by powerful motors. Some people have argued that the Monorail is actually the fastest "ride" in WDW. However, its top speed is only about 55 mph and its normal maximum cruising speed is around 40 mph. Technically speaking, if you want the fastest ride in WDW, you should hop in the seat of a real stock car over at the *Richard Petty Driving Experience* at the WDW Speedway. You can take the wheel or ride shotgun as your car tackles the asphalt at speeds of up to 145 mph.

27. c.) *Cranium Command*
"General Knowledge" is the commanding officer who trains the "Cranium Commandos" — the fellows who are responsible for piloting our brains. His voice is provided by Corey Burton, who has an impressive list of voiceover work, including roles in such Disney animated feature films as *Mulan, Aladdin, Hercules,* and *The Hunchback of Notre Dame.* He can also be heard throughout the WDW theme parks in attractions such as *It's Tough to Be a Bug!, The Timekeeper,* and *Ellen's Energy Adventure.*

Did You Know?

MORE THAN 500,000 CHARACTER WATCHES (MOSTLY MICKEY) ARE SOLD IN THE WDW GIFT SHOPS EACH YEAR.

•

BY 1978, GUESTS VISITING WALT DISNEY WORLD SPENT MORE MONEY ON MERCHANDISE THAN ON FOOD.

28. c.) *Buzz Lightyear's Space Ranger Spin*
Hop into your XP-37 Star Cruiser for your voyage into the Gamma Quadrant to help save the universe! Here's a tip: For the most points, aim at targets far away from your vehicle. For example, the top of the volcano is worth 100,000 points and will erupt when you hit it!

29. b.) A hot air balloon
"Ear Force One" is the name of the hot air balloon shaped like Mickey Mouse that can occasionally be seen over WDW. It is more than 100 feet tall and weighs 330 pounds uninflated and without the basket! Mickey's ears are 35 feet in diameter, while his nose is 33 feet long, and his head about 168 feet around.

30. c.) 120,000
Next time you complain about how much laundry you have to do, think about this. . . if you were to wash and dry one load of laundry every day for 33 years, you'd clean as much as the

folks at the WDW Laundry do in a single day. Some 550 Cast Members (every WDW employee is a Cast Member, regardless of their position onstage or off), launder an average total of 120,000 pounds of clothing and linens each and every day from the parks, resorts, and restaurants. And that doesn't include the 30,000 to 32,000 garments that must be dry-cleaned daily.

31. c.) Disney's Polynesian Resort
A wave machine was installed off the southern shore of Beachcomber Isle in the Seven Seas Lagoon before the Resort opened in 1971. It was shut down a few months later because the waves were severely eroding the beach. Part of the machine can still be seen above the water off the island.

32. a.) *Maelstrom*
Norway's *Maelstrom* ride opened to guests of Epcot's World Showcase on July 5, 1988. *Jim Henson's MuppetVision 3D* opened at Disney-MGM

Studios May 16, 1991; Disney's Fairy Tale Weddings Pavilion, July 1995, and Disney's BoardWalk Inn & Villas, June 30, 1996.

33. b.) Jeremy Irons
Jeremy Irons narrates *Spaceship Earth* and provides the voice for H.G. Wells in *The Timekeeper*. You may recognize his voice as that of "Scar" in *The Lion King* movie.

34. d.) *Jungle Cruise*
Your tour guide in this attraction will point out the Chief, noting that he's your "head salesman." Take a ride on *Jungle Cruise* to see why that's so funny! (OK. . . Can't wait? Well, Chief Nammie makes his living selling shrunken heads. No matter how you slice it, you'll come out "a-head." Get it?)

35. d.) *Big Thunder Mountain Railroad*
As your runaway mine car speeds through the deserted town, you will pass by a volcanic pool and a 30-foot geyser — and experience an earthquake, a flash flood, and an avalanche! That's why it's the wildest ride in the wilderness.

36. d.) Disney's Caribbean Beach Resort
Parrot Cay Island lies in the middle of a 42-acre lake, which is surrounded by the resort. Guests can wander a 1.5-mile nature trail on the island and see

an aviary filled with a variety of exotic birds. Footbridges link the island to the mainland.

37. b.) Magic Kingdom
Magic Kingdom, the original and perhaps most family oriented of WDW's four theme parks, is the only one that doesn't serve alcohol anywhere within its borders.

38. d.) 12 million
The more than 230 buses WDW uses to transport guests cover about 12 million miles per year. Think of it this way — to drive 12 million miles, you would have to circle the equator more than nine times a week for a year!

39. b.) 12 feet
There are more than 2.385 billion gallons of water in Bay Lake and the adjoining Seven Seas Lagoon, WDW's two largest lakes, which together cover over 596 acres. Bay Lake is natural and was on the property when Disney bought it, while the Seven Seas Lagoon is completely man made.

40. b.) Adventurers Club

In 1985, Doug Henning was hired as a consultant by the Walt Disney Company to help it find ways to put more "magic" into its theme parks and exhibits. He is credited with contributing to the special effects at the Adventurers Club. In the late 1980s, Henning proposed a joint venture with Disney to build Henning's own theme park near WDW, to be called VedaLand (from the Eastern term 'veda' which means knowledge). However, nothing came of it.

41. b.) Christmas Day

There are 12,213 parking spaces in the MK parking lot. By 10 a.m. Christmas morning, WDW's busiest day of the year, they are all filled.

42. b.) 10

WDW has a variety of water-based attractions. In the Magic Kingdom, guests board a boat on the *Jungle Cruise*, *Pirates of the Caribbean*, *Splash Mountain*, *Liberty Square Riverboat*, *it's a small world*, and the rafts to *Tom Sawyer Island* (because you have to take a raft to the Island, the ride is considered part of the attraction). In Epcot, there are three boat rides: Norway's *Maelstrom*, *Living with the Land*, and *El Rio del Tiempo* in the Mexico pavilion. Disney's Animal Kingdom has only *Kali River Rapids*, while the Studios offers no water-based attractions at all (though you can get to the Studios via boat

from Epcot and its resort hotels). If you counted 11 attractions, instead of 10, you might make the case that the flying pirate "ships" of *Peter Pan's Flight* offer a "boat" ride.

43. d.) The Wicked Witch in *The Great Movie Ride*

When *The American Adventure* opened in Epcot's World Showcase in 1982, the Benjamin Franklin Audio-Animatronics figure was the most sophisticated in Disney history. His subtle body movements, including the appearance of being able to walk up stairs, were revolutionary at the time. That changed in the late 1980s, when the Imagineers developed what they called the "A-100" technology. A-100 Audio-Animatronics use what is known as "compliance technology." This allows more fluid, realistic movement and requires incredibly painstaking programming. In fact, it takes about eight hours to program one second of animated movement! The Wicked Witch from the "Wizard of Oz" scene in the Studios' *The Great Movie Ride* was the first of these next-generation figures to appear in WDW. She premiered in 1989. She's since been joined by the carnotaurs in *Dinosaur* and Hopper, the nine-foot grasshopper in *It's Tough to be a Bug!* (both in Disney's Animal Kingdom) as well as Bill Clinton and George W. Bush in *The Hall of Presidents* and 9-Eye in *The Timekeeper* (both in the MK).

44. d.) Hollywood Tower Hotel
The Hollywood Tower Hotel in Disney-MGM Studios is the home of *The Twilight Zone Tower of Terror*. You'll see a poster for the Anthony Freemont Orchestra playing the Tip Top Club on the right side of the queue area in the hotel lobby.

45. b.) Walt Disney World Marketplace
WDW's first shopping and dining village opened March 22, 1975, as "Lake Buena Vista Village." Located near the "official hotels," the area had the feel of a village to it and quickly became a popular nighttime dining and shopping place for guests. The Village later changed its name to "Walt Disney World Village" and then in 1989, to "Disney Village Marketplace." Finally, in 1996, it became known as "Downtown Disney Marketplace." In 1989, due to demand for more night-time entertainment — and partially in response to a popular Orlando entertainment complex known as "Church Street Station" — Disney opened its nighttime entertainment complex, Pleasure Island.

46. c.) *Dick Tracy*
The comic-book detective film *Dick Tracy*, starring Madonna and War-ren Beatty, was the very first world premiere to be screened in WDW. Held at Downtown Disney's Pleasure Island in 1990, it coincided with the

Dick Tracy & the Diamond Double Cross show, which opened at Disney-MGM Studios that same year. The show, a 28-minute long production, ran in the Theater of the Stars near the Brown Derby restaurant from May 21, 1990, until February 21, 1991.

47. a.) Phil Simms
"I'm going to Disney World!" This phrase was first spoken immediately after Super Bowl XXI in 1987 by MVP Phil Simms of the New York Giants in answer to a reporter's question of "What's next?" It soon became the catchphrase of a memo-rable series of commercials – 34 to date – featuring such champs as America's Cup skipper Dennis Con-ner, the L.A. Lakers' Magic Johnson, World Series player Frank Viola of the Minnesota Twins, and a number of football stars, among them San Francisco 49ers quarterback Joe Montana (1989 and 1990),

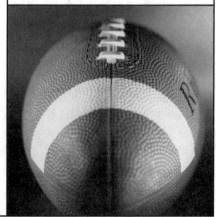

Dallas Cowboys running back Emmitt Smith (1994 and 1997), Denver Broncos quarterback John Elway (1998 and 1999), and New England Patriots quarterback Tom Brady (2002 and 2004). So, what do the players get for appearing in the commercial? Well according to some sports agents, in addition to the free tour of WDW those five words can net a player upwards of $50,000!

48. d.) *Disney Stars and Motorcars Parade*
Star Wars characters join Luke Skywalker and Princess Leia each day in the *Disney Stars and Motorcars Parade* at Disney-MGM Studios.

49. b.) *Test Track*
Along with having the longest ride track in WDW, Epcot's *Test Track* has some of the World's longest wait times!

50. b.) *Jungle Cruise*
Yeah, the jokes on *Jungle Cruise* may seem a little corny, but you can't help but chuckle when your Guide takes you underneath an overhang and behind a waterfall and shows you the "back side of water." It's definitely the "punniest" ride in the Magic Kingdom! (Sorry, I couldn't resist!)

51. b.) 1987
Magic Journeys was a 3D movie that premiered in Epcot's Journey Into Imagination pavilion. It was moved to the Magic Kingdom's Fantasyland Theatre in 1987 and ran there until December 1, 1993, when it was removed in preparation for the *Legend of the Lion King* show. It was replaced in Epcot by Michael Jackson's *Captain EO.*

52. b.) *Pirates of the Caribbean*
Pirates of the Caribbean opened in WDW on December 15, 1973. Walt Disney passed away on December 15, 1966, at St. Joseph Medical Center right across the street from the Disney Studios in Burbank.

53. b.) A broken down attraction
There are two codes that Cast Members use to describe the status of an attraction: "Code 101" means that the attraction has broken down, and "Code 102" means that the attraction is back up and running.

54. b.) 1995
After a relatively slow start in Fall 1971, WDW quickly became the world's most popular vacation destination. In August 1972, cumulative attendance reached 10 million; in March 1976, 50 million; by October 1979, 100 million. Total attendance topped 250 million in July 1987 and reached an incredible 400 million by August 1992. October 13, 1995, marked the milestone 500 millionth visitor, with number 600 million passing through the gates on June 24, 1998.

55. d.) Disney's Animal Kingdom
Radio Disney River Cruise was one of the few rides that was operational on April 22, 1998, the opening day for Disney's Animal Kingdom. But it had a different name then – in fact, it had several during its short life. The first was *Discovery River Boats*, then *Animal Kingdom Water Taxis*, and eventually *Radio Disney River Cruise* (because the music played on its floating tour of the park from docks in Africa and Asia was provided by Radio Disney DJs who broadcast from inside the park). Next, it briefly became *Discovery River Taxis* (Confused by these names yet?), then *Discovery River Boat Tour*, and finally *Discovery River Taxis* again. Then, just 16 months after its original opening, the attraction was shut down for good in August 1999.

56. a.) EPCOT
In February 1967, just two months after Walt Disney's death, Walt Disney Productions announced that it was going to build Walt Disney's dream of a city of tomorrow in WDW. Walt had outlined his plans for that city in a film he narrated. In it, he states that "The most exciting and by far the most important part of our Florida Project — in fact, the heart of everything we'll be doing in Disney World — will be our Experimental Prototype Community of Tomorrow. We call it 'EPCOT'. EPCOT will be an experimental prototype community of tomorrow that will take its cue from the creative centers of American industry. It will be a community of tomorrow that will never be completed, but will always be introducing and testing and demonstrating new materials and systems. And EPCOT will always be a showcase to the world for the ingenuity and imagination of American free enterprise. I don't believe there's a challenge anywhere in the world that's more important to people everywhere than finding solutions to the problems of our cities."

57. c.) 55,000
WDW is the largest employer in Central Florida. In fact, it employs more people on a single site than any other company in the United States. During its busiest times of the year,

(the holidays, for example), there are up to 60,000 Cast Members working at the Resort. That's about half of all of the Disney employees worldwide.

58. b.) By a mouse
In looking back on the success of the Disney Company, Walt Disney once noted, "I only hope that we never lose sight of one thing — that it was all started by a mouse."

59. c.) 175
Mickey Mouse has about 175 different outfits in his wardrobe, including a scuba suit and a tuxedo. Minnie Mouse's massive "walk-in closet" contains about 200 outfits, including a cheerleader costume and various evening gowns.

60. b.) *World of Motion*
When EPCOT's *World of Motion* pavilion was closed in 1995, some of the "homeless" Audio-Animatronics figures were used to renovate (or in some cases, replace) figures from Disneyland's *Pirates of the Caribbean*.

61. a.) Walt Disney World buses
With a top speed (according to local limits) of 50 mph, the WDW buses were, technically, the fastest "ride" in the resort, until *Test Track*, with it's 65 mph speeds, opened in 1999.

62. b.) *it's a small world*
"It's a world of laughter,

A world of tears;
It's a world of hopes
And a world of fears."
Listen, if you didn't get this one, you obviously haven't ridden *it's a small world*. Ever.

63. d.) *The Haunted Mansion*
Each of the other rides has a left and a right queue line.
Here's a tip: You should usually try to take the queue on the left when given a choice. Why? Well, most people tend toward the right side. Thus, the line on the left will usually be shorter.

64. d.) Disney's Grand Floridian Resort & Spa
Children three to ten years old can take a two-hour pirate cruise and search for buried treasure (while their parents get some quiet time for themselves!). The cruise leaves from the Grand Floridian's marina on Seven Seas Lagoon. (I only wish they had one for adults!)

65. c.) *Space Mountain*
In the early 1970s, representatives of NASA and the Soviet Academy of Sciences met to discuss the possibility of a joint space venture and agreed on an Apollo-Soyuz joint mission. After U.S. astronauts visited Moscow, Soviet cosmonauts visited the Johnson Space Center in Florida. During their stay, the two groups of explorers visited the Magic Kingdom

and gave its newest attraction, *Space Mountain*, a "test flight."

66. d.) *Who Wants To Be A Millionaire — Play It!*
If you ever dreamed of being in the Hot Seat, then head on over to *Who Wants To Be A Millionaire — Play It!* in Disney-MGM Studios. It's just like the original TV show, but without Regis and with a slight twist to the lifelines. Two of the three lifelines, "50/50" and "Ask the Audience," are the same as on the show. But instead being able to "Phone a Friend," you actually call a complete stranger who is randomly selected by a Cast Member outside the theater. When you use this lifeline, your host says to the Cast Member, "Hi, could you find us a stranger please?"

67. b.) *It's Tough to be a Bug!*
Flik is your host for the 3D film *It's Tough to be a Bug!* shown in the trunk of *The Tree of Life* in Disney's Animal Kingdom.

68. c.) *Indiana Jones Epic Stunt Spectacular*
In this exciting, live-action stage show, you can be pulled from the audience to help Indiana Jones from the *Raiders of the Lost Ark* film pull off some amazing stunts! The giant sets and stages move to reveal new scenes, including one with a giant rolling boulder. The incredible shifting sets weigh around 100 tons

EACH — making them the largest moving sets in history.

69. b.) DisneyQuest
Located in the Create Zone of Downtown Disney's DisneyQuest, the Animation Academy reveals the secrets of Disney animators by showing guests how to use basic shapes to draw their favorite Disney characters. After they finish, guests can pick up a printed copy of their work, along with a Diploma for completing the course!

70. b.) 5
With the exception of service animals such as guide dogs for the visually impaired, Disney doesn't admit pets into its theme parks. So you will find a kennel outside each of the parks plus one at the Fort Wilderness Campground (pets are welcome at certain locations within Fort Wilderness, such as the full hook-up campsites). The kennels are primarily geared towards dogs and cats, but can accommodate birds, ferrets, non-venomous snakes, and hamsters. Each kennel is a member of the American Boarding Kennel Association.

71. a.) Disney's Polynesian Resort
You can walk to the WDW Transportation and Ticket Center (TTC) from the Polynesian Resort via a designated pathway. Once there, you can pick up a monorail or ferryboat

to the Magic Kingdom and its resort hotels (Disney's Contemporary, Polynesian, and Grand Floridian). You can also catch a four-mile monorail to Epcot at the TTC.

72. c.) 1980
When the Magic Kingdom opened in 1971, guests didn't get in for a flat fee. Each attraction (with the exception of a few freebies) required a ticket, and guests bought ticket books containing A, B, C, D, and E tickets. The best attractions required E tickets. In the early 1980s, in anticipation of the opening of "EPCOT Center," the ticket books were phased out and replaced by "Passports" that offered guests admission and unlimited access to the attractions.

73. d.) *Walt Disney World Railroad*
You hear this line as you approach Tomorrowland. The train ride is a nice relief for tired feet, and offers unique views of the park.

74. b.) September 14, 1999
In anticipation of Hurricane Floyd, WDW closed its theme parks for a day and a half as a safety precaution — the first time in its history that the parks were closed. The parks closed early on Tuesday, September 14 and remained closed through Wednesday, September 15, 1999. The theme parks did close on September 11, 2001, following the early morning attacks. But after extensive

communication with local and state law enforcement officials, Disney reopened them with heightened security at their normally scheduled times the next morning.

75. b.) Disney's Old Key West Resort
The "Gurgling Suitcase" is the Old Key West Resort's pool bar, which serves light meals, snacks, and drinks.

76. b.) "I am not a crook."
Richard Nixon gave his memorable "I am not a crook" speech at Disney's Contemporary Resort on November 17, 1973, to a convention of more than 400 Associated Press newspaper editors, who were holding their annual meeting at the hotel.

77. c.) *Blizzard Beach*
Tike's Peak is a "mini" version of Mount Gushmore, the centerpiece of *Blizzard Beach*, where many of the water slides are located. Tike's Peak features kid-sized water slides, a snow castle, a fountain play area, and an ice pond.

78. a.) *Spaceship Earth*
The shell of *Spaceship Earth* is composed of thousands of triangular panels made of a substance called "alucobond" (from ALUminum COmposite BOND). This light-weight material consists of two aluminum cover sheets and a core made of plastic. It is stable, yet flex-ible, and has a smooth surface that is weather resistant, unbreakable, shock resistant, and absorbs vibrations.

79. d.) 7
Since WDW opened in 1971, a total of seven 3D movies have played at various locations in its theme parks — two in the Magic Kingdom ("Working for Peanuts," which was "Act 1" of the *Magic Journeys* attraction and *Mickey's PhilharMa-gic*), three in Epcot (*Magic Journeys*, which was later moved to the Magic Kingdom, *Captain EO*, and *Honey, I Shrunk the Audience*), and one each in the Studios (*Jim Henson's Mup-petVision 3D*) and Disney's Animal Kingdom (*It's Tough to be a Bug!*).

80. b.) *The American Adventure*
This line is found in *The American Adventure* in World Showcase, where the family with brothers on opposite

sides of the Civil War is getting its picture taken.

81. c.) *Carousel of Progress*
After its debut at the 1964-65 World's Fair, an attraction called General Electric's Progressland was moved to Disneyland, where it was renamed the *Carousel of Progress*. It ran there from July 1967 until September 9, 1973. It reopened in WDW's Tomorrowland on January 15, 1975, with a new song, "The Best Time of Your Life," and a new final scene.

82. b.) *Treasure Island*
Treasure Island, known as "Bay Lake's Tropical Island Paradise," opened April 8, 1974, as a bird sanctu-ary themed to a pirate motif (after Disney's 1950 live action movie of the same name). *Space Mountain* opened January 15, 1975; *Big Thun-der Mountain Railroad*, September 23, 1980. *Spaceship Earth*, along with the rest of EPCOT Center, had its grand opening October 1, 1982.

83. b.) Epcot
MouseGear is the largest merchan-dise store in any of the four Walt Disney World Resort theme parks. However, it is not the largest mer-

Did You Know?

WDW'S THEME PARK AND RESORT CHEFS
USE MORE THAN 50 VARIETIES OF CHEESES.

chandise shop on the property. Can you figure out where that is?

84. a.) Epcot's Future World

The Fountain of Nations, located in Innoventions Plaza in Future World — and operational since Epcot's opening day — is WDW's largest fountain. More than 108,000 gallons of water flow through its pipes, and its 304 nozzles can shoot water over 150 feet into the air (nearly as high as the *Spaceship Earth* globe!). Throughout the day, the fountain comes to life to dance to musical selections. It took the Disney Imagineers three months to program the dancing waters and their music. At night, 1,068 lights create a rainbow of colors to complement the ballet score. The fountain was designed by a team of Imagineers, one of whom went on to found WET Design, the company responsible for such magnificent fountains as the one in front of the Bellagio hotel in Las Vegas.

85. c.) 600

Three 600-passenger, diesel-powered ferryboats navigate the waters of Seven Seas Lagoon between the Transportation and Ticket Center and the Magic Kingdom. They are the "Richard F. Irvine," the "Admiral Joe Fowler," and the "General Joe Potter."

86. c.) *Country Bear Jamboree*

Henry, the show's host, says this line during his opening welcome to the audience. He just wants you to refrain from hibernating and enjoy the show . . . "because we've got a lot to give."

87. b.) Epcot

In the early phases of Epcot's construction, a nest of endangered red-cockaded woodpeckers was discovered in a wooded area that was scheduled to be cleared for future development. To preserve the area's natural state, Disney moved the entire construction site 300 feet. A backstage service road was later named for the woodpeckers.

88. c.) Canada pavilion

A "Beaver Tail" is a fried pastry dessert that can be purchased in the Canada pavilion. It comes in flavors such as Apple & Cinnamon and Maple & Chocolate. MMmmmmm!

89. d.) Disney's Animal Kingdom

Disney's Animal Kingdom, the largest theme park in WDW, encompasses 500 acres of lush landscape, wonderful attractions, and close encounters with exotic wildlife — all with the Disney magic. The park's signature attraction, *Kilimanjaro Safaris*, covers over 100 acres, making it the largest single attraction in any Disney theme park worldwide — big enough to fit the entire Magic Kingdom inside with room to spare for a herd of giraffes!

90. c.) *Peter Pan's Flight*
As you exit Wendy's bedroom window, you fly over Nana the dog, who is barking at the sight of an airborne boat flying out of a little girl's bedroom.

91. a.) *Ellen's Energy Adventure*
During the pre-show, when Ellen's neighbor comes in to borrow some items for an experiment, she tells him to ". . .take whatever you need. I don't wanna miss any of the game."

92. b.) *Rock 'n' Roller Coaster*
The high-speed launch of your limo on the *Rock 'n' Roller Coaster* takes you from zero to 60 mph in just 2.8 seconds. That blows away *Test Track's* 0 to 60 mark of 8.8 seconds.

93. c.) *Spaceship Earth*
OK, I can hear some of you screaming that *Tower of Terror* is the tallest attraction. Let me explain: Although the top of the *Spaceship Earth* sphere reaches only 180 feet above the ground, you forgot about the Mickey hand and wand that was attached to the structure in 1999. The tip of the wand is 257 feet above the ground, far higher than the 199-foot *Tower of Terror*. And if you notice, the tip of the wand features a number of flashing red lights to comply with FAA (Federal Aviation Administration) regulations requiring same on any structure over 200 feet tall. SO, technically, (though not "officially")

Spaceship Earth is the tallest attraction on property.

94. d.) *The Twilight Zone Tower of Terror*
References to Mickey are hidden throughout the attraction. Most people will be able to spot the 1930s' doll held by the little girl getting into the elevator. But can you find references to the Main Mouse in the sheet music in the Library . . . and the Hidden Mickey outside the hotel itself?

95. c.) *Blizzard Beach*
At 120-feet tall, Summit Plummet in *Blizzard Beach* water park is the world's tallest and fastest free-fall water slide. You can reach speeds of up to 60 mph as you drop from the "ski jump" tower on Mount Gushmore straight down to a splash landing at the base of the mountain!

96. c.) *Dinosaur*
The Time Rover is a 12-passenger all terrain vehicle that takes you back through time and space to rescue a dinosaur.

97. c.) *9*
In Circle-Vision attractions, guests are required to stand so that they can easily turn to view all nine screens in the full 360 degrees.

98. b.) **Digital Animation Control System**

The Digital Animation Control System, or DACS, located in the tunnels below the Magic Kingdom, controls the movements, speech, and expressions of the more than 1,600 Audio-Animatronics figures in the park, as well as the sound effects and background music that are synchronized with them. That adds up to more than 72,000 individual functions every second. As if that weren't enough, the system also is responsible for the park's lighting systems, fire detection system, and security systems, as well as opening theater doors.

99. b.) Disney's Polynesian Resort
Disney's Polynesian Resort opened with the Magic Kingdom on October 1, 1971. It has 11 guest room buildings, known as "longhouses," and a main building, known as the Great Ceremonial House. When the longhouses were named, all were given Pacific island-related names (some real, some imaginary). The longhouses were renamed on October 28, 1999, so that the buildings would be in approximately the same geographical relationship to one another as the islands they're named after: Tonga, Niue, Samoa, Tahiti, Rapa Nui, Tokelau, Hawaii, Rarotonga, Aotearoa, Fiji, and Tuvalu. Don't believe me? Take a map of the South Pacific and lay it over a map of the Polynesian Resort to see the correspondence. Niue, by the way, is

located next to the Great Ceremonial House and is the smallest building at the Polynesian Resort.

100. c.) It is awarded to needy families in the Orlando area
All of the money collected from the fountains in WDW is given to DisneyHand, "The Worldwide Outreach for the Walt Disney Company," which uses it to serve needy families in the Orlando area. In fact, you'll see a sign in each of the WDW fountains that reads: "Your Wishes Will Help Us To make Dreams Come True... Thanks for your contribution to DisneyHand - The Worldwide Outreach for the Walt Disney Company."

101. d.) Rainbow Falls
All of the other "features" can be found in WDW. Can you locate them? Hint: "Catastrophe Canyon" is found in Disney-MGM Studios; "Chickapin Hill" in Magic Kingdom, and "Ketchakiddie Creek" in the *Typhoon Lagoon* water park.

102. c.) New York Street in Disney-MGM Studios
Get it? "lacks" security?

103. c.) *Horizons*
Horizons was the first (and arguably only) attraction in WDW where guests could actually choose how the ride was going to end - by water, space, or land.

104. d.) *Peter Pan's Flight*

As you leave the attic scene in *The Haunted Mansion*, your Doombuggy turns backwards as you descend the roof outside to the graveyard. In *Maelstrom* in Epcot's Norway pavilion, you encounter mischievous trolls as you enter the mythical forest. They cast a curse on the boat that causes it to head downriver — backwards. In Epcot's *Spaceship Earth*, as your vehicle reaches the top of the sphere, you will see thousands of stars projected onto the ceiling as your car turns and you begin to descend the sphere backwards towards the exit.

105. b.) *Space Mountain*

Space Mountain opened January 15, 1975, as part of the expansion of the Magic Kingdom's (MK's) Tomorrowland. *Big Thunder Mountain Railroad* opened in Frontierland September 23, 1980, (but celebrated its Grand Opening over a month later on November 15). Disney-MGM Studios' *Rock 'n' Roller Coaster* opened August 1, 1999, while *Primeval Whirl*, in Disney's Animal Kingdom, opened March 18, 2002.

106. d.) The Coral Reef restaurant in Epcot's *The Living Seas*

One of the finest dining experiences in the entire Walt Disney World Resort, the undersea atmosphere of the Coral Reef restaurant complements its excellent food and exceptional

service. (It's very important that you leave enough room for dessert. Be sure to try the "Chocolate Wave" — a warm chocolate cake with white chocolate center, melted cream filling, and dried-cherry compote.)

107. c.) *Ellen's Energy Adventure*

The ride vehicles in *Ellen's Energy Adventure* weigh more than 30,000 pounds each (not including the 96 passengers) but are guided along the concrete floor by a wire only 1/8-inch thick!

108. a.) *The American Adventure*

"Andy" is Andrew Carnegie. In the scene in which you view the Great Hall in Philadelphia — where hundreds of inventions were introduced — four stages rise up. From left to right, you see Mark Twain, Alexander Graham Bell, Andrew Carnegie, and Susan B. Anthony. Andrew Carnegie boasts how Carnegie Steel built Carnegie Hall, but Mark Twain says that Carnegie Hall will never last. Donating libraries, though, is a good idea according to Twain.

109. a.) A proposed ride through the movies in Epcot

Originally planned for Future World as a ride through famous Hollywood movie scenes, the *Movie Pavilion* ended up being the inspiration for what would become Disney-MGM Studios. In addition to featuring great moments from classic films such as *The Wizard of Oz* and *Casablanca*, the proposed *Movie Pavilion* was to have housed a second attraction, *Mickey's Movieland*. Developed by legendary Disney animator Ward Kimball, this would have featured Audio-Animatronics figures giving a behind-the-scenes history of classic Mickey Mouse cartoons. However, not long after they took over as the "head mice" at Disney, CEO Michael Eisner and President Frank Wells met with the Walt Disney Imagineers, who agreed that the possibilities for a movies-based attraction could not be fully explored in just one pavilion. It was at that point that Eisner suggested creating an entire theme park around the idea. . . And Disney-MGM Studios was born.

110. b.) 99

WDW boasts 99 holes on one 9-hole golf course and five championship 18-hole courses (several of them designed by world-renowned architects Tom Fazio and Pete Dye). WDW is home to the PGA Tour's FUNAI Classic and has been recognized three times as a Gold Medal Resort by Golf Magazine. It is one of Florida's largest golf resorts.

111. b.) 1901

Information regarding Walt Disney's personal history can be found throughout WDW. One of the best and most entertaining sources is *Walt Disney - One Man's Dream* in Disney-MGM Studios. During the walk-through exhibit and film, you will learn that Walter Elias Disney was born December 5, 1901, in Chicago, Illinois. His father, Elias Disney, was an Irish-Canadian, while his mother, Flora Call Disney, was of German-American descent. He was one of five children, four boys and a girl. While he was still very young, his family moved to a farm near Marceline, Missouri. It was here that Walt cultivated his interest in art, selling some of his early drawings to neighbors when just seven years of age.

112. b.) *Cranium Command*

In the queue line for the pre-show movie in *Cranium Command*, you will see a sign commemorating inductees into the "Hall of Brains." Its members include Florence Nightingale, Isaac Newton, Shakespeare, Mozart, Thomas Edison, Henry Ford, Walt Disney, and Harry Houdini.

Did You Know?

MORE THAN 200 TOPIARY FIGURES ARE ON SHOW AT WDW.

113. c.) *Spaceship Earth*
More people ride *Spaceship Earth* every year than any other attraction in WDW. In fact, it is the most popular theme park attraction in the entire world, with more riders every year than any other ride in any other park, anywhere.

114. c.) *The Haunted Mansion*
In order of opening, it's *The Haunted Mansion*, *Space Mountain*, *Splash Mountain*, and *Tower of Terror*. Magic Kingdom's *The Haunted Mansion* opened with Walt Disney World on October 1, 1971. *Space Mountain* followed, taking guests on their first "flights" on January 15, 1975. Frontierland's *Splash Mountain* opened on October 2,1992, followed by *Tower of Terror* on July 22, 1994, in Disney-MGM Studios.

115. b.) Disney's Pop Century Resort
Located near Disney's Wide World of Sports Complex, Disney's Pop Century Resort is divided into two sections, the Classic and the Legendary Years. They are separated by "Hourglass Lake" and connected by "Generation Gap Bridge."

116. c.) A sea serpent
For many years, a giant sea serpent has been found in the Magic Kingdom, "guarding" the canals surrounding Cinderella Castle. Need help finding him? (Come on. . . he's a big dragon made out of plants!

How can you miss him?) OK, go to the end of Main Street and take a right at the Plaza Ice Cream Parlor. Look on the grass near the edge of the water, and there you'll find this partially submerged sea creature.

117. d.) Downtown Disney
When Walt Disney announced his "Florida Project" in 1965, he envisioned turning desolate swampland in central Florida into the world's greatest vacation resort, as well as a "city of the future." During a film presenting his "Master Plan" for the project, he referred to a wall-sized illustration of what he and his Imagineers envisioned. Part of this plan included an ice rink, a domed roller-rink, and his signature theme park, Magic Kingdom.

118. a.) *The Haunted Mansion*
The Haunted Mansion is the only attraction to be found in a different themed land in each of the four Disney theme parks worldwide. It is located in Liberty Square at WDW, New Orleans Square at Disneyland, Fantasyland at Tokyo Disneyland, and Frontierland at Disneyland Paris.

119. b.) Central Shops
The Walt Disney World Resort is truly a world unto itself. It has its own government, phone systems, power plants, and transportation system. So where do you think it goes when it needs something built?

Exactly — right to its own backyard. Central Shops is located just north of the Magic Kingdom. It is here, in this 300,000-square-foot manufacturing facility, that the magic is made — literally. If you visit (you can, but only if you take the 7.5 hour "Backstage Magic" behind-the-scenes tour), you might find recently repainted *Peter Pan's Flight* ride cars, signs for a new attraction, character costumes, carousel horses, park decorations, cars, boats, buses, or even some Audio-Animatronics figures in need of repair. The sign over the building's entrance sums it up well: "Home of Excellence."

120. b.) Disney's Animal Kingdom
At over 500 acres, Disney's Animal Kingdom is not only the largest WDW theme park, but the largest theme park Disney has ever created. It is almost five times the size of WDW's Magic Kingdom and 40 percent larger than Epcot, which is approximately 300 acres. In contrast, California's Disneyland is about 160 acres and Tokyo Disneyland, about 115 acres.

121. d.) *Kali River Rapids*
Disney's Coronado Springs Resort's main pool has a five-story Mayan pyramid towering over it. Mexico's pavilion is shaped like an Aztec-inspired pyramid, while the Imagination! pavilion's structure contains two impressive glass pyramids.

122. b.) *Mission: SPACE*
After your ship makes its emergency landing, Misson Control comes in over the intercom and warns you not to move a muscle or the ship will fall over the cliff it's delicately balanced on.

123. b.) *Pirates of the Caribbean*
During the auction scene on the port (left) side of your boat, you will notice a banner offering some of the town's ladies for auction. Originally the banner read, "Take a Wench for a Wife," but it was changed to "Buy a Bride" during the ride's "politically correct" rehab of 1999.

124. c.) *Tom Sawyer Island*
You can explore Harper's Mill on this island in the Magic Kingdom, along with caves, bridges, and trails.

125. b.) *The Enchanted Tiki Room – Under New Management*
During Iago's rendition of "Friend Like Me" from the *Aladdin* soundtrack, he says that the other birds will have him to thank when the guests start linin' up at the door.

126. a.) 5 days
The "refurbishment" required to turn *If You Had Wings* into *If You Could Fly* was little more than removing any reference to Eastern Airlines, the original sponsor by changing the signs and the theme song.

127. d.) *Honey, I Shrunk the Audience*

During the pre-show (presented by Kodak), guests view a montage of photographs while Cyndi Lauper's "True Colors" plays in the background. The images are a tribute to the imagination and include inspirational sayings such as, "Take risks," "Expect the Unexpected," and "Look at the world from a different angle."

128. a.) Restaurant in Fantasyland

Located near Ariel's Grotto, Scuttle's Landing is THE place to get Frozen Coca-Cola and caramel corn!

129. b.) Epcot

During initial testing (long before the attraction opened to guests), one of *Test Track's* empty ride vehicles flipped off its track. Consequently, the Imagineers designed and installed a computer system in each ride car that fits into a cooler-sized compartment yet is so powerful each one could run all the rides and shows in the Magic Kingdom!

130. d.) *The Haunted Mansion*

There may be 999 happy haunts, but only 109 of them are Disney-created Audio-Animatronics figures!

131. c.) A failed wave-making machine

A failed wave-making machine, built off the southern shore of Beach-comber Isle near Disney's Polynesian Resort, was scuttled on the bottom of Seven Seas Lagoon. While original plans called for the machine to make waves large enough for surfing, the waves caused such massive beach erosion that the machine was shut down. It now serves as a reef for fish.

132. c.) *Kilimanjaro Safaris*

Near the end of your journey, you come upon a Game Warden who has successfully captured the poachers and let's you know that the elephant known as "Little Red" is okay.

133. b.) Epcot

You can enter Epcot through the main entrance or via the International Gateway in World Showcase. Located between the United Kingdom and France pavilions, this "back gate" allows guests of the Epcot Resorts (Disney's BoardWalk Inn, Yacht Club, and Beach Club as well as the WDW Swan and Dolphin) to walk or take a Friendship boat directly from the BoardWalk to Epcot.

134. b.) Private in-room baby-sitting

"Kids Nite Out" provides supervised childcare that includes nightly entertainment and an activity center for kids. It also offers in-room childcare and baby-sitting facilities for children between 6 weeks and 12 years of age. The staff is licensed, and the service is sanctioned and approved by Disney.

135. a.) *Test Track*
During the Environmental Chamber Test, Bill (who's up in the GM Control Room) asks Sherry if she remembered to turn off the robots.

136. c.) *Rock 'n' Roller Coaster Starring Aerosmith*
As you travel in this rockin' indoor roller coaster, your limo drives by giant road signs, such as a Santa Monica Blvd. freeway sign and one that reads "Corkscrew Ahead."

137. c.) *Journey Into Imagination*
The Sherman Brothers' song "One Little Spark" was heard in the original *Journey Into Imagination* attraction, which ran from March 5, 1983, until October 10, 1998. Sung by the Dreamfinder and Figment, it was one of the most memorable songs in all of WDW. The song and the characters were removed when the ride closed for renovation in 1998, but when the new (and not very popular) ride closed for a second "renovation" in 2002, Figment and "One Little Spark" were reinstated.

138. d.) *Spaceship Earth*
Sophocles' *Oedipus Rex*, written in about 428 B.C., is "performed" (in part) hundreds of times a day by Audio-Animatronics figures during the Greek theater scene in Epcot's *Spaceship Earth*.

139. c.) Disney-MGM Studios
Dinosaur Gertie's Ice Cream of Extinction is a snack stand located on Echo Lake in Disney-MGM Studios. It offers delicious soft-serve ice cream.

140. a.) *Astro Orbiter*
Located in Tomorrowland in the Magic Kingdom, *Astro Orbiter* travels clockwise.

141. d.) Town Square Exposition Hall on Main Street, U.S.A.
Let's have a moment of silence for the dearly departed *Mr. Toad's Wild Ride*. . . If you miss the ride (like many of us do), you can still find one of the original ride cars in a back corner of Town Square Exposition Hall, on the right side of Main Street as you enter the Magic Kingdom. It doesn't do anything but sit there, but it's a nice place to take a picture because you can hop inside. Although most people walk right by the Exposition Hall, you may want to stop in. It offers lots of photo ops in addition to the Toad car, and it's a nice place to sit and rest in the air conditioning while watching old Mickey Mouse cartoons.

142. b.) *Jim Henson's Muppet Vision 3D*
Only in *MuppetVision 3D* are the

3D glasses called "3D Glasses." *It's Tough to be a Bug!* in Disney's Animal Kingdom's calls them "Honorary Bug Eyes"; *Honey, I Shrunk the Audience* in Epcot calls them "Safety Goggles"; *Mickey's PhilharMagic* in the Magic Kingdom calls them "Opera Glasses."

143. c.) *Maelstrom*
As your narrator takes you into the land of forests and mystery, where trolls still prowl the waters edge, you are spotted by three trolls. They cast a spell on you and cause you to "disappear, disappear... over the falls!"

144. d.) *Pirates of the Caribbean*
The Torre del Cielo ("Tower of the Sky") stands near the entrance to *Pirates of the Caribbean* in Caribbean Plaza. Near the top of this tall tower, you will find a working clock.

145. a.) West Center Street
West Center Street, a side street off the Magic Kingdom's Main Street, U.S.A., was removed when the Emporium shop expanded in 2001. The street was home to Main Street Flower Market, the original Harmony Barber Shop, Livery Stable, and Champion Cyclery, among others.

146. c.) *The American Adventure*
This line is from "New World Bound," a song heard near the beginning of *The American Adventure*. Another wonderful tune from the team of X. Atencio and Buddy Baker, it tells of the Pilgrims' sail to the New World: "You'd think that these landlubbers never would last, This cargo of pilgrims twelve week 'fore the mast. It's land ho, me hearties, at last we've arrived, And praise be to God nearly all have survived."

147. b.) Rafiki's Planet Watch
Rafiki's Planet Watch can only be accessed via the Wildlife Express train in the Africa section of Disney's Animal Kingdom. Once there, you can learn about worldwide conservation efforts, visit a veterinary medical center, journey through outdoor discovery trails, and get up close and personal with friendly animals in a petting yard.

148. d.) *The Many Adventures of Winnie the Pooh*
The legendary Sherman Brothers wrote "Heffalumps and Woozles" in 1968 for the animated *Winnie the Pooh* film, and Buddy Baker arranged the tune. When Baker stated that he wanted silly, crazy sounds in the music, along with the normal orchestra sound, Richard Sherman suggested using a kazoo and ended up playing it for the film score recording. So when Baker re-recorded the score for the WDW attraction, he brought along a kazoo and Sherman played it once again!

CHAPTER TWO

Magic Kingdom

1. It was estimated that 100,000 people would attend Opening Day at the Magic Kingdom in 1971. About how many actually showed up?
- a.) 100,000
- b.) 10,000
- c.) 187,000
- d.) 211,000

2. What color are the walkways as you enter the Magic Kingdom?
- a.) Gray
- b.) White
- c.) Red
- d.) Red, White and Blue

3. About how many Audio-Animatronics figures are there in the Magic Kingdom?

a.) 350
b.) 775
c.) 999
d.) 1,100

4. What person or character is depicted in flowers in front of the train station at the entrance to the Magic Kingdom?
a.) Walt Disney
b.) Mickey and Minnie
c.) Mickey
d.) It varies

5. Who appears in the Magic Kingdom to find the "Temporary Ruler of The Realm"?
a.) Merlin
b.) Sorcerer Mickey
c.) Mickey Mouse
d.) The Genie from *Aladdin*

6. What real-life castle served as one of the inspirations for Cinderella Castle?
a.) Neuschwanstein Castle in Bavaria
b.) Windsor Castle in England
c.) Buckingham Palace in England
d.) Linderhof Castle in Germany

7. How does Magic Kingdom compare in size to Epcot?
a.) Epcot and Magic Kingdom are approximately the same size
b.) Magic Kingdom is about one-third the size of Epcot

c.) Magic Kingdom is twice as large as Epcot
d.) Magic Kingdom is about one-tenth the size of Epcot

8. What is the name of the body of water in front of the Magic Kingdom?
a.) Bay Lake
b.) Discovery Lake
c.) Seven Seas Lagoon
d.) Echo Lake

9. Underneath the Magic Kingdom is a series of underground service corridors used by Cast Members to move around the park. What are they called?
a.) Magic Kingdom Caverns
b.) Utilidors
c.) The Kingdom Corridors
d.) Utilitunnels

10. What is the oldest "mountain" in the Magic Kingdom?
a.) *Splash Mountain*
b.) *Space Mountain*
c.) *Big Thunder Mountain*
d.) *Mount Liberty*

11. During the Opening Day Parade for the Magic Kingdom, the band that played contained how many pieces?
a.) 1,076
b.) 200
c.) 999
d.) 429

12. What secret can be found on each of the floats in the *Share a Dream Come True Parade?*
- a.) There is a hidden Mickey on each of the floats.
- b.) There is a hidden Walt on each of the floats.
- c.) They are all remote controlled by a Cast Member standing among the crowds.
- d.) They all have an American flag painted on them.

13. Which of these attractions was NOT an "E-Ticket" attraction on the park's opening day?
- a.) *Pirates of the Caribbean*
- b.) *The Haunted Mansion*
- c.) *20,000 Leagues Under the Sea*
- d.) *Jungle Cruise*

14. What is the name of the large bronze statute of Walt and Mickey in front of Cinderella Castle?
- a.) Friends
- b.) Father and Son
- c.) Partners
- d.) Magic

15. If you travel through Cinderella Castle to the back exit, what land would you be in?
- a.) Fantasyland
- b.) Liberty Square
- c.) Adventureland
- d.) Tomorrowland

16. Where can you play checkers in the Magic Kingdom?

Did You Know?

THERE IS A FLAG RETREAT CEREMONY EVERY DAY ON MAIN STREET, U.S.A. VETERANS WHO'D LIKE TO PARTICIPATE CAN INQUIRE AT CITY HALL.

- a.) Frontierland
- b.) *Walt Disney World Railroad* station on Main Street, U.S.A.
- c.) Fantasyland
- d.) Columbia Harbor House

17. Which of these attractions closed exactly five years after the same attraction closed in Disneyland?
- a.) *20,000 Leagues Under the Sea*
- b.) *Mr. Toad's Wild Ride*
- c.) *Skyway*
- d.) *Mike Fink Keelboats*

18. Upon entering the Magic Kingdom, what is the first full-service restaurant you come across?
a.) Pecos Bill's Cafe
b.) Crystal Palace
c.) Tony's Town Square Restaurant
d.) The Plaza Restaurant

19. What attraction is located inside Cinderella Castle?
a.) *Cinderella's Ball*
b.) *Mickey's PhilharMagic*
c.) There is no attraction inside the Castle.
d.) *Cinderella's Golden Carrousel*

20. How many sets of stairs are there from the underground service corridors below the Magic Kingdom to the park above?
a.) 9
b.) 18
c.) 29
d.) 33

21. What is the largest living thing in the Magic Kingdom?
a.) The Liberty Tree in Liberty Square
b.) The *Swiss Family Treehouse*
c.) A Mickey Mouse topiary in the Central Plaza
d.) The guy in front of you at the Crystal Palace buffet

22. Who plays the drums in the *SpectroMagic* parade?
a.) Mickey
b.) Goofy
c.) Buzz Lightyear
d.) Woody

23. What is said to have prompted Walt Disney to design the underground corridors in the Magic Kingdom?
a.) While in Disneyland, he saw a Frontierland Cast Member dressed as a Sheriff walking through Tomorrowland.
b.) He did not want utility buildings and offices to be seen by Guests.

Did You Know?

TO KEEP THE 200 OR SO PROPS IN *THE HAUNTED MANSION* LOOKING UNTOUCHED AND DUSTY, DISNEY BUYS FIVE-POUND BAGS OF THEATRICAL DUST, KNOWN AS "FULLER'S EARTH," IN LARGE QUANTITIES. IT HAS LONG BEEN RUMORED THAT ENOUGH DUST HAS BEEN USED SINCE THE ATTRACTION'S OPENING IN 1971 TO BURY THE MANSION COMPLETELY!

c.) He did not want Cast Members to eat with Guests.

d.) He wanted a secure area to store the cash that was taken in during the day.

24. How many gallons of water are there in the moat surrounding Cinderella Castle?
a.) 3,370
b.) 33,370
c.) 3,370,000
d.) 33,370,00

25. Which of these Magic Kingdom attractions has the longest ride?
a.) *The Haunted Mansion*
b.) *Splash Mountain*
c.) *Big Thunder Mountain Railroad*
d.) *Liberty Square Riverboat*

26. What is the "Laughin' Place"?
a.) The Penny Arcade on Main Street, U.S.A.
b.) The stage show at the Galaxy Palace Theater in Tomorrowland
c.) A shop outside of *Splash Mountain*
d.) A children's playground near *Splash Mountain's* exit

27. "Mickey's Birthdayland" opened June 18, 1988, to commemorate?
a.) Walt Disney's 100th birthday
b.) Mickey Mouse's 60th birthday

c.) The opening of EPCOT
d.) The 30th Anniversary of Disneyland

28. What Magic Kingdom attraction was first built at WDW, then later copied at Disneyland in California?
a.) *Space Mountain*
b.) *Big Thunder Mountain Railroad*
c.) *Country Bear Jamboree*
d.) *The Haunted Mansion*

29. Cinderella Castle is made of how many stones?
a.) 365,000
b.) About 1 million
c.) Over 2 million
d.) None; it is made of fiberglass.

30. Which of these characters does NOT and never did have either a shop or a merchandise cart named after him/her?
a.) Madame Leota
b.) Big Al
c.) Winnie the Pooh
d.) Peter Pan

31. What happened to Cinderella Castle in 1997?
a.) It was hit by lightning and a fire broke out in one of the spires
b.) It was hit by a hurricane, damaging some areas of the facade and forcing Disney to close the castle to Guests

Did You Know?

IN *THE HALL OF PRESIDENTS*, FRANKLIN DELANO ROOSEVELT'S FIGURE IS SO DETAILED, THAT IF YOU LOOK CLOSELY, YOU CAN SEE THE BRACES ON HIS LEGS.

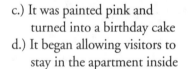

c.) It was painted pink and turned into a birthday cake

d.) It began allowing visitors to stay in the apartment inside

32. The service corridors underneath the Magic Kingdom connect all of the themed lands except?

a.) Fantasyland

b.) Tomorrowland

c.) Mickey's Toontown Fair

d.) You can access each themed area of the park from the tunnels

33. Which of these rides is unlike the others?

a.) *Dumbo the Flying Elephant*

b.) *Astro Orbiter*

c.) *Magic Carpets of Aladdin*

d.) *Peter Pan's Flight*

34. Can you name the area near Cinderella Castle where Belle reads stories to Guests?

a.) Fairytale Garden

b.) Belle's Magic Garden

c.) Ariel's Grotto

d.) Fantasyland Theater

35. What Disney Legend was given the task of designing what became Cinderella Castle?
a.) X. Astencio
b.) Herb Ryman
c.) John Hench
d.) Robert A.M. Stern

36. In which of these lands can you find an arcade?
a.) Fantasyland
b.) Main Street, U.S.A.
c.) Adventureland
d.) Tomorrowland

37. What is the name of the nighttime fireworks display that replaced *Fantasy in the Sky* in October 2003?
a.) *Wishes*
b.) *DreamScapes*
c.) *SpectroMagic*
d.) *Remember the Magic*

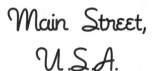

38. What is significant about the windows atop the shops on Main Street, U.S.A.?
a.) They are actually made of plastic, not glass.
b.) Most shield hidden cameras that monitor activity on Main Street.
c.) They contain the names of

Walt Disney Imagineers and others who contributed to WDW in some way.
d.) There are corporate offices behind them.

39. When is the *WDW Railroad* closed to guests?
a.) When it is raining
b.) During the fireworks displays
c.) Between Christmas and New Year's Day
d.) On Sundays

40. How many stops were on the *WDW Railroad* when it opened?
a.) 1
b.) 2
c.) 3
d.) 4

41. What takes place every day at 5:00 p.m. in Town Square?
a.) A parade
b.) Mickey and Minnie come out to sign autographs
c.) A flag ceremony
d.) The barbershop quartet comes out

42. Which restaurant on Main Street, U.S.A. has the same name as a restaurant in one of Disney's animated features?
a.) The Crystal Palace
b.) Casey's Corner
c.) Tony's Town Square Restaurant
d.) The Plaza Diner

43. The Fire House on Main Street, U.S.A. is Number?
  a.) 1
  b.) 71
  c.) 1971
  d.) 999

44. What energy source powers the *WDW Railroad?*
  a.) Wood
  b.) Electricity
  c.) Gas
  d.) Oil

45. Where are the horses that pull the trolleys on Main Street kept?
  a.) In a stable behind Adventureland
  b.) Near Rafiki's Planet Watch in Disney's Animal Kingdom
  c.) Disney's Fort Wilderness Resort
  d.) Off property in a stable used exclusively by Disney

Adventureland

46. How many Audio-Animatronics figures are there on the *Jungle Cruise?*
  a.) None
  b.) 9
  c.) 27
  d.) 47

47. Who provides the voice of "Zazu" in *Mickey's PhilharMagic?*

  a.) Paul Reubens
  b.) Robin Williams
  c.) Rowan Atkinson
  d.) Michael Gough

48. Where were the spitting camels at *The Magic Carpets of Aladdin* ride first used or seen in WDW?
  a.) In a parade
  b.) As decorations in a restaurant
  c.) The entrance to Adventureland
  d.) In the *Backlot Tour* at Disney-MGM Studios

49. On the loading dock of *Jungle Cruise* there is an advertisement for a tour company. What is its name?
  a.) Lotus Tours
  b.) Soupy Sails
  c.) Nile River Cruises
  d.) Jungle Cruise Tours

50. Two pirate skeletons are playing what game in *Pirates of the Caribbean?*
  a.) Checkers
  b.) Chess
  c.) Poker
  d.) Golf

51. What is the "Fuente de Fortuna"?
  a.) The pirate ship in *Pirates of the Caribbean*
  b.) The gift shop in Caribbean Plaza
  c.) A fountain near *Pirates of the Caribbean*
  d.) A drink in the Mexico pavilion in Epcot

52. Guests can pilot their own miniature version of the *Jungle Cruise* boats in what Adventureland attraction?

    a.) *Shrunken Ned's Junior Jungle Boats*

    b.) *Bwana Bob's Boats*

    c.) *El Pirata Y El Perico*

    d.) *Pilots of the Caribbean*

53. Who or what sits atop the center column of *The Magic Carpets of Aladdin* ride?

    a.) The Genie

    b.) The Genie's lamp

    c.) A Spitting Camel

    d.) Apu

54. According to the theme song from *Pirates of the Caribbean,* the pirates, "Kidnap and ravage and ..."

    a.) "even hijack"

    b.) "pillage and plunder"

    c.) "don't give a hoot"

    d.) "drink up me 'earties, yo ho"

55. In the *Swiss Family Treehouse,* what is the bathroom sink made out of?

Did You Know?

THE RIVER IN *JUNGLE CRUISE* IS ACTUALLY DYED BROWN TO GIVE IT AN AUTHENTIC LOOK. IF IT WEREN'T, GUESTS COULD SEE THAT THE "RIVER" IS ONLY 3.5 FEET DEEP.

•

THE ISLANDS YOU PASS ON THE *JUNGLE CRUISE* ARE CALLED CATALINA AND MANHATTAN.

a.) A barrel
b.) A clamshell
c.) A hollow tree
d.) Bamboo

56. What other Magic Kingdom attraction is mentioned during Iago's exit spiel in _The Enchanted Tiki Room – Under New Management?_
a.) *The Haunted Mansion*
b.) *The Hall of Presidents*
c.) *Splash Mountain*
d.) *Swiss Family Treehouse*

57. _Jungle Cruise_ was inspired by?
a.) The movie *The African Queen*
b.) A documentary called *The African Lion*
c.) An attraction Walt saw during the 1964-65 World's Fair
d.) *Tarzan*

58. The _Swiss Family Treehouse_ contains about how many man-made leaves?
a.) 1 million
b.) 100,000
c.) 300,000
d.) 30,000

59. In the opening song of _The Enchanted Tiki Room – Under New Management,_ Iago mentions how many crackers he has in the bank. How many does he have?
a.) A million
b.) A billion
c.) A zillion
d.) A whole lotta

60. What is the name of the private club that can be found near WDW's _Pirates of the Caribbean?_
a.) Club 33
b.) Pirate's Club
c.) Adventurers Club
d.) There is no private club

61. As you ride the _Walt Disney World Railroad_ and pass through Adventureland, you will notice an outpost on the right side of the train. What is the name of the outpost?
a.) Adventurer's Outpost
b.) Desperation
c.) Imagination
d.) Bwana Bob's

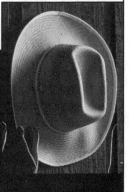

Did You Know?

THE VOICE OF BIG AL IN THE
COUNTRY BEAR JAMBOREE
WAS PERFORMED BY NONE OTHER THAN
TEX RITTER, ONE OF THE BEST-KNOWN
SINGING COWBOYS IN WESTERNS.

Frontierland

62. How much did it cost to build *Big Thunder Mountain Railroad*?
   a.) $3.9 million
   b.) $17 million
   c.) $33 million
   d.) $71 million

63. What is the name of the first drop on *Splash Mountain*?
   a.) Brer Bottom
   b.) Slippin' Falls
   c.) Zipp-A-Dee-Doo-Drop
   d.) Laughin' Falls

64. How many bears perform at the *Country Bear Jamboree*?
   a.) 8
   b.) 11
   c.) 15
   d.) 18

65. According to Cast Members, why should you ride *Big Thunder Mountain Railroad* in the late afternoon?
   a.) The cars are sped up 10%.
   b.) The lines are shorter because that's when people eat lunch.
   c.) The grease on the tracks is thinner thus your train goes faster.
   d.) There are more trains running which moves the lines along faster.

66. What song do the creaks and groans of Harper's Mill on *Tom Sawyer Island* play?
   a.) "Song of the South"
   b.) "Down by the Old Mill Stream"
   c.) "Zip-A-Dee-Doo-Dah"
   d.) "Swanee River"

67. Where does the action take place at the *Frontierland Shootin' Arcade?*
a.) Davey Jones' Locker
b.) Boot Hill
c.) The O.K. Corral
d.) Billy the Kidd's hideout

68. As you make your way through the line at *Big Thunder Mountain Railroad*, what company's "main building" do you enter?
a.) Tetak Logging Company
b.) Mojave Mining Co.
c.) Big Thunder Mining Co.
d.) MM Mining

69. When the attraction is running at full capacity, how many logs are running on the *Splash Mountain* ride at any given time?
a.) 15-17
b.) 20-25
c.) 40-44
d.) 50-54

70. What is the name of the rickety-feeling bridge that connects the two islands of *Tom Sawyer Island?*
a.) Langhorn Bridge
b.) Becky's Bridge
c.) Superstition Bridge
d.) Smuggler's Bridge

71. Where did the idea for the *Country Bear Jamboree* come from?
a.) Lillian Disney
b.) An idea Walt had for a ski resort

c.) A trip Walt and his family took to Canada
d.) A small theme park Walt visited as a child

72. Which of the following is the name of a cave located on *Tom Sawyer Island?*
a.) Huck Finn's Hideout
b.) Injun Joe's Cave
c.) Tom's Hideaway
d.) Big Al's Cavern

73. At the *Frontierland Shootin' Arcade*, what did the rifles shoot before they were refitted to use infrared beams of light?
a.) BBs
b.) Lead pellets
c.) Real bullets
d.) Soft foam balls

Liberty Square

74. In *The Haunted Mansion*, what is the first scene in which you see a ghost?
a.) The ballroom scene
b.) The attic
c.) The seance room
d.) The graveyard

75. How many lanterns hang from the Liberty Tree in Liberty Square?
a.) None
b.) 5
c.) 13
d.) 50

Did You Know?

THE *WDW RAILROAD* ENGINES GET A
WHOPPING 792 FEET PER GALLON OF GAS.

•

THE PORTRAIT IN THE FRONT FOYER IN
THE HAUNTED MANSION SLOWLY CHANGES AS THE MAN
IN THE PICTURE AGES. . . AND BADLY I MIGHT ADD.

---

76. Which of these U.S. Presidents recorded his own voice for *The Hall of Presidents?*
   a.) George H.W. Bush
   b.) Bill Clinton
   c.) Ronald Reagan
   d.) Gerald Ford

77. The illusion of ghosts in the ballroom of *The Haunted Mansion* is created by what technique?
   a.) Smoke and mirrors
   b.) Pepper's Ghost
   c.) Imagineerification
   d.) Ghosting

78. How deep is the "Rivers of America"?
   a.) 1 foot
   b.) 7 feet
   c.) 27 feet
   d.) 47 feet

79. Which of the following statements about Liberty Square is true?
   a.) It was part of Walt Disney's original plan for EPCOT

and was to have had actual residents.
   b.) It was initially conceived as a side street off of Disneyland's Main Street, U.S.A.
   c.) It was not supposed to have had any attractions, only *The Hall of Presidents*, shops, and restaurants
   d.) It was to have been a single attraction about the United States, similar to *The American Adventure* in Epcot.

80. How many ghosts "live" in *The Haunted Mansion?*
   a.) 9
   b.) 99
   c.) 999
   d.) 1001

81. What date is found on top of *The Hall of Presidents* building?
   a.) 1776
   b.) 1971
   c.) 1787
   d.) July 4

82. In *The Haunted Mansion*, when the room with portraits on the wall appears to "stretch," what is actually happening?
    a.) The floor lowers
    b.) The ceiling rises
    c.) Nothing — it is an optical illusion
    d.) The room moves clockwise

83. How much does the Liberty Tree in Liberty Square weigh?
    a.) 13 tons
    b.) 38 tons
    c.) 50 tons
    d.) 100 tons

84. Whose names are the tombstones in *The Haunted Mansion* cemetery?
    a.) Members of Walt Disney's family
    b.) No actual people — they were chosen because they were easy to rhyme
    c.) Walt Disney Imagineers who helped create the attraction
    d.) Pets of Disney Company employees

85. How many ride cars are there in *The Haunted Mansion?*
    a.) 71
    b.) 99
    c.) 160
    d.) 213

Fantasyland

86. What Disney character has a restaurant in Fantasyland, but not an attraction?
    a.) Buzz Lightyear
    b.) Snow White
    c.) Pinocchio
    d.) Winnie the Pooh

87. Who is waving "Good-bye" to you above the exit sign at *Snow White's Scary Adventures?*
    a.) Snow White
    b.) Dopey
    c.) Happy
    d.) All seven Dwarfs

88. In April 1997, the restaurant located in Cinderella Castle changed its name from:

Did You Know?

THE SINGING, ANIMATED PARROT ATOP THE ENTRANCE TO *PIRATES OF THE CARIBBEAN* IS NAMED PEGLEGGED PETE.

a.) Cinderella's Grand Feast
b.) King Stefan's Banquet Hall
c.) Cinderella's Royal Table
d.) King Stefan's Royal Feast

89. When did Mr. Toad's take his last Wild Ride?
a.) July 4, 1996
b.) December 31, 1998
c.) September 7, 1998
d.) October 1, 1998

90. According to the clock tower on *Peter Pan's Flight*, what time is it?
a.) 2:29
b.) 11:18
c.) 9:06
d.) 10:18

91. When was *Cinderella's Golden Carrousel* originally built and by what company?
a.) 1967 by Disney Imagineers
b.) 1917 by Philadelphia Toboggan Co.
c.) 1952 by WED Enterprises
d.) 1880 by Asbury Park Carousel Co.

92. In what type of vehicle do you ride on *Snow White's Scary Adventures?*
a.) A mine cart
b.) A log
c.) A boat
d.) A car

93. How many gallons of water does the 20,000 Leagues Under the Sea Lagoon in Fantasyland hold?
a.) 300,000 gallons
b.) 197,100 gallons
c.) 5.5 million gallons
d.) 11.5 million gallons

94. In *it's a small world,* what nation is represented by figures dressed as chess pieces?
a.) Italy
b.) England
c.) The U.S.
d.) Germany

95. Who or what is seen on the sign above the FastPass return times for *Peter Pan's Flight?*
a.) Captain Hook
b.) Peter Pan
c.) The Crocodile
d.) The Lost Boys

96. What year did *20,000 Leagues Under the Sea* close?
a.) 1993
b.) 1994
c.) 1995
d.) 1996

97. In *The Many Adventures of Winnie the Pooh,* you can find a picture of Mr. Toad giving a deed to the property to:
a.) Winnie the Pooh
b.) Owl
c.) Eeyore
d.) Piglet

98. Which attraction in Fantasyland is closest to Mickey's Toontown Fair?
a.) *Snow White's Scary Adventures*
b.) *Mad Tea Party*
c.) *Dumbo the Flying Elephant*
d.) *Peter Pan's Flight*

99. How many Audio-Animatronics children are in *it's a small world?*
a.) 999
b.) 289
c.) 553
d.) 199

100. What country did *Mr. Toad's Wild Ride* take you through?
a.) America
b.) England
c.) France
d.) Neverland

101. What were the puppets used in *Legend of the Lion King* called?
a.) Animaluppets
b.) Muppets
c.) Humanimals
d.) Audio-Animatronics figures

102. In the "white room" of *it's a small world,* a clown in a balloon is holding up a sign. What does the sign say?
a.) Hello
b.) Peace
c.) Help
d.) Bon Jour

103. What color is Nana's doghouse in *Peter Pan's Flight?*
a.) Blue
b.) Yellow
c.) Red
d.) Green

Mickey's Toontown Fair

104. At Mickey's house in Toontown, there is a Ping-Pong tournament in progress. What is unusual about the game?
a.) The paddles are shaped like Mickey, Donald, and Goofy heads.
b.) They are playing with a basketball.
c.) The score is "1,000,000 to 1,000,000."
d.) The ball is teetering on the top of the net.

105. Minnie Mouse is the editor and publisher of what magazine?
a.) "Disney Today"
b.) "Minnie's MousEars"
c.) "Minnie's Cartoon Country Living"
d.) "The Toontown Weekly Star"

106. What color is the fence at *Mickey's Country House?*
a.) White
b.) Yellow

c.) Red

d.) There is no fence.

107. Before *The Barnstormer at Goofy's Wiseacre Farm* was built, what stood in its place?

a.) A petting zoo

b.) A character meet-and-greet area

c.) Restrooms

d.) *Donald's Boat*

108. Pete's Garage in Mickey's Toontown Fair is:

a.) A restaurant

b.) A restroom

c.) A food station

d.) A storage facility

109. Who is Red Barns?

a.) A Toontown radio DJ

b.) The mayor of Toontown

c.) Mickey's cousin

d.) According to a sign in the train station, the conductor of the *WDW Railroad*

110. According to the book found on the coffee table in the living room of *Minnie's Country House*, what book did Minnie write?

a.) "Famous Mice in History"

b.) "Mickey and Me. . . the First 50 Years"

c.) "How To Win a Mouse in 10 Days"

d.) "Recipes by Minnie"

Did You Know?

KIDS WHO VISIT THE MAGIC KINGDOM ON THEIR BIRTHDAYS CAN STOP BY CITY HALL ON MAIN STREET, U.S.A. AND PICK UP A "TODAY IS MY BIRTHDAY" BUTTON! WEAR IT AND MANY CAST MEMBERS WILL GO WAY OUT OF THEIR WAY TO MAKE YOU FEEL EXTRA SPECIAL!

Tomorrowland

111. What was the original name of *The Timekeeper*?
a.) *Transportarium*
b.) *Magic Journeys*
c.) *Journey Through Time*
d.) *Centorium*

112. Which Tomorrowland attraction was in a development for ten years before it opened?
a.) *The ExtraTERRORestrial Alien Encounter*
b.) *Walt Disney's Carousel of Progress*
c.) *Space Mountain*
d.) *WEDway PeopleMover*

113. In *Walt Disney's Carousel of Progress*, what is the name of the video game they are playing in the last scene?
a.) Space Ranger Spin
b.) Space Pilot
c.) Star Patrol
d.) Alien Encounter

114. How fast do the cars on the *Tomorrowland Indy Speedway* go?
a.) 7 mph
b.) 15 mph
c.) 25 mph
d.) 0 mph — it is a virtual reality ride

115. What powers the *Tomorrowland Transit Authority*?

a.) Solar energy using solar panels on the rooftops of Tomorrowland buildings
b.) Steam engines
c.) Electricity
d.) Propane gas

116. How many laser cannons are there in each ride vehicle on *Buzz Lightyear's Space Ranger Spin*?
a.) 1
b.) 2
c.) 4
d.) 6

117. Which of these was operating on Opening Day?
a.) *Grand Prix Raceway*
b.) *Space Mountain*
c.) *WEDway PeopleMover*
d.) *Star Jets*

118. In 1995, *Astro Orbiter* opened as a new attraction in the New Tomorrowland. What was the name of the original attraction?
a.) *Rocket Jets*
b.) *Astro-Jets*
c.) *Mission to Mars*
d.) *Star Jets*

THE ANSWERS
TO CHAPTER TWO

1. b.) 10,000
Fearing traffic jams and overcrowding, and fueled by media hype, people stayed away from the park on its opening day, making the Florida State Troopers who had been brought in to control traffic jams unnecessary. In November, however, Florida experienced the worst traffic jam in its history, as nearby Interstate 4 was backed up for miles by would-be Disney visitors.

2. c.) Red
Walt Disney wanted his Disney World Guests to feel as if they were entering a movie theater and that everything inside was part of the "show." In keeping with this idea, he wanted his Guests to feel as though Disney was laying down the "Red Carpet" for them. Thus the red walkways at the main entrance to the MK. (And that's also why everyone who works there is "onstage" and part of the "Cast" at all times.)

3. d.) 1,100
There are about 1,100 Audio-Animatronics figures in the Magic Kingdom, all controlled from a central location. The total for all four theme parks is close to 2,000.

4. c.) Mickey
Mickey's face is composed of multicolored flowers in a flower bed in front of the Main Street Train Station.

5. a.) Merlin
Presided over by Merlin the Magician, the Sword in the Stone Ceremony takes place several times daily in Fantasyland in the area behind Cinderella Castle and in front of *Cinderella's Golden Carrousel*. A child is chosen from the audience to pull the magical sword, Excalibur, from the stone. He or she is then appointed "temporary ruler of the realm."

6. a.) Neuschwanstein Castle in Bavaria
Cinderella Castle, the majestic icon of the Magic Kingdom, was inspired by a number of castles and architectural styles, including the French castles and chateaux of Fontainebleau, Versailles, Chenonceau, Chambord, Chaumont, and Usse. In fact, French writer Charles Perrault, the author of the original "Sleeping Beauty" and "Cinderella" (also known as "The Little Glass Slipper"), was said to have been inspired by Usse, the "chateau of dreams," for his fables.

Disney's designers also borrowed a large number of elements from King Ludwig II's Neuschwanstein (or "New Swan Stone") Castle in Bavaria, Germany. Like Neuschwanstein, Cinderella Castle fuses several architectural elements. In the case of Cinderella Castle, the base resembles a 13th century medieval fortress, while the upper portion is lighter and more delicate like a Renaissance palace. In addition to being an inspiration for Cinderella Castle, Neuschwanstein was one of the models for Sleeping Beauty Castle in Disneyland and the castle in the animated film, *Sleeping Beauty.*

7. b.) Magic Kingdom is about one-third the size of Epcot.

Magic Kingdom occupies an area of just 107 acres, while Epcot covers about 300 acres. That means that you could almost fit three Magic Kingdoms inside of Epcot!

8. c.) Seven Seas Lagoon
Disney's Polynesian and Grand Floridian Resorts also face the man-made Seven Seas Lagoon.

9. b.) Utilidors
OK. . . so what are the Utilidors anyway? Simply put, "Utilidor" stands for UTILity corrIDOR. The Utilidors are a series of service corridors and areas directly beneath the Magic Kingdom. Why put everything underground? Well, for a number of very good reasons. But

first, let's clarify: technically the corridors aren't underground — they are on the first floor of the Magic Kingdom. When the park was under construction, the Seven Seas Lagoon in front of it did not exist. The millions of cubic yards of dirt dug up to create the lagoon were used to raise the park's site an average of about 14 feet. Before putting it in place, the Disney Imagineers created a nine-acre system of utility corridors, rooms, and service areas. Then they covered it with the dirt, turning the area into a solid, first-floor foundation for the park. So, what Guests see above the pavement are actually the Magic Kingdom's second and third floors! The underground area accommodates the park's entire infrastructure in one easy to maintain place, out of view of Guests. It houses an intricate series of sewer lines, water pipes, computer networking cable, a state-of-the-art trash disposal system, (which uses pneumatic tubes located throughout the park to move trash to a central collection point), rooms to accommodate everything from Cast Member cafeterias, to offices, rehearsal studios, beauty salons, computer rooms, security, banking and laundry facilities, costuming, merchandise storerooms, and more. Cast Members can travel through the corridors on electric golf carts, giving them easy access to the different areas of the park without having to buck the crowds above. And because these areas are "offstage" (that is, out of view of Guests) Cast Members can relax while there. (Any time Guests can see them, they must be "on stage" and look and behave appropriately.) If you are over 16 years of age and want to take a first-hand look at this amazing Disney secret, you can take one of two behind-the-scenes tours, The "Keys to the Kingdom" or "Backstage Magic." Both let you peek at this "Cast Members-only" area.

10. b.) *Space Mountain*

Space Mountain opened January 15, 1975, while *Big Thunder Mountain Railroad* opened September 23, 1980 (but had its Grand Opening November 15). *Splash Mountain* opened October 2, 1992. There is no "Mount Liberty" in the MK or anywhere else in WDW.

11. a.) 1,076

More than 5,000 performers, (not counting the 500 doves that were released), joined in the Grand Opening Celebration of Walt Disney World at the Magic Kingdom on October 25, 1971. A 1,076-piece band (including 76 trombones) was led by "Music Man" Meredith Willson as part of the Grand Opening parade up Main Street, U.S.A. Meredith Willson was best known as author and composer of *The Music Man*, which premiered on Broadway in 1957. He also composed many memorable songs, such as "76 Trombones," "It's Beginning to Look Like Christmas," "You and I," "May the Good Lord Bless and Keep You" and "Till There Was You," which was a hit for the Beatles in 1963.

12. b.) There is a hidden Walt on each of the floats.
You can find hidden Mickeys throughout the WDW theme parks and resorts, but when designing and building the parade floats, the Imagineers put a hidden image of Walt Disney on each. Many are hard to spot, especially at night, but they include silhouettes, statues, and small portraits. On the Mickey snow globe, for example, look for a silhouette of Walt's face on the left side of the "video projector" on the top of the globe.

13. a.) *Pirates of the Caribbean*
Pirates of the Caribbean did not open in Walt Disney World until December 15, 1973.

14. c.) Partners
Walt Disney Imagineering President Marty Sklar commissioned retired Imagineer and Disney Legend Blaine Gibson to capture Walt and Mickey in a statue. Gibson is also the primary sculptor of the presidents' heads and faces that were used as the bases of the Audio-Animatronics figures in *The Hall of Presidents*. He came out of retirement to sculpt Ronald

Reagan, George H.W. Bush, Bill Clinton, and George W. Bush. The Partners statue was placed in WDW June 19, 1995. There is a second "Partners" in Disneyland, which was unveiled on November 18, 1993, Mickey's 65th birthday.

15. a.) Fantasyland
Cinderella Castle serves as the main entrance to Fantasyland, acting as a gateway to its medieval village. If you look carefully, you will notice that many of the entrances to the attractions look like tents in a medieval fair!

16. a.) Frontierland
You'll find a place to sit and play checkers in front of the *Frontierland Shootin' Arcade*. You can also play checkers in the fort on *Tom Sawyer Island*.

17. c.) *Skyway*
The *Skyway* closed November 10, 1999, five years to the day after its counterpart closed in Disneyland. The Disneyland Tokyo *Skyway* closed 1998, also in November but not on the 10th.

18. c.) Tony's Town Square Restaurant
This full-service Italian restaurant is located on Main Street, U.S.A., on your right as you enter the Magic Kingdom. Here, next to the Town Square Exposition Hall, you can re-

live the romance of the Disney film, *Lady and the Tramp,* complete with checkerboard tablecloths and *Lady and the Tramp* decor.

19. c.) There is no attraction inside the Castle.

Cinderella Castle houses a gift shop and a dining hall, as well as a legendary apartment originally built for Walt Disney and his family. However, no attraction exists inside the Castle. But be sure to walk through it and take the time to view the elaborate mosaic murals that tell the Cinderella story.

20. c.) 29

There are 29 access points to the service corridors below the MK, located throughout the park. While most of the access points are out of sight of Guests, don't be surprised if you happen to see a Disney character seemingly appear out of nowhere. The main corridor travels down Main Street, under the central hub, and directly to Fantasyland. The rest of the utilidors circle the park.

21. a.) The Liberty Tree in Liberty Square

At over 130 years old, the Liberty Tree is the oldest living thing in Walt Disney World. This large oak, the centerpiece of colonial Liberty Square, is more than 40 feet tall, 60 feet wide, and weighs more than 38 tons.

22. b.) Goofy

Goofy, dressed in his yellow overcoat, plays both the drums and the lighted xylophone, while Chip and Dale play piano in the "jazz" section of this parade of music and lights.

23. a.) While in Disneyland, he saw a Frontierland Cast Member dressed as a Sheriff walking through Tomorrowland

In Disneyland, Cast Members have to walk through the park, in full view of Guests, to get to and from

Did You Know?

CINDERELLA CASTLE WAS ELEVATED DURING CONSTRUCTION BECAUSE WALT DISNEY HAD NOTED THAT HE DIDN'T THINK DISNEYLAND'S CASTLE WAS PROMINENT ENOUGH.

•

ONE OF THE FLAGPOLES ON CINDERELLA CASTLE HAS AN ARTIFICIAL FLAG THAT IS ACTUALLY A TRANSMITTING ANTENNA FOR COORDINATING THE MAIN STREET PARADES.

central areas such as costuming. During a trip to Disneyland's Magic Kingdom, Walt Disney reportedly saw a "Sheriff" from Frontierland walking through Tomorrowland. The out-of-place character ruined the illusion of Tomorrowland — which was reportedly the catalyst that prompted Walt to develop the system of underground corridors for WDW.

24. c.) 3,370,000
There are approximately 3.37 million gallons of water in the moat surrounding Cinderella Castle.

25. d.) *Liberty Square Riverboat*
The Liberty Belle steamboat offers a leisurely 17-minute ferryboat ride around the Rivers of America. *Splash Mountain* offers the next longest ride (11 minutes), followed by *The Haunted Mansion* (8 minutes), and *Big Thunder Mountain Railroad* (about 4 minutes).

26. d.) A children's playground near the *Splash Mountain's* exit
The "Laughin' Place" is a great place to occupy children who are too short to ride the attraction.

27. b.) Mickey Mouse's 60th Birthday
"Mickey's Birthdayland" opened in 1988 to celebrate Mickey's 60th birthday (November 18, 1988). It was the first new land added to the Magic Kingdom since the park's opening in 1971 and was intended to be a temporary addition. However, in 1989 Disney decided to keep the new area and renamed it "Mickey's Starland." Four years later, "Mickey's Toontown" opened at Disneyland, outshining its WDW cousin. So a few years later, "Mickey's Starland" was refurbished, expanded, and renamed "Mickey's Toontown Fair" to celebrate WDW's 25th Anniversary. The anniversary additions included *Minnie's Country House, Donald's Boat,* and the kid-friendly coaster, *The Barnstormer at Goofy's Wiseacre Farm.*

28. c.) *Country Bear Jamboree*
Originally planned for a different Disney theme park that never materialized, the *Country Bear Jamboree* opened as one of the original attractions in Walt Disney World in 1971, to an enthusiastic response. Following the success of the Bears in WDW, the *Country Bear Jamboree* opened in Disneyland in 1972, in the park's newest land, Bear Country.

29. d.) None; it's made of fiberglass
Cinderella Castle is the tallest structure in the Magic Kingdom — just as Walt Disney had expected it to be.

Did You Know?

SOME OF THE TILES IN THE WICKED STEPSISTER MOSAIC IN CINDERELLA CASTLE ARE MADE OF REAL GOLD.

While its interior and exterior walls are sculpted to resemble granite rock, no stones or bricks were used in its construction. Instead, it is made of concrete, steel, cement, plaster, and fiberglass — a combination chosen to withstand central Florida's periodic hurricane-force winds. The inner structure is made of 600 tons of steel, covered with a fiberglass facade, while the concrete foundation is filled with foam to reduce its weight. Construction of the Castle began in late 1969 and ended in July 1971.

There are many long-lived rumors about the Castle — for example, that the spires can be removed in the event of a hurricane, that some of the spires are actually water towers, and that there is a guest room on the upper floors. None is true.

30. d.) Peter Pan
Pooh's Thotful Shop is located at the exit of *The Many Adventures of Winnie the Pooh*. Big Al has a cart by the river in Frontierland, and Madame Leota had a cart outside *The Haunted Mansion*. Although Peter Pan doesn't have his own shop, his pal Tinkerbell does; Tinkerbell's Treasures is located in Fantasyland.

31. c.) It was painted pink and turned into a birthday cake
To commemorate Walt Disney World's 25th anniversary on October 1, 1996, Disney transformed Cinderella Castle into an 18-story birthday cake. Complete with red and pink "icing," giant candy canes, and 26 glowing candles, the most photographed building in the world served as the centerpiece for the 15-month long celebration.

This was no small undertaking. Designed by Walt Disney World Entertainment and built by Walt Disney Imagineering, the "cake" required more than 400 gallons of pink paint for the initial "frosting." Then it was decorated with 20- to 40-foot candles, 16 two-foot-long candy stars, 16 five-foot candy bears, 12 five-foot gumdrops, 4 six-foot Life Savers, 30 three-foot lollipops, 50 two-foot gum balls, and multicolored "sprinkles." Finally, more than 1,000 feet of pink and blue inflatable "icing" was added to finish it off. Not everyone was in love with the new look. There were reportedly more than 200 weddings cancelled because the couples didn't want their nuptials celebrated in front of a giant pink castle-cake! On January 31, 1998, the cake. . . I mean, Castle, was transformed back to its original blue- and gold-spired glory.

32. c.) Mickey's Toontown Fair

The service corridors ("utilidors") below the park connect all of the lands in the Magic Kingdom except for Mickey's Toontown Fair, which did not exist when the park opened.

33. d.) *Peter Pan's Flight*

Dumbo the Flying Elephant, Astro Orbiter, and *Magic Carpets of Aladdin* are similar in that the ride vehicles circle around a vertical pole and guests control their up and down movement. *Peter Pan's Flight* runs along a track and Guests have no control of the vehicle.

34. a.) Fairytale Garden

Located in Fantasyland, near the walkway behind Cinderella Castle that leads to Tomorrowland, Fairytale Garden was created in 1999. It is a quiet spot complete with benches and stools. Here, Belle, the lovely bookworm from *Beauty and the Beast,* frequently appears and tells stories to the Guests with the help of a few lucky volunteers.

35. b.) Herb Ryman

Walt Disney wanted a castle to be the centerpiece of Disney World's Magic Kingdom, just as it was in Disneyland's. Imagineer Herb Ryman was given the task of designing the new icon. He started with a rough charcoal sketch, which he later developed into a painting. He received much of his inspiration from various European castles, including France's Chambord, Usse, and Chenonceau chateaux, as well as Ludwig of Bavaria's Neuschwanstein castle. Herbert Dickens Ryman was a 1931 magna cum laude graduate of the Chicago Art Institute. After a two-year tour of the Orient, Ryman joined MGM Studios, where he worked as a production designer, art director, and illustrator on such classic films as *A Tale of Two Cities.* His outstanding work caught the eye of Walt Disney, who lured him to Walt Disney Studios. There, he contributed to such Disney classics as *Pinocchio, Dumbo,* and *Fantasia.* After leaving Disney, he and Walt remained friends. Walt called on Ryman in the early 1950s to design aerial schematics for what would become Disneyland. He later worked on Walt Disney World, Tokyo Disneyland, and Disneyland Paris (formerly known as Euro Disneyland). After 50 years of working with Disney, he passed away in February 1989.

36. d.) Tomorrowland

Walt Disney World sentimentalists (like me) fondly remember the old Penny Arcade on Main Street, U.S.A., not because it had great video games, but for the genuine old games and hand-cranked moving picture machines. For just a penny, you could watch old Mute-o-scopes (which you cranked by hand) and Cail-o-scopes (which rotated the pictures automatically). You could then head over to the Fortune Teller machine to see what the future held for just a few cents, then take a penny and have it impressed with a Disney image. Sadly, the Penny Arcade closed March 19, 1995, and was converted into a part of the Main Street Athletic Company. That left the Tomorrowland Arcade, located at the exit to *Space Mountain*, the only remaining arcade in the Magic Kingdom.

37. a.) *Wishes*

Beginning in October 2003, *Wishes*, the biggest fireworks show ever presented for Magic Kingdom Guests, began its nightly run. Narrated by Pinocchio's conscience, Jiminy

Cricket, the 12-minute show tells the story of making a wish come true by combining moments from classic Disney films with dazzling pyrotechnic effects. The show is several times the size of *Fantasy in the Sky*, the production it replaced.

Main Street, U.S.A.

38. c.) **They contain the names of Walt Disney Imagineers and others who contributed to WDW in some way.**

The windows on the second story of most of the buildings on Main Street, U.S.A. bear dozens of names. They include Disney executives, contributing artists, and members of the Disney family. Here are just a few: Roy E. Disney, his wife Patty, Dick Nunis (the Chairman of Walt Disney Attractions), John Hench (the Executive Vice President of WED Enterprises), and E. Cardon (Card) Walker (the former Walt Disney Productions CEO).

39. b.) **During the fireworks displays**

You can't ride the *WDW Railroad* during the nighttime fireworks displays, because burning embers may land near the tracks. After the fireworks, Cast Members walk through these areas to confirm that no fires

are present before the train can start carrying passengers again.

40. a.) 1
For about eight months after the Magic Kingdom's opening, the only station on the *Walt Disney World Railroad* line was at Main Street, U.S.A., making the ride a "D-Ticket," roundtrip attraction. In 1972, the first Frontierland Railroad Station was constructed near the Pecos Bill Café. It marked the westernmost point of Frontierland for 19 years. It was torn down in 1990 in preparation for building *Splash Mountain*. In December 1991, a new station opened as part of *Splash Mountain*. Meanwhile, a third station was constructed in 1988 as part of the addition of the new Mickey's Birthdayland.

41. c.) A flag ceremony
There is a flag ceremony daily in Town Square. The American flag is taken down for the evening, while the band plays and white doves are released. Veterans can inquire about participating in the ceremony.

42. c.) Tony's Town Square Restaurant
You may remember the restaurant from the famous "spaghetti scene" in *Lady and the Tramp*. In the actual Magic Kingdom restaurant, guests can enjoy great pasta and seafood specialties. And be sure to look for

the paw prints in the cement right outside the entrance!

43. b.) 71
In honor of the year that marked the opening of the Magic Kingdom, the Firehouse on Main Street, U.S.A. is "Engine Co. 71."

44. d.) Oil
The engines used on the *WDW Railroad* were built in the early 1900s. They were discovered by some Walt Disney Imagineers on a trip through Mexico. Originally wood burning, the locomotives were converted to burn oil.

45. c.) Disney's Fort Wilderness Resort

Guests can catch a ride in Town Square or in front of Cinderella Castle near Central Plaza for a one-way, horse-drawn trolley ride down Main Street, U.S.A. The horses used to pull the trolleys make their home at Disney's Fort Wilderness Resort. Their horseshoes are made of plastic, because it was found to be easier on their hooves than metal.

Adventureland

46. a.) None

Believe it or not, there are no Audio-Animatronics figures in the entire *Jungle Cruise*! The animals in the attraction aren't actual Audio-Animatronics, because their "insides" couldn't withstand the water and the elements. Instead, they use a simple system of air pressure and pneumatics. The Audio-Animatronics system uses hydraulics, pneumatics, servo valves, and actuators.

47. c.) Rowan Atkinson

Atkinson, who provided the voice of Zazu in Disney's *The Lion King*, may be best known for his role as "Mr. Bean." Michael Gough provides the voice of Zazu in *The Enchanted Tiki Room*.

48. a.) In a parade

The camels that occasionally "spit" on riders of *The Magic Carpets of*

Aladdin were first used in *Aladdin's Royal Caravan Parade* at Disney-MGM Studios. When that parade ended in 1995, they were relocated to the Soundstage Restaurant in the Studios, which closed in November 1998. Later they became a part of the *Magic Carpets* ride when it opened in 2001.

49. a.) Lotus Tours

You can see a sign for Lotus Tours in the *Jungle Cruise* queue line as you prepare to board. According to the ad, this fictitious tour company can take you to such exotic lands as Malay, Burma, Siam, Cambodia, and the ancient ruins of Bangkok.

50. b.) Chess

Dead men may not tell any tales, but apparently they still play chess, as evidenced by the two skeletons engaged in a stalemate chess match. You can find these two masters of their game if you peek down into one of the dungeon cells in the queue line. Pirates fans have long insisted that the chess game was set up intentionally so that the two pirates were at a stalemate, thus leading to their demise at the table. Others say that the position of the pieces would be impossible in a real chess match.

51. c.) A fountain near *Pirates of the Caribbean*

The "Fuente de Fortuna" fountain is located across from *Pirates*. It is usually filled with coins tossed in by guests who've made a wish there.

52. a.) *Shrunken Ned's Junior Jungle Boats*

Shrunken Ned's is located near the *Jungle Cruise* exit. It lets Guests who pay an extra fee pilot a radio-controlled mini-*Jungle Cruise* boat around islands and obstacles. "El Pirata Y El Perico" is a counter-service Mexican restaurant across from *Pirates of the Caribbean* that features tacos and chili. "Bwana Bob's" is a small, freestanding store in Adventureland, originally called the "Adventureland Kiosk." In 1985, it was renamed Bwana Bob's as a tribute to comedian Bob Hope, star of the 1963 film, *Call Me Bwana*. Bob Hope also took part in WDW's 1971 opening celebration.

53. b.) The Genie's lamp

Located next to *The Enchanted Tiki Room –Under New Management*, and near the Agrabah Bazaar, *The Magic Carpets of Aladdin ride* is themed after the 1992 Disney animated hit, *Aladdin*. Much like Fantasyland's *Dumbo* ride, it features ride cars ("magic carpets") revolving around a vertical central hub, which here resembles the Genie's lamp.

54. c.) "don't give a hoot"

These memorable lyrics were written by Disney legend Xavier Atencio, with music by George Bruns. The song's first chorus is: "Yo ho, yo ho, a pirate's life for me. We pillage, we plunder, we rifle, and loot, Drink up, me 'earties, yo ho. We kidnap and ravage and don't give a hoot, Drink up me 'earties, yo ho!"

55. b.) A clamshell

Desperate times call for desperate measures, and the Robinson family (with a little help from the Disney Imagineers) made the best use of their natural surroundings, and a lot of imagination! With sinks made from clamshells, and bamboo pipes and barrels providing running water, their treehouse has all the comforts of home. . . sort of. Unless, of course, you live in a Banyan tree.

56. b.) *The Hall of Presidents*

At the end of *The Enchanted Tiki Room* show, Iago tells a woman leaving the theater to walk a little faster, as he's off to *The Hall of Presidents* to go take a nap.

Did You Know?

LADY AND TRAMP'S PAW PRINTS CAN BE FOUND ENCLOSED IN A HEART IN THE SIDEWALK IN FRONT OF TONY'S TOWN SQUARE RESTAURANT ON MAIN STREET, U.S.A.

57. b.) A documentary called *The African Lion*

The 1955 Disney True-Life Adventures documentary, *The African Lion*, set in the shadow of Mount Kilimanjaro, follows a pride of lions through the changing seasons. This film inspired Walt and his Imagineers to create *Jungle Cruise*. The 27-foot long boats used in the attraction, however, were modeled after the boat in the motion picture *The African Queen*, starring Humphrey Bogart and Katherine Hepburn.

58. c.) 300,000

The 300,000 polyethylene leaves, which reportedly cost about $1.00

each in 1971, are found on the more than 1,400 branches of the Swiss Family's tree. While the leaves may be fake, the tree is draped with real Spanish moss. Its "roots" are 42 feet deep to support the structure.

59. a.) A million

In his own rendition of *Aladdin's* "Friend Like Me," Iago boasts. . . " 'Cause I'm a very famous movie star, and all of Hollywood drops my name. Who cares about Aladdin or Jafar? I'm the one with all the looks and fame. I got a million crackers in the bank, and I plan to get a zillion more!"

60. d.) There is no private club

"Club 33" is the name of a private, membership-only club in Disneyland's New Orleans Square near its *Pirates of the Caribbean* attraction. The entrance is located next to the Blue Bayou entrance to the Square and its restaurant is on the second floor. It is the only place in Disneyland's Magic Kingdom that serves alcohol. Opened in 1967, it was originally planned as a private restaurant and club in which Walt Disney could entertain corporate attraction sponsors, but it did not open until after his death. Today, it is open to a limited number of corporate and individual members. Thinking of joining this ultra-exclusive Disneyland club? Sure! Just fork over $20,000 for a corporate membership and $7,500 for an individual one. Oh, and don't forget the $2,250 in yearly dues. There is no such club in WDW.

61. b.) Desperation
As your train passes through Adventureland, look for the small shack on the right side with a sign that says, "Desperation." Look quick or you just might miss it!

Frontierland

62. b.) $17 million
OK, if you were around in 1979 and had $17 million in your bank account, what could you have bought yourself? Let's see. . . 113,333,333 stamps, 19,318,181 gallons of gas, or one heck of a roller coaster for your backyard! Or, to put it another way, building *Big Thunder Mountain Railroad* in 1979 cost as much as it did to build all of Disneyland for its 1955 opening!

63. b.) Slippin' Falls
Slippin' Falls is the name of the first drop for *Splash Mountain*. You can see the sign near the stairs on the right-hand side as you approach the drop.

64. d.) 18
You don't have to love (or even LIKE) country music to enjoy this timeless attraction. Located directly across from the *Frontierland Shootin' Arcade*, the *Country Bear Jamboree*

is an hysterical 15-minute stage show performed by various Audio-Animatronics characters. Henry, your host, introduces you to the 18 bears that perform in the show and appear from all around (and above) the theater. Each of the bears has a distinctive personality (You gotta love Big Al), as well as mannerisms and (dare I say?) "style" of dress. They can sing (some of them), laugh, talk, and even play musical instruments.

65. c.) The grease on the tracks is thinner thus your train goes faster.
The sun, which is at it's highest and hottest point at noon, heats and melts the grease on the tracks to its thinnest point as the day wears on; thus the train goes faster. The ride's average speed is about 30 mph, but it can reach speeds of up to 33 mph, which is faster than *Space Mountain*! Be sure to sit in the back of the train if you want to the ride to feel even faster!

66. b.) "Down by the Old MillStream"
Hearing the Mill Wheel on *Tom Sawyer Island* creaking and groaning "Down By the Old Mill Stream" is just one of the many surprises awaiting you on the Island.

67. b.) Boot Hill
The *Frontierland Shootin' Arcade* is set in Boot Hill in the year 1850. Here, you can shoot rifles loaded with infrared light beams at almost 100 animated targets.

Did You Know?

THE ANTIQUE MINING EQUIPMENT IN THE *BIG THUNDER MOUNTAIN RAILROAD* ATTRACTION IS GENUINE AND COST OVER $300,000.00.

68. c.) Big Thunder Mining Co.

Listen to the safety spiel as you board your train for a ride through the rocky Southwest: "Howdy, folks! Please keep your hands and arms inside the train, and remain seated at all times. . . 'cause this here's the wildest ride in the wilderness!" Each of the six trains on *Big Thunder Mountain Railroad* is named. They are I.M. Brave, I.M. Fearless, I.B. Hearty, U.B. Bold, U.R. Daring, and U.R. Courageous.

69. d.) 50-54

There are between 50 and 54 logs on the waters of *Splash Mountain* when it is running at full capacity. Each log is closely monitored by computer not only to prevent it from crashing into other logs but also to pinpoint each log's position in case the ride should need to be evacuated.

70. c.) Superstition Bridge

Take a walk over Superstition Bridge to get to *Tom Sawyer Island*'s fort, wilderness trail, and fishin' pier.

71. b.) An idea Walt had for a ski resort

The idea for *Country Bear Jamboree* was developed for a proposed ski resort Disney wanted to build in the Mineral King area of the Sierra Nevadas during the sixties. Walt came up with the idea for a bear-band show, which would include a variety of talking, singing, and laughing bears, each with its own distinct personality. Studio animator Marc Davis did concept drawings for the characters. When the Mineral King Resort idea was abandoned, Walt wanted the bear show made part of WDW, which was still in its planning stages. The *Country Bear Jamboree* debuted with the park in October 1971, making it one of WDW's original attractions.

72. b.) Injun Joe's Cave

Tom Sawyer Island's other cave is named the Magnetic Mystery Mine. Some of the other areas you can explore on the Island are the windmill, Aunt Polly's, Barrel Bridge, Suspension Bridge, and the Escape Tunnel.

73. b.) Lead pellets

Mosey on up to the *Frontierland Shootin' Arcade* and pick up a genuine refitted .54 caliber Hawkins buffalo rifle. Put in a couple of quarters and take aim at tin cans, gravestones, tree stumps (try and hit the possum that peeks out every so often), and other animated targets. When you hit one of the targets, many of which are moving, they make noise, move, and provide a few other surprises. When the arcade first opened, the rifles fired real lead pellets at the targets. However, they were soon refitted to shoot beams of light. The reason: paint. Paint? Yup. . . because the lead pellets chipped the paint off the props in the attraction, Disney maintenance personnel had to repaint the attraction every night. Over the course of a year, that took over 2,000 gallons of paint—plus all that maintenance time! An extra plus for the light beams: they're safer.

Liberty Square

74. a.) The ballroom scene

If you pay close attention, you will notice that you do not see a ghost until after Madame Leota summons them during the seance scene. If you pay even CLOSER attention, you will see that after you fall out of the attic window (or did the Bride push you?) the ghosts become less transparent. This is because YOU are now a ghost, too! Yes. . . I'm sorry to inform you that that you "died" when you fell. That is why you can see them better . . . and now they can see you, too!

75. c.) 13

The 13 lanterns hanging from the majestic oak, Liberty Tree, represent the first 13 colonies of the United States. Located across from *The Hall of Presidents*, the Liberty Tree commemorates the communal meeting place of Boston's Sons of Liberty who, in 1765, protested the imposition of the Stamp Act. Early patriots in every colonial American town and village designated a tree as their "Liberty Tree," a symbol of their right to freedom of speech and assembly. When British troops recognized the symbolism, they cut the trees down to deflate morale.

76. b.) Bill Clinton

The first serving President to record his voice for *The Hall of Presidents* was Bill Clinton. In 1993, he recorded a short speech for the show in the White House library. In 2001, the Hall was again updated to include our 43rd president, George W. Bush, who recorded a speech written especially for the attraction.

77. b.) Pepper's Ghost

One of the most memorable scenes in *The Haunted Mansion*, the

Did You Know?

YOU CAN HEAR THE SOUND OF TAP SHOES IF YOU LISTEN OUTSIDE THE "DANCE STUDIO" ON MAIN STREET, U.S.A.

ballroom dancing scene, is based on one of the oldest, and simplest, tricks in the book. Known as "Pepper's Ghost," this old magician's illusion is named for John Henry Pepper, a chemistry professor at the London Polytechnic Institute. In 1862, he published "Wonders of Optical Science," which describes an effect that allows ghostly images to be projected quite easily using mirrors. Disney Imagineer, Yale Gracey (for whom "Master Gracey," the Mansion's legendary owner, was named), used this trick in *The Haunted Mansion*. Here's how it works: There is a large pane of glass between you and the ballroom below. The dancing ghosts are actually located above and below the track that your vehicle rides on — the ballroom itself has not a single figure in it. The "ghosts" are carefully lit, and it is their reflections that you see in the glass. If you look closely at the dancing figures, you will notice that they appear to be dancing "backwards," with the ladies leading the men. This is because the Imagineers apparently forgot the reflections would be mirror images of the actual Audio-Animatronics figures.

78. b.) 7 feet
Although the "Rivers of America" may seem quite deep, the depth is only about seven feet. When the water was drained from the river in 1996 and maintenance trucks were able to drive around the dry riverbed, their roofs just reached what would have been the water line! How can a paddle-wheel riverboat like the Liberty Belle traverse such shallow water? Well, believe it or not, the Liberty Belle actually rides along a rail that is attached to the riverbed below.

79. b.) It was initially conceived as a side street off of Disneyland's Main Street, U.S.A.
Many years ago, signs were posted in Disneyland for an upcoming "Liberty Street." There would have been buildings representing the 13 colonies and themed to the period. *Independence Hall* would have been the signature attraction, very much like *The Hall of Presidents* we have today. The idea never materialized in Disneyland, but it was expanded and used as the basis for WDW's Liberty Square.

80. c.) 999

Foolish mortals. . . you enter *The Haunted Mansion* only to be informed by your host that there are 999 happy haunts living here. . . but there's room for a thousand. . . If you wish to volunteer, you can make "final" arrangements at the end of the tour.

81. c.) 1787

1787, the year that the Constitution of the United States was ratified, can be seen on the front of the building in gold numbers, just below the steeple.

82. b.) The ceiling rises

Your tour of *The Haunted Mansion* begins in an eight-sided room, where you see paintings of some of the Mansion's former guests in their "corruptible, mortal state." Soon you notice that the room appears to be stretching upwards, to reveal the true extent of the pictures on the walls. So, is the haunted room actually stretching, or is it your imagination, hmmm? Well, if you are in the WDW *Haunted Mansion,* the ceiling of both of its two "stretching rooms" moves upwards. However, if you visit *The Haunted Mansion* in Disneyland, the room is actually a large elevator that takes you down one level. Why the difference? This effect was originally created out of necessity. When the original *Haunted Mansion* was being built in Disneyland

back in 1963, the empty building it was going into had been constructed years earlier and was too small to fit everything the Imagineers wanted inside. So, they dug a "basement" to the mansion and connected it (by a tunnel that can't be seen by Guests) to a separate attraction building — which, thanks to Disneyland's limited space had to be built literally on the other side of the existing Disneyland Railroad tracks. The Imagineers designed the "stretching room" to take guests down one level, under the tracks, and over to the attraction building. That wasn't necessary in the WDW *Haunted Mansion* where, thanks to the lack of space constraints, Guests can exit directly into the attraction building. But the effect was so popular in Disneyland that the Imagineers decided to include it in the WDW *Mansion.*

83. b.) 38 tons

The Liberty Tree is a living tribute to Boston's original Liberty Tree. While many guests mistakenly believe it is a replica created by Disney, it is actually a southern live oak (quercus virginiana) that is more than 130 years old. It was found about six miles away from where it stands today in Liberty Square and it is likely one of the largest trees ever transplanted. Its root ball had a diameter of over four feet. A unique method was devised to extract and move the tree. While most mature trees are transplanted by wrapping a cable around them and lifting them out of place, that would have severely damaged the bark and cambium layers (thin layers under the bark that give rise to the new cells responsible for secondary growth) of this immense tree. Therefore, two holes were drilled into the tree, and steel rods (dowels) were inserted through the center of its trunk. These rods became the grips for lifting the tree out of place using a 100-ton crane. When the tree was safely in place in Liberty Square, the rods were removed and replaced with the original wood plugs. However, the wood plugs were contaminated, and the tree became infected and began to rot. To save the tree, the plugs and diseased areas were removed, and the holes filled with cement. Additionally, a young southern live oak was grafted into the base of the tree and continues to grow to this day.

84. c.) Walt Disney Imagineers who helped create the attraction

After you pass through the menacing wrought-iron gates surrounding the Mansion, you will encounter the cemetery (conveniently located right outside the entrance). Here you will find a number of witty headstones with epitaphs not to the dearly departed, but in tribute to the many Imagineers who helped develop *The Haunted Mansion*. Here are some samples with notes on the Imagineers who inspired them:

Dear departed
Brother Dave,
he chased a bear
into a cave

This stone was named after Dave Burkhart, who was the model builder for *The Haunted Mansion*.

At peaceful rest
lies Brother Claude,
planted here
beneath this sod

Claude Coats was the Imagineer who came up with the layout of the OmniMover ride track for *The Haunted Mansion*, as well as numerous concept sketches

----

Dear sweet Leota,
beloved by all
In regions beyond now,
but having a ball

Leota Toombs was an artist at WED whose face was the model for the head in the crystal ball in the seance scene, and so the character was named "Madame Leota" in her honor.

85. c.) 160

Each one of the 160 OmniMover ride vehicles can hold "you. . . and one or two. . . 'loved ones.'" *The Haunted Mansion* vehicles travel at about 1.4 mph, and can accommodate up to 3,200 guests per hour. The Disneyland attraction, in contrast, has only 131 vehicles and a capacity of only 2,618 Guests per hour because its track is shorter than the one in WDW.

Fantasyland

86. c.) Pinocchio
Pinocchio's Village Haus is located behind *Dumbo the Flying Elephant* and is a great place to get burgers and fries. Look up from your boat in *it's a small world* at the people eating behind the windows — that's the Haus! The restaurant is divided into seven themed rooms, each named after a character in the film. The rooms are: Blue Fairy, Cleo, Jiminy Cricket, Monstro, Stromboli, Figaro, and Gepetto's Workshop.

87. b.) Dopey
Take a quick look at the *Snow White's Scary Adventures* "exit" sign as you leave this Fantasyland "Dark Ride" to see Dopey (he's the not-so-strong, but silent type), waving good-bye.

88. b.) King Stefan's Banquet Hall
This restaurant was renamed Cinderella's Royal Table on April 28, 1997. Oddly enough, King Stefan was Sleeping Beauty's father, and not Cinderella's.

89. c.) September 7, 1998
Mr. Toad took his last Wild Ride on Monday, September 7, 1998, less than one year after it was announced that the ride would be replaced. Attempts to save the attraction by fans, both online and in the park, proved unsuccessful.

90. c.) 9:06
As you fly over London's Big Ben clock with Peter Pan and the children, you will notice that it's 9:06 — way past your bedtime!

91. b.) 1917 by Philadelphia Toboggan Co.
The carousel was built in 1917 by the Philadelphia Toboggan Co. for use in Olympic Park in Maplewood, New Jersey. Disney Imagineers discovered the neglected ride there and brought it to Florida, where the 60-foot wide platter and hand-carved wooden horses were painstakingly renovated (the meticulous hand-painting alone took about 48 hours per horse and includes 23-karat gold leaf as well as real silver and bronze). Disney also added 18 hand-painted scenes recounting the story of Cinderella to the wooden canopy above the horses. Although only 72 of the horses from the original carousel were salvageable, there are currently 90 wooden steeds on this two-minute musical attraction, each one different from the other 89. The attraction's gentle charm is enhanced by the nostalgic rhythms of classic Disney songs such as "A Dream Is a

Wish Your Heart Makes," "Someday My Prince Will Come," and "When You Wish Upon a Star."

92. a.) A mine cart
Based on the world's first full-length animated feature, you can take a ride aboard a "wooden" mine cart as you follow Snow White through her enchanting fairy tale, complete with the seven dwarfs and the Evil Queen.

93. d.) 11.5 million gallons
One of the most innovative, yet difficult to maintain attractions ever created for the Disney theme parks was *20,000 Leagues Under the Sea*. An "E-Ticket" attraction from its opening day (October 14, 1971), the ride closed in 1994 exactly 23 years to the day after it opened. Guests boarded

Captain Nemo's submarine (remember how they were numbered using Roman numerals?) and traveled under the sea through coral reefs, dark caverns, and into unexpected danger. The tank that housed the attraction held an impressive 11.5 million gallons of water. Sadly, the ride closed with almost no notice to guests, not due to lack of popularity, but because of constant ride breakdowns, loading difficulties (the subs were not handicapped-accessible), long lines, and the high costs of maintenance (including keeping 11.5 million gallons of water clear enough for guests to see through. For years, rumors of a "Little Mermaid" attraction swirled, and in 2003, with the success of the animated feature film *Finding Nemo*, similar yet unsubstantiated rumors began to surface once again.

94. b.) England
Some of the children in the United Kingdom portion of *it's a small world* are dressed to look like dancing chess pieces. To spot them, look at the figures to the left as you approach the large clock tower.

95. c.) The Crocodile
Peter Pan's Flight in the Magic Kingdom is one of the many attractions that use the FastPass reservation system to minimize your wait in line.

96. b.) 1994
20,000 Leagues Under the Sea closed

October 14, 1994, exactly 23 years to the day after it premiered. The former queue area of the attraction is now known as the Fantasyland Character Festival, where you can meet and get autographs from Disney characters. The back of the lagoon area has become Ariel's Grotto, where you can meet the star of *The Little Mermaid*. While rumors persist that many of the old subs have been either dismantled or buried on WDW property, two of them were brought to Castaway Cay, Disney's private island, and opened up for exploration by Disney Cruise Line passengers.

97. b.) Owl

Mr. Toad's Wild Ride, one of the original Magic Kingdom attractions, was removed and replaced by *The Many Adventures of Winnie the Pooh* in the late 1990s. When it was announced in 1997 that Mr. Toad was to be closed in 1998, the announcement met with not just silent objections, but actual protests. "Toad-Ins" became commonplace in Fantasyland, as fans rallied to try and save Mr. Toad from Winnie. Toad supporters were often sighted wearing T-shirts with slogans like, "Ask me why Mickey is killing Mr. Toad." Fans could not understand the removal of this classic attraction in favor of one that was simply more marketable (Disney knew it would sell a lot more Pooh merchandise than it could ever sell in Toads! Not

only that, but Toad's final scene, one in which you are hit by a train and sent to Hell, was fodder for criticism over the years). Perhaps to prevent a major demonstration, Disney gave just one week's notice of the ride's last day of operation. Fans of Mr. Toad can still see their lovable green friend hidden away in the cheerful Pooh attraction. Toad can be seen handing over the deed to the property to Owl on the left wall of the scene in Owl's house (one of the first scenes in the ride). And, in a final gesture of remembrance, Cast Members in the Magic Kingdom have named one of their break rooms the "J. Thaddeus Toad Memorial Room."

98. b.) *Mad Tea Party*

Tucked away between Fantasyland and Tomorrowland, the entrance to Mickey's Toontown Fair is closest to Fantasyland's *Mad Tea Party* ride.

99. b.) 289

There are 289 Audio-Animatronics children in *it's a small world. . .* all singing that same song over, and over, and over again. . . Actually, there are a total of 553 Audio-Animatronics figures in the attraction counting the animals.

100. b.) England

Mr. Toad's Wild Ride took guests on a wild and crazy trip through the 1949 Disney film *The Adventures of Ichabod Crane and Mr. Toad*. During the three-minute ride, guests sat in old cars as they crashed through Toad Hall, barns, a gypsy camp, haystacks, and eventually a train, only to end up in Hell.

101. c.) Humanimals

Disney's larger than life "humanimals" were manipulated by human "animateers" hidden from audience view, and were larger and more lifelike than any other puppets in the park. Unfortunately, the show they were in, *Legend of the Lion King,* no longer plays in WDW.

102. c.) Help

As your *it's a small world* boat circles to the right in the white room celebrating all nations, look up and to the left at the balloon with the two clowns in it. You can clearly see that the sign one is holding up says "Help." (Is it the song playing over and over again for more than 30 years that has finally driven him over the edge?)

103. c.) Red

At the beginning of *Peter Pan's Flight,*

you can look down and see Nana barking outside of her little red doghouse.

Mickey's Toontown Fair

104. a.) The paddles are shaped like Mickey, Donald, and Goofy heads.

As you tour *Mickey's Country House,* you'll notice the den filled with sports memorabilia and a Ping-Pong game that looks like a rout. On the table, you'll see two paddles — one shaped like Mickey's head, the other like Donald's. On the lower left shelf, right next to the trophy, you'll see a third, green paddle shaped like Goofy's head.

105. c.) "Minnie's Cartoon Country Living"

Minnie is one busy lady. . . I mean, mouse. In addition to being the editor of "Minnie's Cartoon Country Living" magazine, she also quilts, paints, and gardens. Her home office

Did You Know?

WHEN *20,000 LEAGUES UNDER THE SEA* WAS OPEN, THE 24 SUBS THAT OPERATED AT WDW AND DISNEYLAND GAVE THE WALT DISNEY COMPANY THE FIFTH LARGEST SUBMARINE FLEET IN THE WORLD!

is full of recipes and photos for the magazine, and her computer screen shows that she is typing the "Letter From the Editor." In her kitchen, you can see that she has been quite busy canning and baking for the Backyard Fair. And we all know she's a good cook — just look at the blue ribbons and other awards she has won for her many entries. If you think there's not much to do in her house, here are a few little "secrets" for you: Check Minnie's messages on the answering machine; turn on the microwave to pop some popcorn; turn the dials on the stove — this will make the coffee pot perk and the utensils hanging above the stove dance to the music. And if you want to cool off, open Minnie's refrigerator door to feel a chilling blast of air!

106. b.) Yellow
Mickey's colorful home has a yellow fence, red roof, and blue and green trim.

107. a.) A petting zoo
Grandma Duck's petting farm was a small petting zoo located where Goofy's *Barnstormer* stands today. In fact, *The Barnstormer* flies through the barn that at one time held real animals! The zoo's main attraction was "Minnie Moo," the cow who had a "hidden Mickey" spot on one side of her body. When the attraction closed, she was moved to the petting farm in Fort Wilderness, where she died in 2001.

108. b.) A restroom
Located near the entrance to Mickey's Toontown Fair is Pete's Garage, where you can make a "pit-stop" before you visit Mickey and Minnie!

109. a.) A Toontown radio DJ
Known as "The Rowdiest Rooster on the Radio," Red can be "heard" on W-A-C-K-Y Radio near Goofy's *Barnstormer*. He was featured in issue 34.7 of "Minnie's Cartoon Country Living" magazine, which is framed and hangs on the wall of *Minnie's Country House*. Red plays all country, all the toon!

110. a.) "Famous Mice in History"
Look around inside Minnie's colorful Country House. On the coffee table in her living room, you can find "Famous Mice in History."

Tomorrowland

111. a.) Transportarium
When the Circle-Vision film starring Timekeeper opened in Tomorrowland in November 1994, it was known as *The Transportarium*. In early 1995, its name was changed to *The Timekeeper*.

112. c.) *Space Mountain*
Although the idea for *Space Mountain* was originally conceived for Disneyland in the 1960s, it wasn't until 1975 that it debuted in WDW

because the technology needed to bring Walt Disney's concept to life didn't exist when he came up with the idea. It took the Imagineers ten years to design, develop, and test the attraction, which was the first roller coaster to open in WDW, It opened as an E-Ticket ride on January 15, 1975, after more than two years of construction. It was the first thrill ride created using computer-aided design.

113. b.) Space Pilot

During the Christmas scene in *Carousel of Progress*, you can see the whole family in the "modern" living room, which is decorated for the holidays. Grandma is sitting near the TV, watching Jimmy play his new video game while wearing his virtual reality (VR) headgear. Grandma also has some VR headgear on, but it is above her eyes and she hasn't started playing yet. Sarah comments on how peaceful everything was, "until Santa brought that new virtual reality Space Pilot game."

114. a.) 7 mph

Huge Briggs & Stratton 9 horsepower engines take these speed demons up to a maximum velocity of about 7 mph (maybe 7.5 if the track conditions are "just right"). And you don't even need a license to drive one!

115. c.) Electricity

The *Tomorrowland Transit Authority* (TTA) premiered in Disneyland on July 2, 1967 as the *WEDway PeopleMover*, and in WDW on July 1, 1975. However, the two attractions were somewhat different. In the Disneyland version, the cars on the track didn't have a motor in them — the motors were on the track itself! About every nine feet was a small Goodyear tire that was turned by an electric motor. As your vehicle passed over the tire, it was pushed forward. The WDW version, though, uses a propulsion method known as "linear induction." Here, rather than having motors rotate tires that push the ride car, the cars are pulled by electromagnets embedded in the track. (The magnets attract and repel the vehicles to move them along.) This clean, quiet system was developed in the early 1970s by MAPO, Disney's electrical engineering group, and is also used at the Houston Intercontinental Airport. While WDW's version of the ride is still operating, Disneyland's closed in 1995 and reopened as the *Rocket Rods*, a faster ride that still uses the original *WEDway* track.

116. b.) 2
Guests can take a trip "To infinity and beyond!" in their Star Cruiser, which is controlled by a joystick and armed with two "laser cannons."

117. a.) *Grand Prix Raceway*
When Walt Disney World opened in 1971, there were slim pickings in Tomorrowland; only the *Grand Prix Raceway* and the *Skyway to Fantasyland* were operational. *America the Beautiful* didn't open until more than a month later on November 25, 1971. *Flight to the Moon* followed it on December 24, 1971, and *If You Had Wings* opened on June 5, 1972, The *Carousel of Progess* was not moved from Disneyland until September 9, 1973. *Space Mountain*
and *Star Jets* opened in 1974, with the *WEDway PeopleMover* following in 1975.

118. d.) *Star Jets*
The original centerpiece of Tomorrowland, *Star Jets* opened on November 28, 1974. This D-Ticket attraction was a large, white rocket surrounded by Guest-controlled jets. When it closed in 1993, the center rocket was removed, painted green camouflage, and used in the TV series, "Thunder in Paradise," which was filmed at Disney-MGM Studios. (It can now be found in the Studios' "Bone Yard.") The Tomorrowland attraction was completely updated and renamed *Astro Orbiter* when reopened in 1995.

CHAPTER THREE

EPCOT

1. About how large is Epcot?
   a.) 200 acres
   b.) 300 acres
   c.) 400 acres
   d.) 520 acres

2. In what year was the plan for Epcot (the theme park and not the city) formally announced to the public?
   a.) 1971
   b.) 1975
   c.) 1977
   d.) 1979

3. What was NOT sold inside Epcot when the park first opened?
   a.) Alcohol
   b.) Beverages in plastic cups, which were deemed environmentally "unfriendly"
   c.) Balloons
   d.) Disney character merchandise

4. Prior to and during Epcot's construction, where was the "EPCOT Preview Center" located?
   a.) Near where *Spaceship Earth* stands today

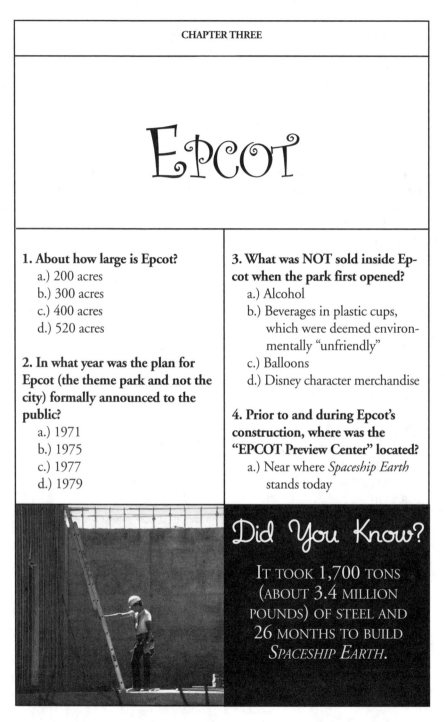

Did You Know?

IT TOOK 1,700 TONS (ABOUT 3.4 MILLION POUNDS) OF STEEL AND 26 MONTHS TO BUILD *SPACESHIP EARTH*.

b.) Near the entrance to the
Transportation and Ticket
Center
c.) On Main Street, U.S.A. in
the Magic Kingdom
d.) In the Disney Village Marketplace

5. The original plans called for Epcot's entrance to open into what?
a.) World Showcase
b.) A museum
c.) The Epcot Resort Hotel
d.) CommuniCore

6. When did Epcot construction begin?
a.) 1971
b.) 1979
c.) 1981
d.) 1983

7. The first company to sign an agreement with Disney to sponsor a pavilion was?
a.) AT&T
b.) HP
c.) GM
d.) GE

8. Where is the First Aid station located in Epcot?
a.) Odyssey Center
b.) Next to the Wonders of Life
pavilion
c.) Near the main entrance
d.) Innoventions West

9. How much was spent on fireworks for Epcot's Millennium New Year's Eve celebration?
a.) $100,000
b.) $250,000
c.) $500,000
d.) $1,000,000

10. What Epcot parade had its final performance on March 1, 2003?
a.) *Tapestry of Nations*
b.) *Tapestry of Dreams*
c.) *Parade of Nations*
d.) *Dream Seekers*

11. In what year was the *Candlelight Processional* first held at Epcot?
a.) 1982
b.) 1971
c.) 1994
d.) 1999

Future World

12. How much does *Spaceship Earth* weigh?
a.) 500,000 pounds
b.) 2,000,000 pounds
c.) 16,000,000 pounds
d.) 29,000,000 pounds

13. In *Cranium Command,* what color is Buzzy's hat?
a.) Green
b.) Red
c.) Blue
d.) Yellow

14. What is unique about the Snow Cat vehicle at "Ice Station Cool"?
- a.) It is fueled by Coca Cola
- b.) The treads are in the shape of Coca-Cola bottles
- c.) It is made out of recycled Coca-Cola bottles
- d.) It has a Jacuzzi in the back

15. How long is the track in *Test Track*?
- a.) 1,457 feet
- b.) 3,255 feet
- c.) 4,976 feet
- d.) 5,246 feet

16. In *Ellen's Energy Adventure*, what is Ellen's first correct response when playing Jeopardy?
- a.) "My name is Ellen."
- b.) "Is this a nightmare, or what?"
- c.) "Who do you think you are, Einstein?"
- d.) "Hey, aren't you Alex Trebeck?"

17. How many "Leave a Legacy" sculptures are there in Epcot's main entrance plaza?
- a.) 12
- b.) 25
- c.) 35
- d.) 48

18. What type of structure is *Spaceship Earth*?
- a.) A geodesic sphere
- b.) A Newtonian globe
- c.) A geodesic dome
- d.) An ecosphere

19. In *Mission: SPACE*, each guest performs a role that is vital to the mission's success. If you wanted to assume the role of legendary Apollo 11 astronaut Neil Armstrong, which seat would you sit in?
- a.) Commander
- b.) Pilot
- c.) Navigator
- d.) Engineer

Did You Know?

WHEN THE PARK WAS STILL IN ITS DESIGN PHASE, A 1/8TH INCH SCALE MODEL OF EPCOT WAS BUILT. IT COVERED OVER 1,428 SQUARE FEET — ABOUT THE SIZE OF AN AVERAGE HOME.

Did You Know?

THE WINDOWS IN THE CORAL REEF RESTAURANT IN
THE LIVING SEAS ARE 18 FEET HIGH, 8 INCHES THICK,
AND MADE OF ACRYLIC.

20. What Future World attraction opened exactly one year after the park's opening?
- a.) *Living with the Land*
- b.) *Test Track*
- c.) *Horizons*
- d.) *World of Motion*

21. The pylons that hold up *Spaceship Earth* are sunk how deep into the ground?
- a.) 200 to 250 feet
- b.) 120 to 185 feet
- c.) 350 to 425 feet
- d.) 5 to 15 feet

22. During the dream sequence in *Ellen's Energy Adventure*, which of these things does Ellen's neighbor, Bill Nye the Science Guy, NOT want to borrow from her?
- a.) Aluminum foil
- b.) Duct tape
- c.) A candle
- d.) A clothespin

23. How many square feet of space do the Innoventions pavilions occupy?
- a.) 10,000
- b.) 30,000
- c.) 50,000
- d.) 80,000

24. What is the name of the research facility in *The Living Seas*?
a.) Disney Seas
b.) WEDWorks Research Labs
c.) The Under Sea Project
d.) Sea Base Alpha

25. Who directed the 3D film, *Captain EO*?
a.) Francis Ford Coppola
b.) George Lucas
c.) Steven Spielberg
d.) John Landis

26. How many theaters are there in The Wonders of Life pavilion's "Fitness Fairgrounds"?
a.) 1
b.) 2
c.) 3
d.) 4

27. What do the names and numbers written on the pipes throughout *The Living Seas* pavilion represent?
a.) The many species of fish located inside the attraction
b.) Names of Disney animated films and the year they were released
c.) Code names of attractions and their opening dates
d.) The names and extension numbers of Imagineers who worked on the attraction

28. If you listen closely as you walk though Future World past *Spaceship Earth*, you will hear the distant sound of a bird. What is significant about that sound?
a.) It is the sound of a bird that's been nesting on the property since Epcot opened
b.) It is a recording of a bird in distress, played to keep other birds out of Future World
c.) It is a recording of birds from Discovery Island used as background noise to soothe guests
d.) Bird? What bird?

29. Where did the idea for "Figment" (from *Journey Into Imagination)* come from?
a.) An episode of "Magnum, P.I."
b.) The movie *Pete's Dragon*
c.) A recurring nightmare suffered by one of the Imagineers
d.) Early concept drawings for Donald Duck

30. What former attraction's theme song was "It's Fun to Be Free"?
a.) *Horizons*
b.) *World of Motion*
c.) *Journey Into Imagination*
d.) *If You Had Wings*

31. How long did it take to develop *Mission: SPACE*?
a.) 1 year
b.) 3 years
c.) 5 years
d.) 9 years

Did You Know?

EACH CAR IN *TEST TRACK*
HAS THREE TIMES
THE COMPUTING POWER
OF THE SPACE SHUTTLE!

32. In which Epcot attraction do you ride in "time machines"?
  a.) *Mission: SPACE*
  b.) *Journey Into Imagination with Figment*
  c.) *Ellen's Energy Adventure*
  d.) *Spaceship Earth*

33. What is the name of the youngest brother in *Honey, I Shrunk the Audience?*
  a.) Adam
  b.) Nick
  c.) Buzzy
  d.) Wayne

34. How many miles per day does each of the *Test Track* vehicles travel?
  a.) 40
  b.) 140
  c.) 240
  d.) 999

35. What can be found at the very top of *Spaceship Earth?*
  a.) A VIP lounge for corporate guests
  b.) A lightning rod
  c.) A hidden camera
  d.) A trap door

36. In what year did the original *Journey Into Imagination* ride open?
  a.) 1982
  b.) 1983
  c.) 1984
  d.) 1986

37. Hanging from the ceiling of The Land pavilion is a large balloon surrounded by four smaller balloons. What do those four represent?
  a.) Earth, air, fire, water
  b.) North, east, west, south
  c.) Winter, summer, spring, fall
  d.) The four corners of the earth

38. Who was an interactive, friendly robot that would talk with guests in *Epcot Computer Central?*
  a.) R2-D2
  b.) REX
  c.) InfoBot
  d.) SMRT-1

39. What famous "space explorer" directed the *Body Wars* ride film?
a.) William Shatner
b.) Leonard Nimoy
c.) Patrick Stewart
d.) Gene Roddenberry

40. In the original *Journey Into Imagination,* what color was Dreamfinder's hair?
a.) Red
b.) Rainbow
c.) Blue
d.) White

41. How much is spent per night on fireworks for the *IllumiNations: Reflections of Earth* display?
a.) $10,000
b.) $35,000
c.) $5,000
d.) $72,000

42. What color are Figment's eyes in the Imagination! pavilion attraction, *Journey Into Imagination with Figment?*
a.) Pink
b.) Green
c.) Yellow
d.) White

43. Which of the following could fit inside The Land pavilion in Epcot?
a.) Typhoon Lagoon
b.) Fantasyland
c.) Discovery Land
d.) World Showcase Lagoon

44. What's the name of the restaurant located in The Wonders of Life pavilion?
a.) Nice and Easy
b.) Pure and Simple
c.) Cheap and Fast
d.) Good Eatin'

45. On the replica of the moon outside *Mission: SPACE,* you'll see red, white, and blue markers. What do the white markers represent?
a.) Unmanned missions to the moon
b.) The first manned mission to space
c.) A commemoration of the lives lost in space exploration
d.) The first lunar landing

46. How long did it take to build *Spaceship Earth?*
a.) 12 months
b.) 17 months
c.) 26 months
d.) 37 months

Did You Know?

WALT DISNEY ORIGINALLY ENVISIONED A DOME OVER EPCOT CITY TO GIVE IT COMPLETE CONTROL OVER THE WEATHER.

47. In addition to the butterfly garden found in World Showcase, there is another one in Future World. Where is it?
a.) The Land pavilion
b.) The Imagination! pavilion
c.) Next to the Odyssey Center
d.) Near MouseGear

48. What was located in the *Test Track* building when Epcot opened?
a.) The building was always used for the *Test Track* ride
b.) *Horizons*
c.) *If You Had Wings*
d.) *World of Motion*

49. How many attractions were operational in Future World when Epcot opened?
a.) 4
b.) 5
c.) 6
d.) 7

50. Why does *Mission: SPACE* take place in the year 2036?
a.) It is 75 years after the first manned space flight
b.) It is exactly 65 years after the opening of WDW
c.) It is 50 years after the first Space Shuttle launch
d.) To commemorate the 50th anniversary of the first landing on Mars

51. In what year was *Test Track* originally scheduled to open?
a.) 1995
b.) 1997
c.) 1998
d.) 1999

52. About how many different creatures inhabit *The Living Seas?*
a.) 500
b.) 8,500
c.) 10,000
d.) 20,000

53. What is the largest pavilion in Epcot?
a.) *Mission: SPACE*
b.) *The Living Seas*
c.) The Land
d.) *Universe of Energy*

54. In *Spaceship Earth,* what Disney cartoon can be seen playing in the Cinema scene?
a.) *Pinocchio*
b.) *Fantasia*
c.) *Sleeping Beauty*
d.) *Snow White and the Seven Dwarfs*

55. How many pounds does each of the ride cars in *Ellen's Energy Adventure* weigh?
a.) 900 pounds
b.) 3,000 pounds
c.) 11,000 pounds
d.) 33,000 pounds

56. What restaurant replaced the Stargate?
a.) Beverage Base
b.) Sunrise Terrace Restaurant
c.) Electric Umbrella
d.) Fountainview Cafe

57. Which of these attractions may be closed during inclement weather?
a.) *Living with the Land*
b.) *Test Track*
c.) *Ellen's Energy Adventure*
d.) *Spaceship Earth*

58. In *The Making of Me* in The Wonders of Life pavilion, where did Martin Short's parents meet?
a.) The 1965 World's Fair
b.) The 1947 Fall Mixer
c.) The opening of Walt Disney World
d.) The unemployment line

59. What is the motto of the *Mission: SPACE* training center?
a.) "To Infinity. . . and beyond!"
b.) "To boldly go. . ."
c.) "We choose to go. . ."
d.) "The final frontier is at hand"

60. About how many times bigger than actual size is the DNA strand in front of the Wonders of Life pavilion?
a.) 1 million
b.) 100 million
c.) 550 million
d.) 5.5 billion

61. If you stand under *Spaceship Earth* during a rainstorm, the water won't run off the globe and drench you. Why not?
a.) It is drained into a children's play area
b.) It is drained into an underground well
c.) It is funneled to the trees surrounding Epcot
d.) It is funneled into the World Showcase Lagoon

Did You Know?

TEST TRACK'S TRACK HAS BEEN ENGINEERED TO WITHSTAND WINDS UP TO 200 MILES PER HOUR.

62. What was the name of the first attraction to be removed from Future World?
a.) *The Astuter Computer Revue*
b.) *Horizons*
c.) *World Of Motion*
d.) *EPCOT Computer Central*

63. Each car in *Test Track* has how many wheels?
a.) None, the cars ride along a rail system
b.) 4
c.) 16
d.) 22

64. In *Kitchen Kabaret,* what type of cheese was "Miss Cheese?"
a.) Cheddar
b.) Swiss
c.) Mozzarella
d.) American

World Showcase

65. Which flag in World Showcase has the most colors in it?
a.) United States
b.) Norway
c.) Mexico
d.) Morocco

66. What is located at the top of the campanile (bell tower) in the Italy pavilion?
a.) An angel
b.) A statue of Jesus
c.) A cross
d.) A statue of St. Mark

67. How many stories high is the pagoda in front of the Japan pavilion?
a.) 3
b.) 4
c.) 5
d.) 6

68. What character(s) can you sometimes find signing autographs in full sombrero and serape near the Mexico pavilion?
a.) Mickey
b.) Goofy
c.) The Three Caballeros
d.) Donald

69. About how far have you traveled if you walk from the Canada pavilion all the way around the World Showcase Lagoon to the Mexico pavilion?
a.) .7 miles
b.) 1.2 mile
c.) 2.1 miles
d.) Exactly 10,182 feet - which stands for 10-1-82, Epcot's opening day

70. How many nations in World Showcase have at least one star on their flag?
a.) 1
b.) 2
c.) 3
d.) 5

71. Which of these former U.S. Presidents is NOT represented by an Audio-Animatronics figure in *The American Adventure?*
a.) George Washington
b.) Thomas Jefferson
c.) Theodore Roosevelt
d.) Abraham Lincoln

72. In what pavilion might you be able to meet Pinocchio?
a.) Germany
b.) United States
c.) Italy
d.) United Kingdom

73. What is special about the flag on top of the The American Adventure pavilion?
a.) It once flew over the White House in Washington, D.C.
b.) It has only 15 stars
c.) It was recovered from the World Trade Center site
d.) It was hand stitched by a direct descendant of Betsy Ross.

74. By comparison, about how large is the World Showcase Lagoon?
a.) 85 football fields
b.) 20 baseball diamonds
c.) 90 tennis courts
d.) 3 Ping-Pong tables

75. How many nations are represented in World Showcase?
a.) 15
b.) 11
c.) 14
d.) 9

76. What is the maximum height of any building in World Showcase?
a.) 3 stories
b.) 5 stories
c.) 99 feet
d.) 199 feet

77. Who does the statue outside the Germany pavilion represent?
a.) St. George
b.) A dragon slayer

Did You Know?

MORE THAN 30 TONS OF THE FRUITS AND VEGETABLES SERVED IN WDW RESTAURANTS ARE GROWN IN THE LAND PAVILION.

c.) Saint Nicholas

d.) Saint Michael

78. During the *IllumiNations* nighttime show, all of the pavilions in World Showcase are illuminated except one. Which is it?

a.) Italy

b.) China

c.) Japan

d.) Morocco

79. How many torches outline the shores of World Showcase Lagoon?

a.) 11

b.) 19

c.) 71

d.) 99

80. What is unique about the storefronts in the France pavilion?

a.) They contain living quarters for some of the Cast Members from France.

b.) Behind them is a VIP lounge.

c.) They are "themed" even in areas guests can't see.

d.) Behind them are rooms containing most of the computers that control the attractions in World Showcase.

81. The facade of The American Adventure building is made of approximately how many bricks?

a.) 10,000

b.) 110,000

c.) 1,000,000

d.) None. It is made completely of fiberglass painted to look like brick.

82. The name of the boat ride in the Mexico pavilion is:

a.) *Cerveza y Cantina*

b.) *Mexico - Giver of Life*

c.) *El Rio del Tiempo*

d.) *Muchas Gracias*

83. What is the first spoken line in *The American Adventure*?

a.) "We the people"

b.) "Four score and seven years ago"

c.) "I have a dream"

d.) "America did not exist."

84. The French Gothic "Hotel du Canada" in the Canada pavilion was modeled after a chateau in what Canadian city?

a.) Toronto

b.) Ottawa

c.) Manitoba

d.) Niagara Falls

85. What are the names of the water taxis in World Showcase?

a.) The Friendship Launches

b.) Epcot Water Taxis

c.) World Water Taxis

d.) There's one named for each of the countries in World Showcase

86. In *The American Adventure*, which Audio-Animatronics figure twirls a lasso?
   a.) Roy Rogers
   b.) Wyatt Earp
   c.) Will Rogers
   d.) Ronald Reagan

87. What was the inspiration for the beautiful gardens of the Canada pavilion?
   a.) Various gardens in Ottawa
   b.) Butchart Gardens
   c.) Victoria Garden
   d.) Rose and Crown Gardens

88. The first World Showcase nighttime show was?
   a.) *Fantasmic!*
   b.) *Carnival de Lumiere*
   c.) *IllumiNations*
   d.) *A New World Fantasy*

89. How does the Eiffel Tower in the France pavilion compare in size to the original?
   a.) It's half the size
   b.) It's one quarter the size
   c.) It's one-thirteenth the size
   d.) It's the same size

90. "Port of Entry" is the name of one of the two Plaza merchandise shops that mark the entrance to World Showcase from Future World. What is the name of the other?
   a.) Disney Traders
   b.) MouseGear
   c.) Centorium
   d.) Showcase Shops

91. What color is found on the flag of every nation with a pavilion in World Showcase?
   a.) Red
   b.) White
   c.) Blue
   d.) Green

92. Outside what nation's pavilion might you find "Living Statues"?
   a.) Japan
   b.) France
   c.) China
   d.) Italy

93. What is the first pavilion on the left when you enter World Showcase from Future World?
   a.) China
   b.) Morocco

Did You Know?

THE EARTH GLOBE IN *ILLUMINATIONS* IS THE WORLD'S FIRST SPHERICAL VIDEO DISPLAY SYSTEM. ITS OUTER SHELL IS WRAPPED IN 15,000 LEDS (LIGHT-EMITTING DIODES).

c.) Mexico
d.) Canada

94. In what year did *IllumiNations* begin?
a.) 1982
b.) 1988
c.) 1989
d.) 1993

95. Name the only government-sponsored World Showcase pavilion.
a.) Italy
b.) Norway
c.) United Kingdom
d.) Morocco

96. What was the empty stone building next to Germany built to house?
a.) A boat ride planned for Germany
b.) An Israel pavilion
c.) The control center for the *IllumiNations* fireworks show
d.) Lounges and a restaurant for VIPs

97. Can you name the shop in Norway that specializes in toys, games, and trolls?

a.) Norway Novelties
b.) Viking Traders
c.) Puffin's Roost
d.) Troll Treasures

98. The first country to be added to World Showcase after Epcot's opening on October 1, 1982, was?
a.) Norway
b.) Morocco
c.) Canada
d.) China

99. What Tokyo Disneyland attraction was originally planned for the Japan pavilion but never built there?
a.) *Mount Fuji Roller Coaster*
b.) *Matterhorn Bobsleds*
c.) *Expedition Everest*
d.) *Meet the World*

100. What is the nickname given to the mechanism used to move the sets of Audio-Animatronics figures in *The American Adventure*?
a.) "Mount Movemore"
b.) "Uncle Sam"
c.) "The War Wagon"
d.) "The People Mover"

101. What is the name of the horticultural tour through the gardens and pavilions of World Showcase?
a.) "World Garden Tour"
b.) "Gardens of the World"
c.) "Behind the Seeds"
d.) "Wild about Plants"

102. Can you name the boat moored on World Showcase Lagoon in front of The American Adventure pavilion?
a.) "The Adventurer"
b.) "Freedom"
c.) "The Golden Dream"
d.) "Miss Liberty"

103. Which of the following famous Americans is NOT featured in *The American Adventure*?
a.) Maya Angelou
b.) Ben Franklin
c.) Susan B. Anthony
d.) Samuel Clemens

104. What city's buildings are replicated in the Italy pavilion in World Showcase?
a.) Rome
b.) Venice
c.) Florence
d.) The Vatican

105. The Norway pavilion houses a special house of worship. What is it?
a.) A stave church
b.) A Buddhist temple
c.) A Viking temple
d.) A Gothic cathedral

106. Who is honored with a statue near the rear of the piazza in the Italy pavilion?
a.) Caesar
b.) Neptune
c.) St. Jude
d.) Frank Sinatra

107. Which of these was a proposed concept for World Showcase?
a.) Circus International
b.) A railroad circling the pavilions
c.) International Food Court
d.) House of Cheese

108. What two countries in World Showcase at Epcot have restaurants on the lagoon side of the walkway?
a.) United States and United Kingdom
b.) United Kingdom and Mexico
c.) Mexico and Norway
d.) Japan and Canada

109. Where can you find a statue of marathon champion Greta Waitz?
a.) Germany
b.) United Kingdom
c.) Norway
d.) United States

110. According to the menu in Italy's "Pasticceria Italiana di Alfredo di Roma" restaurant, who brought spaghetti to the U.S.?
   a.) Amerigo Vespucci
   b.) Thomas Jefferson
   c.) Christopher Columbus
   d.) Fiorello H. LaGuardia

111. How many Audio-Animatronics figures are found in *The American Adventure*?

   a.) 35
   b.) 19
   c.) 47
   d.) 9

112. In which country can you find a person making animals out of candy?
   a.) China
   b.) Italy
   c.) Japan
   d.) Germany

Did You Know?

THE CIRCLE OF LIFE FILM IN THE LAND PAVILION
INCLUDES SCENES FILMED IN MORE THAN
30 NATIONS ACROSS THE GLOBE.

113. The Cast Members who work in the pavilions in World Showcase are:
a.) Actors
b.) Natives of the countries they represent
c.) College students looking to study overseas
d.) Cast Members from Disneyland Paris and Tokyo here on an exchange program

114. What is the name of the amphitheater located in front of The American Adventure pavilion in World Showcase?
a.) American Dreams
b.) Theater of the Americas
c.) America Gardens Theater
d.) Hollywood Hills Amphitheater

115. Between France and Morocco there is something different about the pavement. What is it?
a.) It is a different color.
b.) It is made of cobblestone.
c.) It is filled with hidden Mickeys.
d.) It is a wooden bridge.

116. What is the only pavilion without a table service restaurant?
a.) Canada
b.) The American Adventure
c.) Germany
d.) United Kingdom

117. Where in World Showcase can children learn to make masks that reflect each pavilion's culture?

a.) Epcot Junior Imagineering Stations
b.) Imagineering Stops
c.) Kidcot Fun Stops
d.) Epkid Stations

118. Which of the following historical events is NOT represented in *The American Adventure* show by a scene using Audio-Animatronics figures?
a.) The signing of the Declaration of Independence
b.) Philadelphia Centennial Exposition
c.) Valley Forge
d.) The Civil War

119. How many islands are in World Showcase Lagoon?
a.) 0
b.) 1
c.) 2
d.) 3

120. What is the name of the toy shop in the UK pavilion?
a.) The Little Toy Shoppe
b.) The Toy Soldier
c.) Tikes and Bikes
d.) Lads and Lasses

121. Where was World Showcase originally to have been located?
a.) On the site that is now Disney-MGM Studios
b.) Behind the Magic Kingdom
c.) Exactly where it is today
d.) Beside the Seven Seas Lagoon

THE ANSWERS
TO CHAPTER THREE

1. b.) 300 acres
Covering more than 300 acres, Epcot occupies only about 1/100th of WDW's approximately 30,000-acre site.

2. b.) 1975
1975 was a big year for Walt Disney World. After almost four years of success with the Magic Kingdom, attention was turned to Walt Disney's ultimate dream — his "Experimental Prototype Community of Tomorrow," or EPCOT. In July 1975, during a press conference at the Contemporary Resort Hotel, Disney President and Chief Operating Officer, Card Walker, announced plans to build it. However, the project would fulfill Walt's plans in name alone. Instead of an actual working city, EPCOT Center (as it was then called) would be an educational theme park, idea showcase, and multinational exhibit.
Still, two key points of Walt's master plan remained: First, there would be an emphasis on exploring the possibilities of future technologies. Second, there would be an "international neighborhood" where nations from around the world could showcase themselves in an environment

of peace and understanding. They became the bases for Epcot's two major "lands," Future World and World Showcase, which continue to entertain, inform, and inspire Epcot visitors to this day.

3. d.) Disney character merchandise
In an attempt to keep the parks separate and distinct from one another, no Disney character merchandise was sold in Epcot when it opened. In fact, after Mickey Mouse showed up for the park's Grand Opening in 1982, he was not seen or heard there again for two years! That's right — there were no Disney characters seen anywhere in the park in its early days. That all changed when the "Eisner Era" began. Not long after he took over as chairman of The Walt Disney Company, Michael Eisner paid a visit to EPCOT Center and spent a great deal of time playing tourist. When he visited the Centorium store in CommuniCore, he was unhappy with the quality and selection of merchandise. He felt its serious tone made it seem too museum-like and there was too little for children. He also questioned why there were no Disney characters in the park or on the merchandise. The designers told him that Mickey

and his friends belonged in the Magic Kingdom, not in Epcot. Not according to the new Head Mouse they didn't! So, quicker than you could say Mickey, the "Fab 5" — Mickey, Minnie, Donald, Pluto, and Goofy — began to make appearances in Future World (usually in shiny, silver space suits for some reason). And shortly thereafter, classic character merchandise began to appear in shops and on carts throughout the park, right next to toys based on Disney's newest creation Figment, whom children loved.

4. c.) On Main Street, U.S.A. in the Magic Kingdom

The EPCOT Preview Center replaced the *Walt Disney Story* on Main Street, U.S.A. in 1979. The Center included a film, concept art, and construction photographs. When the new monorail track to EPCOT Center was finished, guests were able to ride through the construction site to watch its progress.

5. a.) World Showcase

World Showcase, originally designed as two connected semicircles, was intended to be the main draw for what would become EPCOT Center. It would contain a "Courtyard of Nations," an Observation Tower that would rise high above a promenade, and 30 international pavilions. Future World, originally known as the "EPCOT Theme Center," was to be added later and contain three major pavilions plus smaller, satellite pavilions that would focus on such things as energy, agriculture, transportation, technology, and the arts. After a lukewarm response from foreign nations to the proposal that they sponsor pavilions for the flagship World Showcase project, Disney decided not only to build "Future World" at the same time as World Showcase, but also to make it the main entrance to the new theme park. Why the change of heart? Partly because it was relatively simple to get major corporations to finance the construction of the Future World pavilions in return for exclusive sponsorship deals.

6. b.) 1979

Groundbreaking for Epcot took place October 1, 1979, not far from the Magic Kingdom. It took exactly three years to the day to clear the land and build the entire infrastructure for Future World and World Showcase, including all of the attractions, restaurants, shops, and gardens!

The process involved nearly 3,000 designers, 22 general contractors, 500 subcontractors, and a total of more than 10,000 workers from 18 labor unions, including 4,000 construction workers. At the time, it was the largest construction project in the entire United States. Think they had to move around a little dirt? You bet — try about 54 million cubic feet.

7. c.) GM

General Motors was the first company to sign on with Disney as a corporate sponsor for the planned EPCOT Center. In December 1977, GM signed a ten-year agreement to sponsor the World of Motion pavilion, which opened on October 1, 1982. When the company's contract expired, it renewed its sponsorship for only one year. But prior to the expiration of that agreement, it signed another contract to continue sponsoring the pavilion while a new attraction (which it agreed to sponsor) was designed and built.

Did You Know?

THE EXPERIMENTAL PROTOTYPE COMMUNITY OF TOMORROW, AS EPCOT WAS KNOWN WHEN WALT DISNEY DREAMED IT UP, WAS TO BE LAID OUT LIKE A "WHEEL AND SPOKES," VERY MUCH LIKE THE MAGIC KINGDOM. INSTEAD OF A CASTLE, HOWEVER, THE CENTER WOULD HAVE BEEN THE CITY'S BUSTLING DOWNTOWN AREA.

8. a.) Odyssey Center
The First Aid Center, staffed by registered nurses, is located at the Odyssey Center in Future World. Close by you'll find the Baby Care Center, which is furnished with rocking chairs for tired or nursing moms. Guests can also purchase disposable diapers, formula, and baby food there.

9. c.) $500,000
Following the final *Tapestry of Nations* parade of 1999, the incredible *IllumiNations 2000: Reflections of Earth* lit up the skies over the World Showcase Lagoon. For 15 minutes, the lagoon was awash with flames and pyrotechnics, all choreographed to a musical score. Toward the end, a massive Earth globe appeared in the center of the lagoon. Its continents, acting as three-story-high video screens, portrayed images of unity throughout the world. As the spectacle reached its finale, the Globe unfolded like a Lotus flower, releasing a 40-foot flaming torch. The video screens on the globe then counted down to the dawn of the new century.

10. b.) *Tapestry of Dreams*
The 30-minute *Tapestry of Dreams* parade opened October 1, 2001, in honor of WDW's "100 Years of Magic" Celebration commemorating the 100th anniversary of the birth of Walt Disney. The show — a slightly altered version of the earlier *Tapestry of Nations* parade — ran from Mexico to Morocco in World Showcase. Both it and its predecessor celebrated the human spirit and children's dreams with 150 performers and puppets along with huge floats. Among the most impressive were 15 that measured 19-feet tall by 16-feet wide and carried giant drums called "Millennium Clocks."

11. c.) 1994
The *Candlelight Processional* began in 1958 at Disneyland in California. When Walt Disney World opened in 1971, Rock Hudson narrated the very first *Candlelight Processional* there, which took place in the Magic Kingdom (the only park open at the time). In 1994, the Processional was moved to Epcot's America Gardens Theatre in World Showcase. It is now one of the most popular attractions at Epcot during the holiday season. So, what exactly is the *Candlelight Processional?* It is a retelling of the

Christmas story that includes readings by celebrity narrators, music by a massed choir and 50-piece orchestra, and a total of nearly 400 performers, including Cast Members, local musicians, and high school and community groups from across the country. Each guest narrator usually performs for only one or two days. Over the years, the narrators have included acclaimed actors, singers, sports figures, and astronauts. The show usually runs from the last week in November until the last week in December, with three, 40-minute performances daily. While you need reservations to get in, it's included in the price of park admission.

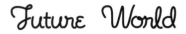

Future World

12. c.) 16,000,000 pounds
Spaceship Earth's estimated weight is 16 million pounds - more than three times that of a Space Shuttle fully fueled and ready for launch!

13. a.) Green
Buzzy is the rookie pilot on your adventurous trip through the human brain.

14. b.) The treads are in the shape of Coca-Cola bottles
Located just outside Innoventions West, Ice Station Cool offers guests the opportunity to sample (for free!)

Coca-Cola beverages from around the world. But be careful. . . some of the drinks taste absolutely terrible! Still, it's a great place to cool off during the sweltering summer months!

15. d.) 5,246 feet
With 5,246 feet (I counted) of track, *Test Track* has WDW's longest ride track (although doesn't it seem as though *it's a small world* just goes on forever?). 2,600 feet of that track is located outside the show building. The track is 0 to 12 feet off the ground inside the pavilion, and 12 to 24 feet off the ground outside.

16. b.) "Is this a nightmare, or what?"
This correct answer actually takes Ellen from a negative score back to zero. Alex Trebeck states that at the end of the first round, Judy has a commanding lead with $17,800, Ellen has a negative score, and Dr. Einstein is nowhere, "relatively speaking," as he has zero points. When Ellen answers "Is this a nightmare, or what?" Alex replies, "Oh, Ellen, your first correct response!"

17. c.) 35
Disney's "Leave A Legacy" program was introduced in 1999 as part of Epcot's Millennium Celebration. The 35 sculptures range from 3 to 19 feet high and are engraved with inch-square images of guests. Guests who want to participate can have

their photos taken at one of five Photo Capture Stations near *Spaceship Earth*. The photo is etched onto a steel tile, which is affixed to one of the stones, usually within 48 hours. To locate the photo, guests can check Epcot's on-site computers or visit Disney's Leave a Legacy web site.

18. a.) A geodesic sphere
Although it is somewhat oblong, thus not a perfect sphere, *Spaceship Earth* is considered the world's first geodesic sphere (or "geosphere"). Its outside surface is 150,000 square feet and its inside volume, 2.2 million cubic feet. The concept of the geodesic sphere came from Buckminster Fuller, who also coined the term "spaceship earth" in his 1969 book, *An Operating Manual for Spaceship Earth*.

19. a.) Commander
Neil Armstrong commanded the historic Apollo 11 space flight. Other noteworthy Commanders include Jim Lovell (Apollo 13) and Alan Shepard (Apollo 14). Famous pilots include John Glenn (Friendship 7) and Buzz Aldrin (Apollo 11). One of the most notable Engineers (or Mission Specialists) was Dr. Sally Ride of the Space Shuttle Challenger.

20. c.) *Horizons*
Horizons opened on October 1, 1983 — exactly one year to the day after EPCOT Center opened — as part of "Phase II" of the park's development. Although the ride promised, "If we can dream it, we can do it," it closed permanently in 1999. The attraction was believed to be unprofitable after it lost its corporate sponsor in 1993. Sadly, the attraction building

was demolished to make room for a completely new ride.

21. b.) 120 to 185 feet
The massive icon that marks the entrance to Epcot is held up by six legs, each of which is supported by pylons sunk 120 to 185 feet into the ground. At its lowest point, the slightly imperfect sphere stands 18 feet off the ground.

22. b.) Duct tape
Bill Nye stops by Ellen's apartment before her dream sequence begins to borrow some aluminum foil, a clothespin, and a candle for an experiment he is working on.

23. c.) 50,000
Innoventions, the high-tech playground located in the center of Epcot's Future World, offers guests exciting live shows, demonstrations, and interactive displays. Presented by a variety of corporate sponsors, Innoventions occupies two pavilions totaling 50,000 square feet.

24. d.) Sea Base Alpha
In *The Living Seas* pavilion, take an elevator down to "Sea Base Alpha," a futuristic ocean research center. Here you will find excellent views of the aquarium. You can explore the facility, learn more about marine life, and even watch marine biologists caring for the inhabitants.

25. a.) Francis Ford Coppola
Captain EO had everything going for it: it was a sci-fi, 3D film; it starred worldwide pop sensation Michael Jackson; it was developed by George

Did You Know?

Lucas, directed by Francis Ford Coppola, and funded by Disney. What else could you ask for? Located inside the Kodak "Magic Eye Theater," this 17-minute film featured the King of Pop as the lead character, who sought to deliver a message of love and peace to an evil Supreme Leader (played by Anjelica Huston). It opened in 1986 and reportedly brought guests in to Epcot just to see it. So, what do you do with a popular attraction with all this going for it? You replace it, of course. *Honey, I Shrunk the Audience*, a 3D movie starring Rick Moranis, replaced *Captain EO* when it closed July 11, 1994, after an eight-year run.

26. c.) 3
In the Fitness Fairgrounds area of The Wonders of Life pavilion, you can test your senses and athletic abilities at various, interactive exhibits. There are also three theaters which house the films, *The Making of Me* and *Goofy About Health* as well as performances by the Anicomical Players.

27. d.) The names and extension numbers of Imagineers who worked on the attraction
If you look closely while walking through the pavilion, you will notice that many of the interior pipes in Sea Base Alpha have names and numbers written on them. There are similar "signatures" left by Imagineers throughout WDW — in attractions, shops, restaurants . . . just about anywhere!

28. b.) It is a recording of a bird in distress, played to keep other birds out of Future World
Most guests don't notice the sound. However, soon after Future World opened, Cast Members and Imagineers noticed that birds were making nests in signs, eaves, and on buildings. Needless to say, it caused a little bit of a mess, and the birds often swooped down near guests to pick up food that had fallen to the ground. To alleviate the bird dilemma naturally, without actually having to go in and evict the "new tenants," Disney installed a series of hidden speakers to broadcast the recorded sound of a bird in distress. The sound is an alert to other birds that there may be danger in the area, which causes them to

stay away. Have no fear, though…no birds were harmed in the making of this recording.

29. a.) An episode of "Magnum, P.I."
Believe it or not, the inspiration for Figment actually came from an episode of "Magnum, P.I." (Yes, the Tom Selleck detective show from the eighties)! Tony Baxter, the Disney Imagineer who came up with the concept, stated that he watched a "Magnum P.I." episode that mentioned a "figment of the imagination" as a real object ("Figments don't eat grass…" is the actual line). He felt the idea of a "figment of the imagination" was never visualized, and thus found the main character for the Imagination pavilion's main attraction. "Figment" began as a rough sketch by artist Steve Kirk,

which Disney legend Xavier Atencio developed into the loveable character we know today.

30. b.) *World of Motion*
Even park guide maps from the 1980s promised, "It's Fun to be Free," as you took a ride through the evolution of transportation in Epcot's *World of Motion* building. This 15-minute ride (quite long by Disney standards) was created in large part by classic Disney animator, Ward Kimball, narrated by legendary voice-over artist, Gary Owens, and featured the classic theme song, "It's Fun to be Free." The lyrics were written by Xavier Atencio and the music by Buddy Baker. The song was heard in both the queue line and the attraction itself, with slightly different lyrics in each area.

31. c.) 5 years
More than 650 Disney Imagineers
spent over 350,000 hours (about 40
man-years) in the development of
Mission: SPACE.

32. d.) Spaceship Earth
Reference is made to the ride vehicles
when the narrator says, "Attention
time travelers! Your Time Machine
is about to rotate for your return to
Earth. Please remain seated at all
times."

33. a.) Adam
Accompanied by his older brother,
Nick, Professor Szalinski's youngest son, Adam, has some fun with
the audience in this incredible 3D
adventure!

34. b.) 140
Each *Test Track* vehicle travels 50,000
miles in a year and is built to last for
about a million miles. That's like driving to the moon and back four times.
You think the drive with the kids to
Florida was rough? Imagine hearing,
"Are we there yet?" every five minutes
over a one-million mile trip!

35. d.) A trap door
Old commercials and print ads for
Epcot show Mickey Mouse standing
on top of the *Spaceship Earth* sphere.
He got there by climbing up through
a trap door at the top (and being
secured to a pole to keep him from
falling off!).

36. b.) 1983
Although the pavilion opened on
October 1, 1982 with the *Magic
Journeys* movie, the *Journey Into
Imagination* attraction featuring
Dreamfinder and Figment didn't
open until March 5, 1983. In 1998,
the ride and pavilion closed for refurbishment. The pavilion (renamed
simply Imagination!) reopened
that same year and was themed to
resemble the Imagination Institute
from the then-new *Honey, I Shrunk
the Audience* film (showing in the
Magic Eye Theater). The updated
ride lacked Dreamfinder, Figment,
and fun. The only things that weren't
missing were complaints from guests.
Before mass rioting and hysteria
broke out, Disney closed the attraction in late 2001, did some retooling,
and reopened it in June 2002 as *Journey Into Imagination with Figment*,
bringing back our purple pal.

**37. c.) Winter, summer, spring,
fall**
The large, center balloon represents
the different cultures of the world.
The "rain" that falls from this balloon symbolizes the many nations
nourishing the earth, which tops
the fountain below. The balloons
surrounding the center balloon represent the four seasons. If you look
closely, you will see that the colors of
the balloons reflect the seasons. Also,
if you look from the second floor
to the umbrellas in the food court

below, you will see that the tops of the umbrellas are all decorated with images of the sun as it is represented in different cultures. It's another incredible example of Disney's attention to detail and theme-ing in everything they do.

38. d.) SMRT-1
SMRT-1 (Smart One) was a small, purple robot located in *Epcot Computer Central*, where you could take a look "behind the scenes" at the computers that ran Epcot. Located on a revolving pedestal surrounded by telephones, he would challenge guests with trivia questions (kind of like what I'm doing now. . .) and would occasionally sing and tell jokes (many of them quite bad). Visitors could compete against one another by speaking their answers into the phones surrounding the pedestal.

39. b.) Leonard Nimoy
Fans may know him as "Mr. Spock" from the *Star Trek* TV shows and movies, but Mr. Nimoy, who has directed numerous feature films, also directed the *Body Wars* attraction movie. *Body Wars* takes guests on a

quick tour through the human body to pick up Dr. Cynthia Lair, who is investigating white-cell response time to a splinter. After being sucked down a capillary, guests chase after her in this action-packed ride.

40. a.) Red
Dreamfinder, accompanied by his lovable little dragon friend Figment, was your red-headed (and red-bearded) host through the quest to fill up your "Idea Bag" with things that inspire imagination. Unfortunately, he did not make the cut when the updated *Journey Into Imagination with Figment* opened on June 1, 2002.

41. b.) $35,000
Disney spends about $35,000 per night for the more than 2,800 shells used in the spectacular *IllumiNations* fireworks show in World Showcase.

42. c.) Yellow
As heard in the original theme song, Figment is: "Two tiny wings, eyes big and yellow. Horns of a steer, but a lovable fellow. From head to tail, he's royal purple pigment. And there—

Did You Know?

THE EXTENSIVE MOSAICS IN THE MOROCCO PAVILION WERE EXECUTED BY 19 MAALEMS (MOROCCAN ARTISANS) SENT OVER BY THE KING OF MOROCCO.

Viola!—you've got a Figment!" A longtime favorite of the original attraction, *Journey Into Imagination*, Figment was almost completely removed when the ride was closed for renovations in 1998 and reopened as *Journey Into Your Imagination*. But after criticism from fans and bad reviews of the attraction itself, it closed once again. It reopened in 2002 as *Journey Into Imagination with Figment*, and our pal Figment got his old job back. Not quite the same (or as good) as the original, but we're happy to have the little fella back in Epcot. As for his friend, the Dreamfinder, I hear he fell on hard times and can now be seen pumping gas on I-4.

43. b.) Fantasyland
At over six acres in size, The Land pavilion could contain the Magic Kingdom's Fantasyland.

44. b.) Pure and Simple
Pure and Simple offers healthy snack and meal choices in keeping with The Wonders of Life pavilion's theme of physical fitness. Guests can enjoy yogurt smoothies, salads, fruits, and more. A nice break from the typical burger and fries menu!

45. a.) Unmanned missions to the moon
The model of the moon located at the entrance to *Mission: SPACE* contains colored markers that indicate the 29 landing sites of manned and unmanned missions to the moon by the United States and Soviet Union between 1959 and 1976.

46. c.) 26 months
At 180 feet tall, without the hand, wand, and glistening "Epcot" addition, *Spaceship Earth* took 1,700 tons of steel and 26 months to build. It opened with the park on October 1, 1982.

47. d.) Near MouseGear
There is a little-known butterfly garden outside the rear entrance to MouseGear (on the way to *Test Track*), complete with benches and a small walking path. The butterfly garden in World Showcase is located in the United Kingdom pavilion, near the hedge maze and live entertainment stage. Both are wonderful, quiet places to sit and take a rest.

48. d.) *World of Motion*

General Motors originally sponsored the pavilion when it opened as *World of Motion*. It continued its sponsorship when the attraction was replaced by *Test Track*.

49. c.) 6

Future World, the area of Epcot showcasing new technologies through educational and interactive attractions and rides, opened with *Spaceship Earth, Universe of Energy, World of Motion, Journey Into Imagination*, The Land, and CommuniCore. Since then, some attractions have been replaced and numerous others have been added.

50. a.) It is 75 years after the first manned space flight

Disney chose the year 2036 for your *Mission: SPACE* training to commemorate the first manned space flight by Russian cosmonaut Yuri Gagarin in 1961. The ride's "International Space Training Center" screens candidates to fly on missions to Mars (a not-so subtle tribute to the former Magic Kingdom attraction of the same name?).

51. b.) 1997

Test Track replaced *World of Motion*, which closed in January 1996. The GM *Test Track* Preview Center opened in February 1996, with a scheduled opening date of May 1997 for the attraction. Everything worked fine

— except for the ride vehicles! The attraction finally opened to the public for limited previews on December 19, 1998, but its grand opening wasn't until March 17, 1999, nearly two years after the projected opening.

52. b.) 8,500

There are more than 8,500 inhabitants in *The Living Seas*, representing over 100 different species of marine life. In order to keep all its residents comfortable, the tank is closely monitored to keep the water temperature between 74 and 78 degrees Fahrenheit. The tank, which is 203 feet in diameter, is 27 feet deep and contains a man-made coral reef, similar to one that would be found in the Caribbean. The windows are made of a special acrylic that does not distort or magnify objects in the aquarium and are anywhere from six

to eight inches thick. Each window measures 8- by 24-feet and weighs about 9,000 pounds.

53. c.) The Land

The Land pavilion measures 253,780 square feet and covers six acres. Its main building holds up to 3,600 people and currently includes two attractions, along with a guided behind-the-scenes tour, a great little food court, and a wonderful character-meal restaurant. It will have a third attraction when *Soarin'* opens in 2005. As you enter The Land, you will pass the largest flower bed on property. It measures 20,000 square feet and contains about 20,000 plants. Working greenhouses and labs are also housed in this pavilion.

54. d.) *Snow White and the Seven Dwarfs*

Right after the Telephone Operators scene, look to the right at the Cinema screen to see Snow White dancing with Dopey and the rest of the seven dwarfs.

55. d.) 33,000 pounds

Weighing more than 15 tons, each of the ride cars in this Universe of Energy attraction is guided through the attraction on a wire that is a mere 1/8-inch thick!

56. c.) Electric Umbrella

Stargate was located in CommuniCore East (now Innoventions

East) when Epcot opened in 1982. It served salads, chicken sandwiches, and other fast foods. It closed on April 10, 1994, and reopened as the "Electric Umbrella" on June 24 of that same year.

57. b.) *Test Track*

Because part of the track is outdoors, the ride may temporarily be shut down in inclement weather. No, not the blistering, humid, middle-of-the-summer Florida heat, but events such as lightning and the oh-so-friendly Florida hurricanes.

58. b.) The 1947 Fall Mixer

According to the movie, Martin's parents met at the "State College Fall Mixer of '47." You can see the banner above the dance floor after they first meet.

59. c.) "We choose to go. . ."

The motto of the "International Space Training Center" is taken from a speech by President John F. Kennedy: "We choose to go to the moon … not because it is easy, but because it is hard." If you want to go "To Infinity… and beyond!" head on over to *Buzz Lightyear's Space Ranger Spin* in the Magic Kingdom's Tomorrowland!

60. d.) 5.5 billion

The 72-foot tall double helix DNA tower at the entrance to Epcot's Wonders of Life pavilion is 5.5 billion times actual size. That strand of DNA would be just the right size for a human who stands about 6 million miles tall.

61. d.) It is funneled into the World Showcase Lagoon

Spaceship Earth's drainage system absorbs rainwater into a gutter system that channels it to underground drains, where it is funneled into the World Showcase Lagoon.

62. a.) *The Astuter Computer Revue*

The Revue (also spelled Review) took place in CommuniCore East, on the second floor of the *Epcot Computer Central* attraction. It was located in an area that overlooked the computers that ran Epcot, and the show explained the role of computers in WDW. Much of the show used a projected image of the actor Ken Jennings dancing on top of these giant computers (Funny, they don't look anything like today's modern PC.) while singing a Sherman Brothers' tune called "The Computer Song." Mercifully, it closed January 2, 1994. *EPCOT Computer Central* closed just 28 days later.

63. d.) 22

Although there are only four visible wheels on the outside of each of the cars, there are a total of 22 wheels on each *Test Track* vehicle. The wheels require a total of six distinct braking systems on board each ride car.

64. b.) Swiss

You may not remember *Kitchen Kabaret*, but for 12 years, beginning in 1982, this show about the four food groups "rocked" The Land pavilion. Sponsored first by Kraft and then (starting in November 1992) by Nestle, the show featured Audio-Animatronics food characters and one human character, your host, Bonnie Appetit. *Kitchen Kabaret* was fun and colorful like Fantasyland's *Country Bear Jamboree*, but it was also informative. "Mr. Dairy Goods" introduced his "Stars of the Milky Way," including "Miss Cheese," a well-dressed … well, piece of Swiss cheese. She was joined by "Miss Yogurt" and "Miss Ice Cream" and sang lyrics like: "Your taste buds, I'll appease. I know how to please. It's known that I'm too good for words. Oh, isn't that right, big boy?"

World Showcase

65. c.) Mexico

Although the main colors of the Mexican flag are red, white, and green, the coat-of-arms in the center, featuring an eagle eating a rattlesnake, includes numerous other colors, such as brown, aqua, yellow, and various shades of green. The flag was adopted in 1821 when the Independence movement ended victoriously. The central shield recalls Mexico's Aztec heritage.

Did You Know?

THE 108,000-GALLON FOUNTAIN OF NATIONS IN FUTURE WORLD USES AS MUCH POWER IN A DAY AS IT TAKES TO RUN A SINGLE HOUSE FOR SIX MONTHS. WHY? BECAUSE IT TAKES AN INCREDIBLE AMOUNT OF PRESSURE TO CREATE ITS BEAUTIFUL WATER BALLET.

66. a.) An angel
The 83-foot bell tower in World Showcase's Italy is a replica of the "campanile" in St. Mark's Square in Venice. The angel atop Epcot's bell tower was created using a model of the original and, like the original, is covered with real gold leaf. Unlike the Venetian angel, however, the Epcot replica is also topped with a lightning rod.

67. c.) 5
The 83-foot tall, blue-roofed Goju-no-to pagoda, the icon of the Japan pavilion, was inspired by the seventh century Horyuji Shrine at Nara. The levels of the five-tiered pagoda represent the five elements from which Buddhists believe all things in the universe are produced: earth, water, fire, wind, and sky. Atop the pagoda is a bronze, nine-ringed spire, known as a "sorin," with gold wind chimes and a water flame.

68. d.) Donald
Donald is not often seen in the parks, so be sure to get his autograph and say hello (or "hola") when you

and say hello (or "hola") when you see him outside the Mexico pavilion. (Oh, and a "sombrero" is a tall straw hat, while a "serape" is a long, multicolored shawl worn by Mexican men.

69. b.) 1.2 miles
The promenade surrounding the World Showcase Lagoon is about 1.2 miles long, and is more than just a way to get from one pavilion to another. It is filled with shops and restaurants and acts as a stage for the parades and performers from the World Showcase nations. At night, the promenade becomes your seat for one of the best nighttime shows in WDW, *IllumiNations: Reflections of Earth*.

70. c.) 3
The World Showcase nations with one or more stars on their flags are the United States, Morocco, and China.

71. d.) Abraham Lincoln
The four Presidents represented in *The American Adventure* are George Washington, Thomas Jefferson,

Theodore Roosevelt, and Franklin D. Roosevelt. Washington is seen in Valley Forge, Jefferson as he pens the Declaration of Independence, Theodore Roosevelt during the founding of Yosemite National Park, and Franklin D. Roosevelt delivering the famous, "The only thing we have to fear" line from his first inaugural address. Abraham Lincoln is featured prominently in *The Hall of Presidents* in the Magic Kingdom.

72. c.) Italy
You may see Pinocchio in Italy with Gepetto. The two may even break into song (in Italian, of course). That makes sense because *Le Avventure di Pinocchio* ("The Adventures of Pinocchio") was written by Tuscan author Carlo Lorenzini (under the pen name "C. Collodi"), and was first published in Rome in 1881. Pinocchio means "pine eyes" in Italian.

73. b.) It has only 15 stars
The flag which adorns the top of The American Adventure pavilion has only 15 stars on it. That's because when the U.S. was first formed, the flag had the same number of stars

Did You Know?
THE THATCHED ROOFS IN THE UNITED KINGDOM PAVILION ARE MADE OUT OF PLASTIC BROOM BRISTLES BECAUSE REAL THATCH WOULD BE A FIRE HAZARD.

nation. As more states joined the union, it became impossible to add a stripe for each one. That is why the current U.S. flag has 50 stars, one for each state, but just 13 stripes representing the original 13 colonies.

74. a.) 85 football fields
The World Showcase Lagoon is about 37 acres in size — roughly the size of eighty-five 100- by 50-yard football fields.

75. b.) 11
World Showcase has 11 national pavilions, each staffed by natives of the country and each offering distinctive merchandise, ethnic cuisine, shows, entertainment, and architecture representative of the nation's culture. Even the landscaping changes from country to country around the promenade encircling the World Showcase Lagoon. It was Disney Imagineer Harper Goff, an art director on *20,000 Leagues Under the Sea* and a Disneyland attraction designer, who came up with the concept of individual pavilions showcasing each participating country's architecture and customs.

76. b.) 5 stories
The maximum height of any World Showcase pavilion is five stories. This includes the Eiffel Tower in France and the temple in Japan, though both look taller thanks to the designers' use of "forced perspective."

Forced perspective is a filmmaking technique used to alter the viewer's perception of an object's size. For example, to make a building look taller than it is, the ground level is constructed at "normal" size and the upper stories made progressively smaller. This makes the upper stories appear higher than they actually are when seen from below. In contrast, The American Adventure pavilion uses forced perspective in reverse. It appears to be three stories tall, when it is actually five, giving it more visual impact at a distance without sacrificing the colonial look the designers wanted.

77. a.) St. George
Atop a fountain in the center of St. George Platz (plaza) in the Germany pavilion, St. George is immortalized on horseback, slaying a dragon. St. George is the patron saint of soldiers, chivalry, and Germany, and monuments to him are common throughout Bavaria.

78. d.) Morocco
Because the buildings in the Morocco pavilion are replicas of structures with great religious significance, they are not lit.

79. b.) 19
As part of the *IllumiNations 2000: Reflections of Earth* fireworks show celebrating the coming of the new millennium, 19 gas-powered torches

were erected around the lagoon. These 27-foot torches represent the first 19 centuries of the common era. The "torch" representing the 21st century rises up each night out of the Earth globe during the show's finale.

80. c.) They are "themed" even in areas guests can't see
Unlike many of the attractions and buildings in WDW theme parks, the false storefronts in France are themed even "backstage," out of view of park guests. Why? Well, the real reason is that some guests of the Epcot resorts can see the rear of the France pavilion from their hotel rooms. Since the area can be seen by guests, it must be themed in every detail; WDW visitors should never be able to see the non-themed "back" of a building.

81. b.) 110,000
The 110,000 red bricks used on the colonial-style structure were all hand made from Georgian clay, then tinted and aged to add to the building's appearance of authenticity. The bricks were used on the entire structure — even "backstage" out of view of guests. Not only that, but the entire structure was constructed at a slightly higher elevation than the pavilions that surround it — a wonderful beacon for Epcot visitors across the lagoon in Future World.

82. c.) El Rio del Tiempo
The main attraction in the Mexico

pavilion, "the River of Time" takes guests on a leisurely, nine-minute boat ride through the "Three Cultures of Mexico," from the ancient jungles of the Yucatan to present day Mexico City. It includes Audio-Animatronics figures, film clips, and a wonderful musical score..

83. d.) "America did not exist."
Benjamin Franklin opens *The American Adventure* with those emotional words. They come from John Steinbeck's 1966 work, *America and Americans*, a book of essays on the American people combined with pictures of the 50 states. The excerpt continues: "Four centuries of work, bloodshed, loneliness, and fear created this land. We built America, and the process made us Americans, a new breed, rooted in all races." Don't miss this attraction.

84. b.) Ottawa
The "Hotel du Canada" is the towering landmark that leads guests into the Canada pavilion. The distinctive building is modeled after the French Gothic design of the 19th-century "Chateau Laurier," located in Canada's capital city of Ottawa. It is another example of "forced perspective," in that although it looks six stories high, it is actually only three. The building was designed to represent the entire nation of Canada, as the top portion of the building represents French Canada, while the

Did You Know?

LOCATED JUST TO THE WEST OF INNOVENTIONS WEST
(ON THE PATH THAT LEADS STRAIGHT TO THE LAND) IS A
MARKER THAT PINPOINTS THE EXACT CENTER OF EPCOT.

lower half is patterned after the hotels built around the turn of the twentieth century by the Canadian railroad as it pushed west toward the Rockies. The Hotel du Canada is home to "a Boutique des Provinces," a small shop with handcrafted items from Canadian artists, as well as pewter and decoupage (the art of cutting out pictures and pasting them on furniture or home accessories to simulate painting).

85. a.) The Friendship Launches
Eight 100-passenger water taxis known as Friendship Launches take guests across the World Showcase Lagoon. Docks are located near Mexico, Canada, Germany, Morocco, and World Showcase Plaza. The launches also transport guests to the Epcot Resort hotels, the BoardWalk, and Disney-MGM Studios.

86. c.) Will Rogers
Demonstrating the incredible advances in and realism of Disney's Audio-Animatronics technology, the Will Rogers figure can actually twirl a rope lasso.

87. b.) Butchart Gardens
The Canada pavilion gardens were inspired by Butchart Gardens on Vancouver Island, British Columbia. Located on Canada's West Coast, the 55-acre site attracts over a million visitors a year from around the world.

88. b.) *Carnival de Lumiere*
The first World Showcase nighttime show was the *Carnival de Lumiere*, which debuted October 23, 1982. It included music, fountains, and floating barges on which images were projected from behind. Unfortunately, the projection technology allowed guests in only certain viewing areas around the lagoon to see the show. *Carnival de Lumiere* was followed by *A New World Fantasy* in the summer of 1983 and *Laserphonic Fantasy* the following summer.

89. c.) It's one-thirteenth the size
There are just a few things that distinguish the Tower in Epcot from the original in Paris. Constructed using a copy of Gustav Eiffel's blueprints for the original tower, the Epcot version is exactly one-thirteenth the size of the original. It appears taller thanks

to the use of forced perspective. Visitors who have seen the original in Paris will also note that the Epcot tower is brownish pink while the original, thanks to years of oxidation, is greenish. Since the Disney pavilion was created to represent Paris in the late 1800s, its Eiffel tower was painted to be representative of that period. A final discrepancy between the original and the replica is one you would likely never notice. To discourage birds from perching on or making nests in the Epcot tower, it is covered with a sticky substance. This also prevents the forced perspective illusion from being ruined: birds perched near the top of the Epcot Eiffel would look enormous!

90. a.) Disney Traders
"World Showcase Plaza," located at the entrance to World Showcase after you cross the bridge from Future World, contains two stores and a small snack shop. (It is also a great place to watch *IllumiNations!*) The stores, "Port of Entry" (to the right) and "Disney Traders" (to the left), are located in the Plaza Towers. "Disney Traders" opened April 9, 1987, and contains Disney character merchandise with World Showcase themes. "Port of Entry," which opened March 28, 1987, sells children's clothing, toys, and giftware. The "Refreshment Port" has a limited McDonald's menu — a far cry from the frozen yogurt and fruit snacks

it sold prior to the menu change on August 8, 2001.

91. a.) Red
All of the nations represented in World Showcase have red in their flags.

92. d.) Italy
As you meander through the Italy pavilion, be sure to keep an eye out for the "Living Statues." These mime performers have an incredible resemblance to real marble and instantly draw a crowd into their silent "theater." Stand next to one and have your picture taken . . . if you dare. These talented performers can be a little mischievous given the chance! Don't take them for "granite," these performers are "marblous." (Sorry. . . I couldn't resist!) But do keep your eyes peeled for them. They used to perform in France and may well move to another country in the future.

93. c.) Mexico
The Mexico and Canada pavilions are located directly to the left and right, respectively, of the entrance to World Showcase from Future World. Their placement represents each country's physical relationship to the continental United States. Here's how: The American Adventure pavilion is in the center of World Showcase, just across the lagoon from the bridges to Future World. When you stand at the American pavilion's

entrance, facing the lagoon, Mexico is to your right (south) and Canada to your left (north).

94. b.) 1988
On January 30, 1988, General Electric partnered with Disney to unveil the original *IllumiNations* fireworks and light show in World Showcase.

95. d.) Morocco
Added to World Showcase in 1984, the Morocco pavilion features beautiful mosaic art and stonework commissioned by the King of Morocco. It is the only national pavilion sponsored by a government rather than by one or more of the nation's domestic corporations.

96. a.) A boat ride planned for Germany
The stone building located alongside the Biergarten Restaurant was to have been the home of a "Rhine River" ride, which would have taken guests on a cruise through the German countryside. It was to offer both education and entertainment by showcasing the cultural heritage of Germany's past and present. The building, which still stands, has been used at various times as a workshop, for prop and float storage, and as a rehearsal studio for performers.

97. c.) Puffin's Roost
At The Puffin's Roost "Curios and Collectibles" shop, guests can purchase authentic Norwegian gifts such as sweaters, clothing, jewelry, leather goods, pewter, and "troll dolls."

98. b.) Morocco
Only two countries have been added to World Showcase since Epcot opened, Morocco (September 7, 1984) and Norway (May 6, 1988). Three north African cities are represented in Morocco, Casablanca, Fez, and Marrakesh, and the pavilion is divided by the "Bab Boujouloud gate." The "ville nouvelle" (new city) lies on one side and the Medina (old city) on the other.

99. d.) *Meet the World*
Originally designed to be part of the Japan pavilion, *Meet the World* is a

Carousel of Progress-type attraction that was a feature in Tokyo Disneyland until it closed June 30, 2003. This 19-minute attraction featured Audio-Animatronics figures of scholars, well-known samurai, and statesmen. It was narrated by a talking crane (the bird, not the machine), who explained a simplified version of Japanese history to a young boy and girl. The plan for Epcot was to house the attraction in the replica feudal castle that is located at the rear of the Japan pavilion. A Mt. Fuji roller coaster was also planned for the pavilion, but never came to pass.

100. c.) "The War Wagon"
Named after the 1967 John Wayne/

Kirk Douglas comedic western of the same name, the "War Wagon" is a massive, high-tech scene changer located behind and below *The American Adventure* theater. This movable device is the length of a railroad boxcar and twice as wide (about 65 x 35 x 14 feet). It weighs 175 tons, moves on a system of computer-controlled tracks, and takes up more space in the pavilion than does the actual seating area for guests! The number of Audio-Animatronics figures and scene changes in the show forced the Disney Imagineers to invent this behemoth, which not only moves the 11 sets backwards and forwards, but up and down as well.

101. b.) "Gardens of the World"
This guided tour is hosted by one of Disney's horticultural experts. The expert takes guests around the promenade to review the plants and share the secrets and technologies that Disney's horticulturists use to acclimate a diversity of plant life from around the globe to the harsh Florida weather.

102. c.) "The Golden Dream"
You may not notice this ship, but it is docked out in the lagoon behind the America Gardens Theatre. "Golden Dream" is also the name of a song by Randy Bright and Robert Moline that is part of *The American Adventure* soundtrack. The song has been part of the attraction since it opened,

but in 1992, it was given a new finale and the song lyrics were changed.

103. a.) Maya Angelou

Ms. Angelou is not featured in *The American Adventure*, but she was the narrator of *The Hall of Presidents* in the Magic Kingdom until 2000. When the attraction was renovated to add George W. Bush, it reopened with a male narrator.

104. b.) Venice

The Italy pavilion is inspired by the romantic city of Venice. Architectural elements of the city are found in the scaled-down reproductions of the city's campanile (belltower) and Doge's Palace. There are also Venetian-style bridges and sculptures, an open-air market surrounded by olive, kumquat, and citrus trees and Mediterranean plant life, and gondolas on the lagoon.

105. a.) A stave church

Stave refers to a construction technique for wooden structures that was perfected by Norwegian artisans in the Middle Ages and helped to ensure the building's longevity. Researchers believe there may have been as many as 2,000 stave churches in existence at the end of the 13th century. Today fewer than 30 original stave churches remain.

The stave church found in the Norway pavilion is a scaled down, detailed replica of the Gol stave church, located in the Norsk Folkemuseum in Oslo, Norway. The church contains a fascinating exhibit on Norwegian culture and the history of the stave churches. It is probably the most visited stave structure in the world.

106. b.) Neptune

Located in the central plaza of the Italy pavilion, known as the "Plaza del Teatro," you can find the "Fontana de Nettuno." This fountain contains the image of Neptune, the God of the Sea, and was inspired by Gian Lorenzo Bernini's Fountain of Trevi in Rome. If it looks vaguely familiar, you may be remembering the Trevi fountain from Federico Fellini's classic film, *La Dolce Vita*.

107. d.) House of Cheese

Disney artist Herbert Ryman, who sketched the original Cinderella Castle concepts, created concept drawings for a "House of Cheese" (don't laugh...OK...you can laugh). At one point, this House of Cheese was to have been part of an "International Food pavilion." MMMmmm... Would have smelled GREAT in the middle of the summer, huh?

108. b.) United Kingdom and Mexico

The United Kingdom's Rose and Crown Pub & Dining Room is located on the lagoon side of the World Showcase promenade, across from The Toy Soldier and The Tea

Caddy shops. Mexico's Cantina de San Angel is also on the edge of the lagoon and serves burgers, tacos, and chili. Both restaurants are great places to watch *IllumiNations*.

109. c.) Norway
Nine-time New York City Marathon winner Greta Waitz is immortalized in a statue located on the grounds of the Norway pavilion. (No other woman has won more than two New York Marathons.) The Greta Waitz Lopet (road race), the largest run for women in the world, is held annually in her home country of Norway.

110. b.) Thomas Jefferson
According to Alfredo's menu, Jefferson brought spaghetti to America in 1786. However, commercial production didn't begin until the mid-1800s, and its popularity wasn't fully established until the turn of the 20th century. (Tip: If you want the best fettucine Alfredo this side of Rome, the Pasticceria can't be beat. It's the signature dish. Buon appetito!)

111. a.) 35
The American Adventure uses some of the Disney Imagineers' most advanced designs and effects. Among them are 35 lifelike Audio-Animatronics figures, which are used in a variety of historical scenes — Plymouth Rock, Valley Forge, the Civil War, and more. Although they are no longer the most advanced Audio-

Animatronics in WDW, these figures execute some amazing movements. For example, Mark Twain blows smoke from his pipe and Ben Franklin appears to walk up stairs.

112. c.) Japan
"Miyuki" is the name of the candy artist found in the Japan pavilion. She creates incredible (and FREE) candy treats by sculpting little edible animals out of rice dough with amazing speed and grace. Using nothing but her hands and a small pair of scissors, she creates detailed animals such as horses, rabbits, cats, monkeys, eagles, dragons, birds, and flowers. She is one of only 20 people in the world (and the only female anywhere) to perform this rare Japanese art, which dates back over 250 years. Miyuki was trained by her grandfather, one of the most renowned candy artists in Japan.

113. b.) Natives of the countries they represent
Each of the World Showcase pavilions is staffed by young men and women who are natives of the countries they represent or first generation Americans whose parents were natives. Disney has an International Staffing office whose representatives travel the globe recruiting these international Cast Members. Some come as part of a 6- to 12-month exchange program. Others spend a year and combine work in the pavilion with

formal education in tourism management and operation.

114. c.) America Gardens Theater
This outdoor stage and amphitheater on the shores of the World Showcase Lagoon offers guests free live entertainment year-round. Acts range from the Temptations and Michael Flatley's *Lord of the Dance* to the *Candlelight Processional* during the Christmas season.

115. a.) It is a different color.
An area of the pavement between France and Morocco is painted a different color from the rest of the dark-red ground. Why? The color change is supposed to suggest a waterway, representing the Straits of Gibraltar, which divides Europe and Africa — the continents that are home to

France and Morocco respectively.

116. b.) The American Adventure
Surprisingly, the United States pavilion does not have a table-service restaurant. Located directly in front of The American Adventure, the Liberty Inn is a counter-service restaurant that features traditional American fast-food such as cheeseburgers, chicken sandwiches, hot dogs, chicken strips, and French fries (along with a couple of healthy choices such as Veggie Burgers and Fruit Cups). Guests can dine inside (ahhhh…air conditioning) or under umbrella-covered tables outside the pavilion.

117. c.) Kidcot Fun Stops
At Epcot's Kidcot Fun Stops, children can interact with a Cast Mem-

ber from the pavilion's native country who will help them create a mask decorated with artwork that reflects the country along with the word "dream" written in that country's native language. The Fun Stops are a great way to keep children occupied and interested while touring World Showcase, which doesn't have much else in the way of entertainment for young guests.

118. a.) The signing of the Declaration of Independence
Although there is a scene with Benjamin Franklin and Thomas Jefferson discussing the famous document, the conversation takes place while Jefferson is drafting the Declaration, not while it is being signed.

119. d.) 3
The 40-acre World Showcase Lagoon contains three small, man-made islands. They are not open to guests and do not house any buildings, attractions, or displays. During the 1999 Millennium Celebration, the islands were decorated with fountains and lights for the nightly *IllumiNations* show.

120. b.) The Toy Soldier
This quaint shop in the United Kingdom pavilion sells a variety of British toys and games, including a large selection of Winnie the Pooh merchandise.

121. d.) Beside the Seven Seas Lagoon
Epcot's World Showcase was originally to have been a separate theme park from Future World. In fact, it was going to be built before Future World. The initial concept art created in 1975 by Disney artist Carl Diniz, shows World Showcase located adjacent to the Seven Seas Lagoon, between the Polynesian and Contemporary Resorts and near the Transportation and Ticket Center. The plans called for two large semicircular buildings to house the participating nations' exhibits rather than the individual pavilions we have today. These crescents would have faced one another across a central plaza that contained a high-rise observation tower. The desire for more distinctive architecture for each country and an enjoyable outdoor street scene for guests were among the factors that caused Disney to change the concept.

CHAPTER FOUR

DISNEY-MGM STUDIOS

1. Disney-MGM Studios ("the Studios") covers how many acres?
  a.) 154
  b.) 213
  c.) 339
  d.) 427

2. How long did it take for the parking lots to reach capacity on the Studios' opening day — possibly due to the rain that marked the occasion?
  a.) Half an hour
  b.) 4 hours
  c.) 6 hours
  d.) They didn't reach full capacity that day

3. What is special about the Mickey Mouse statue located on top of the Crossroads of the World tower?
  a.) His right finger points in the direction of Hollywood, California
  b.) His ear is a lightning rod
  c.) He houses a hidden security camera
  d.) He sings and dances

4. About how many pounds of pasta are served every day at Mama Melrose's Ristorante Italiano?
  a.) 150
  b.) 375
  c.) 720
  d.) 1100

Did You Know?

THE COASTER TRACK FOR *ROCK 'N' ROLLER COASTER STARRING AEROSMITH* WAS BUILT FIRST. THEN THE BUILDING WAS CONSTRUCTED AROUND IT.

5. Which of the following license plate numbers is NOT found on one of the limousine ride cars in *Rock 'n' Roller Coaster*?
a.) 2FAST4U
b.) LUVSPEED
c.) UGOGIRL
d.) 10KLIMO

6. In the queue of *Star Tours*, what is the license plate number of the Star Speeder that is paged because it is parked in a "no hover zone"?
a.) THX 1138
b.) WDW-ILM
c.) LUCAS1
d.) N234MM

7. The nightly *Fantasmic!* show seats how many guests?
a.) 900
b.) 2,900
c.) 4,900
d.) 6,900

8. What children's song can be heard in *The Twilight Zone Tower of Terror*?
a.) "It's a Small World"
b.) "Itsy Bitsy Spider"
c.) "It's Raining, It's Pouring"
d.) "Five Little Pumpkins"

9. According to the directory in the queue area of *Jim Henson's MuppetVision 3D*, who is the head of the "Sartorial Accumulation Division"?
a.) Statler and Waldorf
b.) Miss Piggy
c.) The Great Gonzo
d.) Fozzie Bear

10. How many attractions were running on the Studios' opening day?
a.) 5
b.) 7
c.) 9
d.) 11

11. In *Sounds Dangerous—Starring Drew Carey*, what is the name of the fictional TV show Carey is working on?
a.) "The Monster Sound Show"
b.) "One Saturday Morning"
c.) "Undercover Live"
d.) "Doug: Live!"

12. The *Tower of Terror* has how many identical elevator drop shafts?
a.) 1
b.) 2
c.) 4
d.) 6

13. When taking a trip on *Star Tours*, what flight number are you on?
a.) THX 1138
b.) ST-45
c.) SUCAL 7
d.) Jawa-9

14. What color is the "hot seat" in *Who Wants to Be a Millionaire - Play It!?*
  a.) Black
  b.) Red
  c.) Blue
  d.) Purple

15. On what day did Mickey, Minnie, Roger Rabbit, Goofy, and Donald sign their names and put their prints into the cement in front of *The Great Movie Ride?*
  a.) 1-May-89
  b.) 1-Oct-90
  c.) 15-May-85
  d.) 1-Oct-71

16. How many table-service restaurants are located in the Studios?
  a.) 5
  b.) 6
  c.) 7
  d.) 11

17. What is the name of the boat where you'll find Min and Bill's Dockside Diner?
  a.) SS Minnie
  b.) SS Daisy
  c.) SS Down the Hatch
  d.) SS Lilly

18. Where would you find the Disney Radio Studios?
  a.) Mickey Avenue
  b.) Inside *The Great Movie Ride*
  c.) Sunset Boulevard
  d.) None of the above

19. Who played the "lucky" piano teacher whose winning lottery ticket flew out the window in the pre-show film for *Backstage Pass?*
  a.) Madonna
  b.) Barbara Streisand
  c.) Bette Midler
  d.) Rosie O' Donnell

20. In *Voyage of The Little Mermaid,* **how many live actors are in the show?**
  a.) 0
  b.) 1
  c.) 2
  d.) 5

21. What is stored in the "Earful Tower" in Disney-MGM Studios?
  a.) Water
  b.) Hidden cameras to monitor the park
  c.) Old props
  d.) Nothing

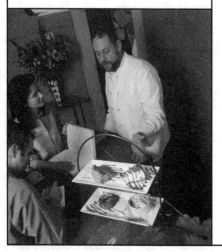

22. The Miss Piggy statue in the fountain in front of *MuppetVision 3D* wears a sash. What does it say?
a.) Ms. Liberty
b.) Miss Piggy
c.) Miss America
d.) Queen for a Day

23. Which Soundstage was home to *Bear in the Big Blue House?*
a.) Soundstage 3
b.) Soundstage 4
c.) Soundstage 5
d.) Soundstage 6

24. What is the name of the detective that Drew Carey plays in *Sounds Dangerous?*
a.) Drew Nancy
b.) Charlie Foster
c.) Sherlock Hardy
d.) Detective Drew

25. Why is *The Twilight Zone Tower of Terror* built to a height of 199 feet and no taller?
a.) It was supposed to be 200 feet, but the builders made a mistake when finishing the building
b.) The actual Hollywood Tower hotel is 199 feet tall.
c.) Disney wanted it to be shorter than Cinderella Castle
d.) If it were one foot higher it would have to have red lights on top

26. How tall is the mountain in *Fantasmic!?*
a.) 39 feet
b.) 59 feet
c.) 99 feet
d.) 129 feet

27. On *Star Tours,* there is a red tag attached to your Pilot. What does it say?
a.) "Experimental Prototype Pilot of Tomorrow"
b.) $1.99
c.) "Scrap Metal"
d.) "Remove Before Flight"

28. What was the first full-length animated feature developed at Disney-MGM Studios?
a.) *Mulan*
b.) *Lilo & Stitch*
c.) *Hercules*
d.) *Tarzan*

29. Where can the back half of the plane from the final scene of the classic film *Casablanca* be found?
a.) In *The Great Movie Ride*
b.) In the *Indiana Jones Epic Stunt Spectacular*
c.) On the *Backlot Tour*
d.) Nowhere

30. In the gangster scene of *The Great Movie Ride,* the license plate on the car is 021-429. What does that number signify?

a.) 21429 was the address of the original Walt Disney Studios on Hollywood Blvd.

b.) It is Walt Disney's Birthday backwards - 09-24-14

c.) It is the date of the St. Valentine's Day Massacre

d.) It was Walt's office telephone extension (21429)

31. Approximately how much does the Sorcerer Mickey hat in the center of the park weigh?
a.) 11 tons
b.) 59 tons
c.) 156 tons
d.) 229 tons

32. What famous comedian cut the ceremonial ribbon to open Disney-MGM Studios?
a.) Robin Williams
b.) Bob Hope
c.) John Ritter
d.) Jerry Lewis

33. Which Muppet character disguises himself as Mickey Mouse during the pre-show to *MuppetVision 3D*?
a.) Kermit
b.) Beaker
c.) Fozzie
d.) Rizzo the Rat

34. Who or what is pictured on the license plate of the fire truck that arrives at the end of *MuppetVision 3D*?
a.) Mickey Mouse
b.) Jim Henson
c.) Cinderella Castle
d.) A Dalmatian

35. The Studios' very first parade was based on which animated film?
a.) *Aladdin*
b.) *Toy Story*
c.) *Mulan*
d.) *Hercules*

Did You Know?

ONE OF THE IDEAS THAT LED TO THE DEVELOPMENT OF DISNEY-MGM STUDIOS ORIGINATED WITH WALT DISNEY MORE THAN 40 YEARS AGO! ALTHOUGH HE LIKED THE IDEA OF "BACKLOT TOURS," HE DIDN'T LIKE THE FACT THAT THEY WERE LIMITED TO A PRIVILEGED FEW. HE WANTED THE MASSES TO SEE AND APPRECIATE THE MAGIC BEHIND THE MOVIES — AND THAT'S JUST WHAT THE STUDIOS LETS YOU DO.

Did You Know?

IN *MUPPETVISION 3D*, AFTER GRABBING YOUR 3D GLASSES, LOOK TO YOUR RIGHT WHERE YOU SEE THE "SECURITY OFFICE." YOU'LL SEE A SIGN THAT READS, "BACK IN 5 MINUTES. KEY IS UNDER MAT." IF YOU STOP AND LOOK DOWN, YOU'LL ACTUALLY FIND A MAT WITH A KEY UNDERNEATH THAT'S EMBEDDED IN THE CARPET!

36. What is the only Disney film represented by Audio-Animatronics figures in *The Great Movie Ride?*
   a.) *Fantasia*
   b.) *Mary Poppins*
   c.) *The Wizard of Oz*
   d.) *20,000 Leagues Under the Sea*

37. In the grand finale of *Fantasmic!*, Disney Characters cruise across the water aboard a replica of:
   a.) The ship in *Steamboat Willie*
   b.) A pirate ship
   c.) A riverboat like in the Magic Kingdom
   d.) A ship from the Disney Cruise line

38. An eviction notice is posted outside The Hollywood Tower Hotel, home of the *Tower of Terror*, for October 31 of what year?
   a.) 1935
   b.) 1937
   c.) 1939
   d.) 1940

39. What popular ride located in Disneyland's Magic Kingdom is in Disney-MGM Studios at WDW?
   a.) *Star Tours*
   b.) *Indiana Jones Epic Stunt Spectacular*
   c.) *MuppetVision 3D*
   d.) *Voyage of The Little Mermaid*

40. How many guests can the Sci-Fi Dine-In Theater Restaurant seat?
   a.) 100
   b.) 150
   c.) 200
   d.) 250

41. In the *Disney Stars and Motor Cars Parade*, what does the license

plate on the black car driven by Hades say?
a.) EVIL
b.) HADES 1
c.) I M BAD
d.) FLAMES

42. Who can you find hidden in the hieroglyphs in the Indiana Jones scene of *The Great Movie Ride?*
a.) Walt Disney
b.) Charlie Chaplin
c.) Kermit The Frog
d.) Donald Duck

43. Your ship's pilot in *Star Tours* repeats a line that can be heard in all *Star Wars* movies. What is it?
a.) "May the Force be with you."
b.) "Leia, what are those things on the side of your head?"
c.) "Use the Force."
d.) "I've got a bad feeling about this."

44. What animals make up the orchestra in *MuppetVision 3D?*
a.) Rats
b.) Frogs
c.) Penguins
d.) Gonzo-thingies

45. Where is Disney-MGM Studios in relation to Epcot?
a.) North
b.) South
c.) East
d.) West

46. In *Disney-MGM Studios Backlot Tour,* what was the name of the boat that was hit by the big, man-made waves?
a.) Miss Tilly
b.) SS Minnow
c.) Miss Fortune
d.) SS Minnie

47. A film shown at the conclusion of *Walt Disney: One Man's Dream* shows Mickey Mouse wearing what kind of character watch?
a.) Walt Disney
b.) Minnie Mouse
c.) Michael Eisner
d.) Donald Duck

48. How deep is the lagoon used in the *Fantasmic!* show?
a.) 1.5 feet
b.) 5 feet
c.) 10 feet
d.) Up to 20 feet in some places

49. What is the main street of Disney-MGM Studios?
a.) Sunset Boulevard
b.) Hollywood Boulevard
c.) Disney Drive
d.) Studio Street

50. In the Wizard of Oz Munchkinland scene in *The Great Movie Ride,* what is hanging by the Wicked Witch of the East's feet?
a.) Her Certificate of Death
b.) Her shoes

c.) Flowers

d.) A picture of Dorothy

51. What was the second full-length animated feature developed at the Studios?

a.) *Toy Story*

b.) *Hercules*

c.) *Tarzan*

d.) *Lilo & Stitch*

52. Which evil creature confronts Mickey at the conclusion of *Fantasmic!?*

a.) Maleficent

b.) Ursula

c.) Jafar

d.) Scar

53. Contestants in the hot seat of *Who Wants to Be a Millionaire — Play It!* need to reach what point level to win a polo shirt?

a.) 8,000

b.) 16,000

c.) 32,000

d.) 64,000

54. How many people were in the *Tower of Terror* elevator when it was struck by lightning?

a.) 3

b.) 4

c.) 5

d.) 6

55. Which of these statements about *The Great Movie Ride* is true?

a.) Gene Kelly's daughter brings her children to visit "grand-pa" (his Audio-Animatronics figure)

b.) Isabella Rossellini, Ingrid Bergman's daughter, brings her children to see "Grandma."

c.) Julie Andrews visits the attraction every few months to be sure her figure from *Mary Poppins* is kept in proper shape

d.) The children of Ray Bolger (the Scarecrow from *The Wizard of Oz*), visit every year on his birthday to see their father.

56. What live show was replaced by *Voyage of The Little Mermaid?*

a.) *Legend of the Lion King*

b.) *Hercules*

c.) *Here Come the Muppets*

d.) *Muppets on Location: Days of Swine & Roses*

57. In *Star Tours,* what is the name of the robot pilot of the Starspeeder 3000?

a.) R5-D4

b.) George (after George Lucas)

c.) C-3PO

d.) Rex

58. From what room of the hotel do guests board the ride elevators on *The Twilight Zone Tower of Terror* (aka *"Tower of Terror")?*

a.) The lobby
b.) The library
c.) The boiler room
d.) Storage rooms

59. What is the registration number on Walt's plane (now on display in the bone yard)?
a.) N234MM
b.) MICKEY1
c.) MM1
d.) WALT71

60. At what gas station in the Studios do you make a pit stop to rent a stroller?
a.) Super Star Service
b.) Goofy's Gas N' Go
c.) Oscar's Super Service Station
d.) Sal's Stroller Station

61. In the original designs of Disney-MGM Studios, the center of

the park formed the shape of what when viewed from above?
a.) A movie camera
b.) Mickey Mouse's head
c.) A castle
d.) The Sorcerer's Hat

62. What year did *Fantasmic!* debut?
a.) 1998
b.) 1991
c.) 1989
d.) 2002

63. A *Star Tours* Starspeeder has how many seats?
a.) 10
b.) 20
c.) 30
d.) 40

64. What size is the rolling ball which threatens to crush Indy in

Did You Know?

THE SAME COMPANY THAT DESIGNED THE *ROCK 'N' ROLLER COASTER* ALSO DESIGNED GOOFY'S *BARNSTORMER* IN MICKEY'S TOONTOWN FAIR.

•

WHEN AEROSMITH CAME TO WDW TO PREVIEW *ROCK 'N' ROLLER COASTER*, STEVE TYLER AND JOE PERRY RODE IT 12 TIMES IN A ROW.

the *Indiana Jones Epic Stunt Spectacular?*
a.) 10 feet in diameter
b.) 12 feet in diameter
c.) 14 feet in diameter
d.) 20 feet in diameter

65. The jewel that is "guarded by a curse" on *The Great Movie Ride* is:
a.) White
b.) Blue
c.) Yellow
d.) Red

66. Goofy wrote what on his cement block near Mann's Chinese Theater?
a.) "I'm Stuck"
b.) "Thanks!"
c.) "Gawrsh"
d.) Nothing - he just left his hand (paw?) prints

67. How much does each ear on the Studios' giant water tower weigh?
a.) 200 pounds
b.) 2,500 pounds
c.) 5,000 pounds
d.) 7,700 pounds

68. What song is playing as the cars are being loaded and you begin your journey through the movies on *The Great Movie Ride?*
a.) "Singin' in the Rain"
b.) "Hooray for Hollywood"
c.) "Follow the Yellow Brick Road"
d.) "The Sorcerer's Apprentice" from *Fantasia*

69. Can you name the disc jockey who is broadcasting "live" from the concert at the beginning of the *Rock 'n' Roller Coaster Starring Aerosmith* ride?
a.) Big Joe Henry
b.) Uncle Joe Benson
c.) Uncle Floyd
d.) Casey Kasem

70. In the *Voyage of The Little Mermaid,* what is the Captain's name?
a.) Captain Horatio Hornblower
b.) Captain Stubing
c.) Captain Horatio Witherspoon
d.) Captain Jack Sparrow

71. What was placed in the center of the Studios to commemorate the 100 Years of Magic Celebration?
- a.) A really big hat
- b.) A statue of Mickey Mouse
- c.) A statue of Walt Disney
- d.) A museum of Disney World memorabilia

72. The *Osborne Family Spectacle of Lights* moved to the Studios from what city?
- a.) Killington, Vermont
- b.) Point Pleasant, New Jersey
- c.) Villanova, Pennsylvania
- d.) Little Rock, Arkansas

73. Which famous Hollywood restaurant that is re-created at the Studios appeared in Disney's animated film, *Fun and Fancy Free?*
- a.) Min & Bill's Dockside Diner
- b.) Mama Melrose's Ristorante Italiano
- c.) The Hollywood Brown Derby
- d.) Hollywood & Vine

74. What attraction was originally intended for Epcot?
- a.) *Backlot Tour*
- b.) *The Great Movie Ride*
- c.) *Sounds Dangerous*
- d.) *Fantasmic!*

THE ANSWERS
TO CHAPTER FOUR

1. a.) 154
At 154 acres (plus an additional 75 acres for parking), the Studios is the second smallest of WDW's four theme parks. Do you know what the smallest is?

2. b.) Half an hour
Although it rained throughout the Studios' opening day, May 1, 1989, traffic was backed up for miles hours before the park opened. Just half an hour after guests were allowed in, the new park was mobbed and the parking lot closed. It's not surprising they turned up. The opening press event for the Studios was the largest in Walt Disney World history and there had been plenty of pre-opening publicity, including an extensive cover story in *Newsweek* magazine a few weeks earlier.

3. b.) His ear is a lightning rod
The Crossroads of the World tower is a replica of the original tower on Hollywood's Sunset Boulevard. A quiet office complex today, it was

Did You Know?

WHEN *THE TWILIGHT ZONE TOWER OF TERROR*
WAS BEING BUILT, IT WAS STRUCK BY LIGHTNING.

once a retail shopping center. The Studios' tower, unlike the original, is topped by Mickey Mouse and a rotating globe. Mickey's right ear (slightly higher than his left) is made of copper and acts a lighting rod.

4. c.) 720
Mama Melrose's Ristorante Italiano serves 720 pounds of pasta every day.

5. b.) LUVSPEED
The five *Rock 'n' Roller Coaster* limos have personalized plates. They are:
1. 10KLIMO
2. UGOGIRL
3. BUHBYE
4. 2FAST4U
5. H8TRFFC

6. a.) THX 1138
THX 1138 was the name of George Lucas's first film, released in 1971. References to it can be found in all his subsequent films, including *Star Wars,* the film on which *Star Tours* is based.

7. d.) 6,900
The theater where *Fantasmic!* plays holds almost 10,000 guests, with seats for 6,900. The other 3,000 have to stand.

8. c.) "It's Raining, It's Pouring"
You can hear the little girl singing this nursery rhyme during the pre-show movie as she boards the elevator for its journey into. . . *The Twilight Zone* (cue music. . .).

9. b.) Miss Piggy
Miss Piggy's title is "Diva." She can be found in the "Very Suite," "Room 4444." Take a minute and look at some of the other offices on the directory in the *MuppetVision* queue area if you have a chance – they're hysterical!

10. a.) 5
The Studios opened May 1, 1989, with just five attractions and an exhibit. They included *The Monster Sound Show*, *SoundWorks* (the exhibit), and *SuperStar Television* (all presented by Sony), plus *The Great Movie Ride*, *The Magic of Disney Animation*, and *The Backstage Studio Tour* (later split into two attractions, a walk and tram tour called *Disney-MGM Studios Backlot Tour* and a walking tour called *Backstage Pass*).

11. c.) "Undercover Live"
Comedian Drew Carey is working in a fictional TV show, "Undercover Live," in *Sounds Dangerous*, which opened in 1999 at the ABC Sound Studios near Echo Lake. It is the third sound effects show in that space, after the original attraction, *The Monster Sound Show*, and *ABC Sound Studio*. *The Monster Sound Show*, starring comedians Martin Short and Chevy Chase, opened with the park on May 19, 1989. It involved audience members becoming "foley" sound artists. The film was first shown without sound, then replayed with the audi-ence providing the sound effects. Late-night comedian David Letterman hosted the pre-show queue video, while the post-show, *SoundWorks*, allowed visitors to create their own sound effects. In 1997, *The Monster Sound Show* was replaced by the *ABC Sound Studio*. Although the concept of the attraction remained identical (audience members added sound effects to a pre-recorded film sequence), the new show featured Disney's "One Saturday Morning" lineup, and seven guests were chosen to create sound effects for "101 Dalmatians: The Series." After running about two years, *ABC Sound Studio* was retired in favor of *Sounds Dangerous*.

12. b.) 2
There are only two elevator shafts in the *Tower of Terror*, but there are four lift shafts. They're used to move the ride vehicles into position to ascend the elevator shafts.

13. b.) ST-45
Star Tours' Flight ST-45 is scheduled for a nonstop flight to the moon of Endor. You can hear your flight being called during the pre-show in the queue line. Pay close attention, as there are some pretty funny lines in the background narration, as well as some classic *Star Wars* references.

14. c.) Blue
Located on Soundstages 2 and 3 on Mickey Avenue, *Who Wants To Be*

A Millionaire — Play It! is a faithful, interactive reproduction of the popular game show, *Who Wants to Be a Millionaire?* You may not get to see Regis Philbin, but audience members get to play in their seats for a shot at the "hot seat." Once there, they can use their brains (and a few "lifelines") to answer questions and win prizes.

15. a.) 1-May-89

Not surprisingly, May 1, 1989, was opening day for Disney-MGM Studios. The full-size replica of Mann's Chinese Theater wouldn't be complete without the hand, foot, and paw prints of famous celebrities out front.

16. a.) 5

The sit-down restaurants at Disney-MGM Studios include: The Hollywood Brown Derby, 50's Prime Time Cafe, Sci-fi Dine-In Theater Restaurant, Hollywood & Vine, and Mama Melrose's Ristorante Italiano.

17. c.) SS Down the Hatch

The "SS Down the Hatch" is docked on Echo Lake. It's a great place to stop for snacks or dessert.

18. d.) None of the above

The Disney Radio Studios, located near Echo Lake right around the corner from *Sounds Dangerous*, is a real, working radio station. It broadcasts the nationally syndicated "Super Gold with Mike Harvey," as well as other Radio Disney shows, such as "Mickey and Minnie's Tune Time" starring B. B. Good.

19. c.) Bette Midler

During the queue line prior to the tram portion of the *Backstage Pass* tour, guests looking at the overhead monitors might see "The Lottery," a 2.5-minute film in which Bette Midler chases a pigeon that has stolen her winning $1 million lottery ticket. The mini-movie took five days and 100 people to create.

20. c.) 2

In *Voyage of The Little Mermaid*, only Ariel and Eric are played by live actors. Film clips and masterfully created puppets provide the rest of the entertainment, which is filled with songs from the original Disney animated film, *The Little Mermaid*. Tip: The front row is not the best place to sit here! Try to sit toward the back of the theater, in the middle of a row (I know, I know. . . "please move all the way to the end of the row to accommodate. . ." blah blah blah). OK, try to time it just right, so half the row is filled before you move in. This way, you will experience everything this don't-miss production has to offer.

21. d.) Nothing

The 130-foot high Earful Tower is modeled on the water tower at the entrance to the Disney Studios in Burbank, California. However, unlike its California counterpart, the WDW tower has never held water.

22. a.) Ms. Liberty

The Miss Piggy statue in front of *Jim Henson's MuppetVision 3D* pays homage to the Statue of Liberty. But unlike the original statue, Miss Piggy wears a sash and has water spouting from her crown.

23. c.) Soundstage 5

Bear in the Big Blue House ran from June 7, 1999, to August 4, 2001, on Soundstage 5 in Animation Courtyard. It was aimed primarily at small children, who sat on the carpeted floor in front of the stage. *Bear* was replaced by *Playhouse Disney Live!* on October 1, 2001.

24. b.) Charlie Foster

In *Sounds Dangerous*, the director of the fictional TV show, *Undercover Live,* says that you'll be following undercover officer Charles Foster, who is wearing the latest in spy technology, including a spy cam and super sensitive microphones.

25. d.) If it were one foot higher it would have to have red lights on top

The Federal Aviation Administration (FAA) requires structures 200 feet and taller to be topped with red, blinking lights to warn away planes. So if The Hollywood Tower Hotel that houses the *Tower of Terror* were a foot higher, it would have to sport the warning lights, and the Imagineers did not want to spoil the 1930s look of the hotel. Back then, there were no regulations requiring warning lights on tall buildings.

Did You Know?

WHEN THE *ROCK 'N' ROLLER COASTER STARRING AEROSMITH* WAS BEING BUILT, THERE WAS A GREAT DEAL OF CONCERN AMONG DISNEY ENGINEERS THAT THE NEARBY *TWILIGHT ZONE TOWER OF TERROR'S* TWO ELEVATOR DROPS, COUPLED WITH THE ENERGY NEEDED FOR THE ROLLER COASTER'S LAUNCH, MIGHT ACTUALLY BRING DOWN THE ENTIRE STUDIOS' POWER GRID! SO A NEW ELECTRICAL SUBSTATION WAS BUILT JUST TO POWER THE COASTER.

26. b.) 59 feet
The 59-foot tall, man-made mountain in *Fantasmic!* is the fourth tallest "mountain" in Walt Disney World.

27. d.) "Remove Before Flight"
Look for the small red tag on Rex, your *Star Tours'* Pilot!

28. a.) *Mulan*
Mulan was the first full-length film to be produced primarily by Walt Disney Feature Animation – Florida at the Studios. The film is based on a Chinese story that's been in circulation for over 2,000 years.

29. d.) Nowhere
OK. . . this is one of those "Urban Legends" that just won't die. I'm sorry to say, the *Casablanca* plane won't be found in WDW. In fact, you won't find it anywhere. . . because it never existed. Contrary to popular belief, the aircraft used in the final scene of the movie classic, where Rick and Ilsa part, wasn't real. The filming took place not long after the bombing of Pearl Harbor, when shooting "on location" at airports was prohibited. Therefore, the entire movie was shot on sound stages at the Warner Bros. studios in Burbank, California. The soundstage used for filming the last scene was too small to accommodate a full-sized airplane. So the studio built half- and quarter-size replicas of a Lockheed Electra 12A out of plywood and balsa wood. No one knows exactly how the rumor started that the plane in *The Great Movie Ride* was the "real" one from *Casablanca*. (I'll give you one guess, though. . . what better way to help hype your new movie-themed park than to tell the world you have a one-of-a-kind, legendary movie prop?) It's said that Disney bought a real Lockheed 12A plane and chopped it in half, putting the front in *The Great Movie Ride* and the back in the Studios' *Backlot Tour*.

30. c.) It is the date of the St. Valentine's Day Massacre, February 14, 1929.

Did You Know?

IN 1966, WALT DISNEY WAS DIAGNOSED WITH LUNG CANCER, CONTRACTED AFTER YEARS OF SMOKING CIGARETTES. HIS ILLNESS AND ITS CONNECTION TO CIGARETTE SMOKING PROMPTED THE IMAGINEERS TO REMOVE ROD SERLING'S SIGNATURE CIGARETTE FROM THE PRE-SHOW VIDEO IN THE *TOWER OF TERROR*.

The St. Valentine's Day Massacre, a violent, gangster-related killing of seven men ordered by famous crime boss Al Capone, took place in Chicago on 02/14/29.

31. c.) 156 tons
With the hat alone standing 100 feet tall, Mickey Mouse would have to be 350 feet tall and wear hat size 605 7/8 to wear the Sorcerer Mickey hat in the center of the Studios!

32. b.) Bob Hope
Entertainment legend Bob Hope cut the ceremonial ribbon, and chairman Michael Eisner proudly read the words on the dedication plaque: "The World you have entered was created by The Walt Disney Company and is dedicated to Hollywood — not a place on a map, but a state of mind that exists wherever people dream and wonder and imagine, a place where illusion and reality are fused by technological magic. We welcome you to a Hollywood that never was — and always will be. We welcome you to Disney-MGM Studios."

33. d.) Rizzo the Rat
You'll find some of the best fun in *MuppetVision* in the pre-show "comedy warehouse," an area often overlooked by guests as they hurry into the main auditorium. This area is filled with hilarious sight-gags and also offers a pre-show movie with

Scooter and Fozzie that "sets up" the 3D portion of the show next door. Be sure to look around the room, read everything you can, watch the movie, and look out for "Rizzo the Rat" doing his best Mickey Mouse impression.

34. c.) Cinderella Castle
The Disney Fire Truck that enters the theater when the screen explodes at the end of the *MuppetVision* film has a picture of Cinderella Castle on its red license plate. Look very carefully and you will see it near the bottom right bumper.

35. a.) *Aladdin*
Aladdin's Royal Caravan Parade opened December 21, 1992, and ran until August 27, 1995. Floats included the genie, spitting camels and, of course, Aladdin and Princess Jasmine, who rode in grand style upon an elephant float. What about Jafar and Iago, the villains? They were there, too. . . at the end. . . sweeping up after the elephant!
The *Toy Story* parade ran in 1996 and offered numerous opportunities for guests to meet and get autographs from Buzz, Woody, and a variety of other *Toy Story* characters. *Hercules Zero to Hero Victory Parade* meandered through the park twice a day starting on June 27, 1997. It included a number of floats, headed by a lucky "Theban Family of the Day," selected from the crowd. There were

also giant balloons and cheerleaders (well, the balloons were giant, not the cheerleaders). The parade closed less than a year later in anticipation of the upcoming *Mulan* parade, which ran for three years from June 19, 1998. It included characters from the movie, as well as Chinese elements, such as a 150-foot long dragon and performers who represented the Great Wall of China.

36. b.) *Mary Poppins*
Follow Bert onto the rooftops and watch Mary Poppins with her magical umbrella. The lifelike recreations of Dick Van Dyke and Julie Andrews from the Disney film sing "Chim Chim Cher-ee" in this *Great Movie Ride* scene.

37. a.) The ship in *Steamboat Willie*
The *Steamboat Willie* ship in *Fantasmic!* is 80 feet long with a 16-foot beam. It weighs approximately 70,000 pounds.

38. c.) 1939
As you approach the open gates at the entrance to the *Tower of Terror* ride, you will find an eviction notice dated October 31, 1939 - the same fateful night that lightning struck the hotel.

39. a.) *Star Tours*
Star Tours is located in Tomorrowland in Disneyland and in the Studios in WDW.

40. d.) 250
The Sci-Fi Dine In Theater is all about atmosphere. The tables look like 1950s' cars complete with tail fins and whitewall tires and all of them face a "drive-in" movie screen showing old monster flicks. Take a look at the license plates on all the "cars" . . . they have letters and numbers representing initials and birth-dates of the Imagineers who designed the restaurant! Oh, and be sure to try the "Cheesecake that Ate New York" and the "Cookie Monster" for dessert! (With names like those, who could resist!?)

41. a.) EVIL
Hades drives a slick black convertible with flames painted on its front in the parade. His license plate, "EVIL," is yellow with red writing.

42. d.) Donald Duck
Look for a "Hidden Donald" in the hieroglyphics of *The Raiders of the Lost Ark* scene having lunch with Mickey Mouse. (Look fast, it is on the last stone pillar on the left). Other hidden characters in this scene are C-3PO and R2-D2, from *Star Wars*.

43. d.) "I've got a bad feeling about this."
Avid fans of the *Star Wars* movies will recognize (and likely chuckle) when they hear their *Star Tours'* pilot say, "I've got a bad feeling about this." This quote appears (often more than

Did You Know?

NEARLY A MILE OF NEON LIGHTS ARE USED OUTSIDE THE *ROCK 'N' ROLLER COASTER* ATTRACTION

once) in each of the first five *Star Wars* movies.

44. c.) Penguins
A full orchestra, conducted by Nicki Napoleon and including his Emperor Penguins, performs *MuppetVision*'s funny musical numbers. They play in the orchestra pit at the front of the theater.

45. b.) South
The Studios is located south (and a little bit west) of Epcot.

46. c.) Miss Fortune
Disney-MGM Studios Backlot Tour takes you through real production facilities and illustrates how a variety of special effects is created for the movies. Prior to the tram portion of the attraction, there is a live demonstration that shows you (and a few lucky volunteers), how special effects are created. One such demo involved thunderstorms and included a "tidal

wave" that hit a small fishing boat, the "Miss Fortune."

47. c.) Michael Eisner
In the film shown at the end of *Walt Disney: One Man's Dream*, there is a scene in which Mickey Mouse chats with Michael Eisner. At the end of their conversation, Mickey and Eisner both check their watches. First, Eisner checks his Mickey Mouse watch. Then Mickey checks his watch - it's a Michael Eisner!

48. a.) 1.5 feet
Although the water is treated and filtered, algae is left in the lagoon used for *Fantasmic!* so guests can't see how deep (or shallow), it really is.

49. b.) Hollywood Boulevard
In Disney-MGM Studios, Sunset Boulevard intersects with Hollywood Boulevard, although in Hollywood, California the two streets run parallel to each other.

Did You Know?

DISNEY-MGM STUDIOS' SUPERSTAR TELEVISION, WHICH CLOSED SEPTEMBER 26, 1998, ALLOWED SELECTED GUESTS TO PARTICIPATE IN A FEW SCENES FROM SUCH POPULAR TV SHOWS AS "I LOVE LUCY," "CHEERS," AND "GILLIGAN'S ISLAND."

50. a.) Her Certificate of Death
During the Wizard of Oz sequence of *The Great Movie Ride*, if you look closely at Dorothy's house, you will see the striped socks of the Wicked Witch sticking out from under the bottom. Hanging nearby is her Certificate of Death. Ding Dong, that witch is toast!

51. d.) *Lilo & Stitch*
Disney's 41st animated feature film stars a Hawaiian girl who adopts a strange pet (actually an extraterrestrial fugitive from the law). This was the second of the three animated films produced by the Feature Animation studios in Orlando, which closed in late 2003. The third and last was Disney's *Brother Bear*, which was released in November 2003.

52. a.) Maleficent
Maleficent, the villain brought to the screen by Disney in the animated

film, *Sleeping Beauty*, appears in *Fantasmic!* first in a flowing black cape and menacing horned headdress. She reveals her true colors in the show's grand finale when she transforms herself into an evil, fire-breathing dragon.

53. c.) 32,000
Prizes (sorry, no cash) are awarded for reaching different levels in the fast-paced game show, *Who Wants To Be A Millionaire — Play It!*. Prizes range from collectible pins and hats to a grand prize of a cruise on the Disney Cruise Line!

54. c.) 5

The five people who boarded the doomed elevator during the storm were a bellhop, two "movie stars," their child, and her nanny.

55. b.) Isabella Rossellini, Ingrid Bergman's daughter, brings her children to see "Grandma."

The Great Movie Ride includes the classic final scene in *Casablanca* in which Rick Blaine (Humphrey Bogart) and Ilsa Lund (Ingrid Bergman) say their final good-byes, ("Here's looking at you, kid.") and go their separate ways. The Audio-Animatronics figures of Bogart and Bergman are amazingly lifelike.

56. c.) *Here Come the Muppets*

The Muppets have had three shows at the Studios since 1990 — in fact, it's a little-remembered fact that they had two running simultaneously from 1990 to 1995. *Here Come the Muppets* opened May 25, 1990, and closed September 2, 1991. *Jim Henson's MuppetVision 3D* opened May 16, 1991, and is still running, and *Muppets on Location: Days of Swine & Roses* (an outdoor show and autograph session based on the premise that the Muppets were shooting a movie) opened September 16, 1991, and closed in the summer of 1995. Why so many Muppet shows? Well, back in 1990 Disney and Muppet creator Jim Henson were discussing a merger. They even co-produced a

TV special, "The Muppets at Walt Disney World" to serve as an introduction to the happy marriage of the Muppet and the Mouse. It aired on May 6, 1990. Ten days later Henson died of a virulent virus, and just nine days after that *Here Come the Muppets* opened — an act that many Henson fans considered unfeeling and disrespectful on Disney's part. That merger proposal ultimately fell apart, but Disney finally landed Kermit and the gang in 2004 when it acquired the Muppets, ending more than a decade of rumors and false starts.

57. d.) Rex

Your rookie pilot's "full name" in *Star Tours* is RX-24, but you can call him "Rex" for short. Recognize his voice? It's none other than actor/comedian Paul Reubens, better known for his role as Pee-Wee Herman, the quirky, gray-suited, red bow tie-wearing geek.

58. c.) The boiler room

After seeing the pre-ride video in the library, you make your way to the boiler room. When you get to there, the line splits — the left line gets you on the elevator more quickly, while the right one gives you a somewhat longer tour of the boiler room.

59. a.) N234MM

The N in the registration number (or "call letters") for Walt Disney's company plane identified it to air traffic controllers as an airplane. The MM stood for Mickey Mouse.

Walt owned three aircraft over time and all used the same call letters. The last, a Gulfstream which he purchased in 1963, is the plane seen on *Backlot Tour*. It was retired to WDW October 8, 1992.

60. c.) Oscar's Super Service Station

The station where you rent a stroller is named for the "Oscar," the statuette given out at the annual Academy Awards ceremony for excellence in all aspects of movie making.

61. b.) Mickey Mouse's head

Considered the largest "hidden Mickey" ever, the central plaza and surrounding areas in front of Mann's Chinese Theater in the Studios form the famous mouse head when seen from the air. Although it was obscured by the addition of Sunset Boulevard and the Sorcerer's Hat after the park's opening, you can still see the shape if you take a park map and turn it upside down. Can't see it? OK... take your map, turn it upside-down, and follow along. . . Mickey's head is formed by the central hub area, while the right ear is formed by the small lake. The left ear is made up of the Brown Derby and the surrounding walkway. (That's where the boulevard and the hat now break up the ear.).

62. a.) 1998

Fantasmic! opened in October 1998 in the Hollywood Hills Amphitheater. This amazing, half-hour spectacle includes lights, lasers, and animation — all set against a backdrop of water screens. Sorcerer Mickey battles classic Disney villains, and dozens of other Disney characters are also found in this not to be missed show. (Yes, you really should get to the theater two hours before showtime to get a good seat!)

63. d.) 40

According to the folks at *Star Tours*, the Starspeeder 3000 is the most advanced transport of its kind in existence. It has a high speed hyper-drive and can travel over one billion light years. With its 40 seats, it makes for a very comfortable transport vehicle. Plus, with those reliable droids at the helm, what could go wrong?

64. b.) 12 feet in diameter

The 12-foot ball that threatens to crush Indy in the *Epic Stunt Spectacular* weighs only about 440 pounds. It is made primarily of roofing material.

65. d.) Red

As you enter the creepy chamber filled with mummies and ancient artifacts, your "tour guide" notices the red jewel in the chest of a statue, and can't bear to leave it behind. You'll have to take *The Great Movie Ride* to see what happens next...

66. a.) "I'm Stuck"
Goofy also wrote "Hsrwag." That's "Gawrsh" spelled backwards.

67. c.) 5,000 pounds
This tower was built in 1988, prior to the opening of the Studios, so guests driving by on World Drive could see this new park icon, which sported the sign, "Opening Spring of '89." While there is no water in it, it is patterned after a real water tower at the Disney studios in California.

68. b.) "Hooray for Hollywood"
As you prepare to embark on *The Great Movie Ride*, "Hooray for Hollywood" can be heard. The song, with lyrics by Johnny Mercer and music by Richard Whiting, was written for the movie, *Hollywood Hotel.*

69. b.) Uncle Joe Benson
"Uncle Joe Benson" is a famous classic rock DJ from Los Angeles. He reassures you that if you're late for the Aerosmith concert, you don't have to worry — his station will be broadcasting live from the show.

70. c.) Captain Horatio Witherspoon
Located in Animation Courtyard, the lively 17-minute *Voyage of The Little Mermaid* features actors, puppets, film, special effects, and music from the original animated film.

71. a.) A really big hat
To commemorate Walt Disney's 100th birthday, the Sorcerer Mickey hat was created for the Studios and located in front of the replica of Mann's Chinese Theater. This giant version of the hat Mickey wore in the animated classic, *Fantasia*, is made of fiberglass, painted with "chameleon paint" that makes the color appear to change as you walk around it, and decorated with two enormous moons and giant stars. It was formally unveiled on September 28, 2001.

72. d.) Little Rock, Arkansas
The *Osborne Family Spectacle of Lights* is an incredible display of holiday lights that has been seen on Residential Street at the Studios since Disney purchased it in 1995.

Did You Know?

IT TAKES 21,000 HOURS AND 10 WEEKS TO INSTALL THE FIVE MILLION LIGHTS USED IN *THE OSBORNE FAMILY SPECTACLE OF LIGHTS.*

The spectacle was born in 1986 when Jennings Osborne created a 1,000-light display as a Christmas gift to his six–year-old daughter, Breezy. By 1993, this little Christmas gift had grown to a display of more than three million lights and could be seen by planes flying 80 miles away. Well, three million lights might make a few people stand up and take notice. . . and they did. Droves of folk came from miles away to visit the lights, making neighbors just a bit perturbed. In fact, they took legal action to make Osborne take the lights down. The case went all the way to the Arkansas Supreme Court (an appeal to the United States Supreme Court was denied by Justice Clarence Thomas). After fighting the good fight and paying multiple fines (one of which was ten thousand dollars), Osborne figured he'd have to pack them in. Step up and take a bow, Mickey Mouse. . .

In 1995, WDW purchased the entire display and brought it to the Studios. That holiday season, more than four million lights adorned Residential Street, making it the third largest attraction in the park! Since then, the show has grown to over five million lights, and Disney has enhanced the spectacle with free holographic glasses and nightly "snowfalls"!

73. c.) The Hollywood Brown Derby

Guests can return to the glamour and elegance of Hollywood in the thirties and forties at this upscale WDW restaurant. Hundreds of framed celebrity caricatures of stars such as Bob Hope, actress Lauren Bacall, and singer/actor Frank Sinatra were a trademark of the original restaurant, and copies of them hang here. The restaurant appeared in Disney's 1947 film, *Fun and Fancy Free*, which was hosted by Jiminy Cricket and featured two animated shorts: "Bongo," about a circus bear escaping to the wild, and "Mickey and the Beanstalk," an adaptation of the original fairy tale.

74. b.) *The Great Movie Ride*

A "Movie Pavilion" was originally planned for Epcot, on a site between the Imagination! and The Land pavilions. Its façade can be seen in early concept drawings. Like *The Great Movie Ride*, it would have taken guests through various scenes from classic films. Instead, the concept ended up prompting Disney to create an entire theme park based on the movies.

CHAPTER FIVE

Disney's Animal Kingdom

1. How many animals live in Disney's Animal Kingdom?
- a.) 250
- b.) 700
- c.) 1,700
- d.) 2,700

2. About how many man-made leaves are on The Tree of Life?
- a.) 25,000
- b.) 100,000
- c.) 200,000
- d.) 300,000

3. When did Disney's Animal Kingdom officially open to the public?
- a.) April 22, 1998
- b.) May 1, 1998
- c.) October 15, 1998
- d.) April 22, 1995

4. Which of these lands was originally proposed for Disney's Animal Kingdom?
- a.) Beastly Kingdom
- b.) The Pyramids of Egypt
- c.) Disney Sea
- d.) The Outback

5. In the *DINOSAUR* queue area, what does it say on the red and yellow pipes that you can see as you descend the stairs and approach the ride vehicles?
- a.) Hot and cold
- b.) Smoking and non-smoking
- c.) Ketchup and mustard
- d.) Mickey and Minnie

6. How many pounds of food are consumed each day by the animals in the park?
- a.) 500 pounds
- b.) 2,000 pounds
- c.) 3,000 pounds
- d.) 6,000 pounds

7. "Guano Joe" can be found in:
a.) *Kilimanjaro Safaris*
b.) Rafiki's Planet Watch
c.) *Maharajah Jungle Trek*
d.) *Flights of Wonder*

8. There are four character greeting trails at Camp Minnie-Mickey. Which of the following is NOT one of them?
a.) Rainforest
b.) Arbor
c.) Jungle
d.) Mickey

9. How large is the *Kilimanjaro Safaris* attraction?
a.) 5 acres
b.) 50 acres
c.) 100 acres
d.) 150 acres

10. Animal Kingdom opened with how many attractions?
a.) 3
b.) 5
c.) 7
d.) 9

11. The first attraction to open in the Asia section was:
a.) *Maharajah Jungle Trek*
b.) *Kali River Rapids*
c.) *Tiger River Rapids*
d.) *Flights of Wonder*

12. How many Audio-Animatronics dinosaurs can be found on *DINOSAUR?*
a.) 9
b.) 11
c.) 19
d.) 29

13. What was the original name of *Kali River Rapids?*
a.) *Tiger River Rapids*
b.) *Kingdom Quest*
c.) *Disney's Kali Adventure*
d.) *Asia Adventures*

14. The *Kilimanjaro Safaris* takes guests through which wildlife reserve?
a.) Kilimanjaro Reserve
b.) Harambe Wildlife Reserve
c.) Pangani Forest Trail
d.) Mombasa Reserve

15. What is the seating capacity of the theater in which *It's Tough to be a Bug!* is shown?
a.) 120
b.) 276
c.) 370
d.) 430

16. How much did it cost to build Disney's Animal Kingdom?
a.) $400 million
b.) $800 million
c.) $250 million
d.) $975 million

17. Asia is represented by a fictitious village known as "Anandapur." What does this name mean?
a.) "Land of the Unknown"
b.) "Peace"
c.) "One People"
d.) "City of Delights"

18. DinoLand U.S.A.'s *DINO-SAUR* was originally called:
a.) *T-Rex*
b.) *Jurassic Park - The Ride*
c.) *Countdown to Extinction*
d.) It has always been called *DINOSAUR*

19. Which of these lands was not one of those present at the opening of Disney's Animal Kingdom?
a.) Oasis
b.) DinoLand U.S.A.
c.) Asia
d.) Rafiki's Planet Watch

20. On *Kali River Rapids*, what river do you traverse?
a.) Kali River
b.) Tigress River
c.) Chakranadi River
d.) Amazon River

21. *Pangani Forest Exploration Trail* was originally known as:
a.) *Gorilla Falls Exploration Trail*
b.) *Beastly Kingdom Nature Walk*
c.) *Wild Animal Kingdom Walk*
d.) *Maharajah Jungle Trek*

22. Prior to *Tarzan Rocks!*, a show based on what film was performed in Theater in the Wild?
a.) *Beauty and the Beast*
b.) *Hercules*
c.) *Mulan*
d.) *The Jungle Book*

23. The area representing Africa is a fictitious village known as Harambe. In the Swahili language, what does "harambe" mean?
a.) "Peace"
b.) "Animal Kingdom"
c.) "One land, many people"
d.) "Coming together"

24. What item used extensively throughout WDW, but never in Disney's Animal Kingdom, was patented on January 3, 1888?
a.) The gas engine
b.) The drinking straw
c.) Plastic
d.) Styrofoam cups

25. *Kilimanjaro Safaris* **is named after what?**
  a.) An extinct African tribe
  b.) A mountain in Tanzania
  c.) A village in Kenya
  d.) The name has no meaning

26. Camp Minnie-Mickey is designed to evoke which part of the country?
  a.) West Virginia
  b.) Washington State
  c.) The Adirondack Mountains
  d.) New England

27. Safari Village is now called:
  a.) Discovery Island
  b.) Conservation Station
  c.) The Oasis
  d.) Harambe Village

28. In what land is the show *Tarzan Rocks!* **presented?**
  a.) Asia
  b.) The Oasis
  c.) Camp Minnie-Mickey
  d.) DinoLand U.S.A

29. On what is the fictional town of Harambe based?
  a.) A town in Kenya
  b.) Plans for a pavilion originally designed for Epcot's World Showcase
  c.) The real town of Harambe in Ethiopia
  d.) A compilation of photographs taken by Walt Disney during his trips to Africa

30. The marooned truck in *Kali River Rapids* **is hauling what type of cargo?**
  a.) Boats
  b.) Logs
  c.) Statues
  d.) Animals

31. Can you name the 65 million year old T-Rex found in Dino-Land U.S.A.?
  a.) Gertie
  b.) Elias
  c.) Rex
  d.) Sue

32. Where in the Asia section can guests find tigers and Komodo dragons?
  a.) *Kilimanjaro Safaris*
  b.) *Kali River Rapids*
  c.) *Maharajah Jungle Trek*
  d.) *Conservation Station*

33. What is the name of the baby elephant featured in the *Kilimanjaro Safaris?*
  a.) Big Ben
  b.) Little Red
  c.) Big Red
  d.) Tonga Tommy

34.You reach DinoLand U.S.A by crossing what bridge?
  a.) Olden Gate Bridge
  b.) Crooklyn Bridge
  c.) Bridge to the Past
  d.) Dinorama Drawbridge

Did You Know?

DISNEY'S ANIMAL KINGDOM CONTAINS
LIVE PLANTS FROM EVERY CONTINENT
ON EARTH EXCEPT ANTARCTICA.

35. Who is the director of Harambe National Park on the *Kilimanjaro Safaris?*
- a.) Wilson Matua
- b.) Dr. Catherine Jobson
- c.) Dr. K. Kulunda
- d.) Dr. Seeker

36. The Caravan Stage is home to what live show?
- a.) *Festival of the Lion King*
- b.) *Flights of Wonder*
- c.) *Pocahontas and her Forest Friends*
- d.) *Tarzan Rocks!*

37. How many animals/creatures are found on the Animal Kingdom logo?
- a.) 3
- b.) 4
- c.) 5
- d.) 6

38. What logging company is featured in the *Kali River Rapids?*
- a.) Luie Logging Co.
- b.) Mojave Logging Co.
- c.) Maharajah Logging Co.
- d.) Tetak Logging Co.

39. The roller coaster in Dino-Land U.S.A. is:
- a.) *Triceratop Spin*
- b.) *Primeval Whirl*
- c.) *Flights of Wonder*
- d.) *Dinosaur Rocks!*

40. The trunk of The Tree of Life is covered with carved animals. How many are there?
- a.) 125
- b.) 225
- c.) 325
- d.) 425

41. In *DINOSAUR* your vehicle is chased by an angry dinosaur. What kind is it?
- a.) Carnotaurus
- b.) T-Rex
- c.) Allosaurus
- d.) Velociraptor

42. What new land opened on March 18, 1999?
- a.) Discovery Island
- b.) Asia
- c.) DinoLand U.S.A.
- d.) Camp Minnie-Mickey

43. Discovery Island is encircled by what river?
- a.) Anandapur River
- b.) Chakranadi River
- c.) Discovery River
- d.) Nahtazu River

44. The *DINOSAUR* ride is set in which prehistoric time period?
- a.) Jurassic
- b.) Cretaceous
- c.) Triassic
- d.) Mesozoic

45. What animal was the first to take up residence at Disney's Animal Kingdom?
- a.) Giraffe
- b.) Hippo
- c.) Elephant
- d.) Lion

46. The Wildlife Express train is powered by what type of engine?
- a.) Steam
- b.) Natural Gas
- c.) Propane
- d.) Diesel

47. What was the original name of Disney's Animal Kingdom?
- a.) Disney's Animal Adventure
- b.) Wild Animal Kingdom
- c.) Discovery Island
- d.) AnimaLand

48. *Primeval Fair* was the working name for what attraction?
- a.) *Conservation Station*
- b.) Camp Minnie-Mickey
- c.) Chester and Hester's Dino-Rama!
- d.) Boneyard Playground

Did You Know?

THERE ARE FEEDERS FOR THE ANIMALS IN THE OASIS THAT ARE DESIGNED TO LOOK LIKE TREES.

The Answers
TO CHAPTER FIVE

1. c.) 1,700
Disney's Animal Kingdom, the largest of the four Walt Disney World theme parks at over 500 acres, has a population of over 300 species of animals, consisting of more than 1,700 birds, mammals, reptiles, insects, amphibians, and fish. Think 300 species sounds like a lot? How about 4,000? That's the number of different species of trees, plants, grasses, vines, and shrubs in the park — more than 4,000,000 plantings in all. They come from every continent on earth except Antarctica.

2. b.) 100,000
The massive Tree of Life, the majestic centerpiece of Disney's Animal Kingdom, has 102,583 leaves. Each is over a foot long, was attached by hand, and actually blows in the wind. Some are transparent, while others are any one of five different shades of green. At 145 feet tall, the tree is several yards shorter than WDW's tallest attraction building, the 199-foot *Tower of Terror*. It's also shorter than Cinderella Castle (189 feet).

3. a.) April 22, 1998
Disney's Animal Kingdom is the fourth WDW theme park. It opened on Earth Day, April 22, 1998, and is clearly NAHTAZU (get it, not a zoo) as Disney likes to put it.

4. a.) Beastly Kingdom
"Beastly Kingdom," the oft-rumored third phase of Disney's Animal Kingdom, was to feature dragons, unicorns, and other mythical creatures. The main attractions were to be a stand-up, dragon-themed roller coaster called "Dragon Tower" and a hedge maze called "Quest For The Unicorn."

5. c.) Ketchup and mustard
The red pipe has the chemical name and formula for ketchup (lycopersicon lycopericum is also known as the tomato) and the yellow pipe has the chemical name and formula for mustard. And how about the white pipe? Well, that's mayonnaise of course!

6. d.) 6,000 pounds
Like cheeseburgers? Can you eat 24,000 quarter-pound cheeseburgers in a day? You'd have to in order to equal what Disney feeds the animals in Animal Kingdom every day. It takes about four tons of food a day to keep the more than 1,700 animals happy. That would last the average human being about 4.5 years.

Did You Know?

IT TOOK 500 SKILLED WORKERS AND CRAFTSMEN TO
CONSTRUCT THE MILLION SQUARE FEET OF ROCK WORK IN
THE PARK'S LANDSCAPING. TO PUT IT IN PERSPECTIVE, YOU
COULD BUILD A SCULPTURE 10 FEET WIDE BY 10 FEET DEEP
BY TWO MILES HIGH WITH THAT MUCH ROCK.

7. d.) *Flights of Wonder*
Flights of Wonder, a fun, yet informative bird show, can be found at the Caravan Stage in Asia. "Guano Joe" is the name of your wacky "tour guide" as you learn about conservation while witnessing the beauty of a variety of exotic birds.

8. a.) Rainforest
The four character greeting trails in Camp Minnie Mickey are: Forest, Arbor, Mickey, and Jungle, and guests can meet Mickey and his pals there every day.

9. c.) 100 acres
The fun, educational *Kilimanjaro Safaris* attraction spans more than 100 acres of savanna, forests, and rivers. Unlike any previous Disney attraction, this massive re-creation of Africa is filled with live animals that are allowed to roam freely.

10. b.) 5
Animal Kingdom opened in 1998 with 5 attractions, 9 exhibits, 12

shows with live entertainment, 8 food locations, 11 merchandise locations, and 6,000 parking spaces which were filled in less than an hour on opening day.

11. d.) *Flights of Wonder*
Animal Kingdom's Asia opened with a single attraction, *Flights of Wonder*. This expanding land now includes the *Kali River Rapids*, a white-water rafting adventure which opened March 18, 1999, and the *Maharajah Jungle Trek*, a walk-through attraction, that opened the same year.

12. c.) 19
There are a total of 19 Audio-Animatronics dinosaurs on the *DINOSAUR* attraction, which uses a ride system modeled after the *Indiana Jones and the Temple of the Forbidden Eye* attraction at Disneyland Resort in California.

13. a.) *Tiger River Rapids*
Formally known as the *Tiger River Rapids Run*, this early name for what

is now *Kali River Rapids* was reportedly changed because there were no tigers to be seen during the entire ride!

14. b.) Harambe Wildlife Reserve
According to Disney's story line, the Harambe Wildlife Reserve was established in 1971, and covers over 800 square miles. The *Kilimanjaro Safaris* ride re-creates an an open-air African safari through acres of savanna, rivers, and rocky hills on which the animals freely roam.

15. d.) 430
Located in the Bug's Life Theater, the 430 seats from which you watch *It's Tough to be a Bug!* aren't your ordinary theater seats, my friend. So be on the lookout for a few "surprises" during the show!

16. b.) $800 million
Disney Imagineers spent over $800 million and 10 years designing and building Disney's fourth theme park. That's about twice as much as it cost to open the entire Walt Disney World Resort in 1971!

17. d.) City of Delights
Anandapur means "place of all delights" in Sanskrit. As with most things found in WDW, this fictional village has a "backstory," a made-up narrative used to guide and inspire the Imagineers (who drew their inspiration from many nations in creating the village rather than from any specific country). Anandapur was supposedly established in 1544 as a royal hunting reserve. In time, a village grew in the area. Although the royal hunting reserve has now been

converted into a conservation area, the surrounding village still thrives to this day.

18. c.) *Countdown to Extinction*
The name of this attraction was changed just weeks before the movie *Dinosaur* was released. This is not uncommon for Disney, which changed the name of Snow White's Castle in Disneyland to Sleeping Beauty Castle in 1955, just a few years before the *Sleeping Beauty* movie premiered. You can still see the letters CTX (*Countdown To eXtinction*) on the *DINOSAUR* ride vehicles.

19. d.) Rafiki's Planet Watch
Animal Kingdom opened with the Oasis, Safari Village (later renamed Discovery Island), Camp Min-nie-Mickey, Africa, Conservation Station (later renamed Rafiki's Planet Watch), DinoLand U.S.A, and a small portion of Asia.

20. c.) Chakranadi River
Kali River Rapids takes you on a wild ride on the Chakranadi River through a lush jungle that is being ravaged by illegal logging. Chakrana-di is Thai for "river that runs in a circle."

21. a.) *Gorilla Falls Exploration Trail*
The Gorilla Falls name for the Pan-gani Forest Exploration Trail lasted only a few months after Animal

Kingdom's 1998 opening. Pangani is Swahili for "place of enchantment," a perfect way to describe this lush, tropical, five-acre, walk-through land.

22. d.) *The Jungle Book*
Journey into the Jungle Book was the opening attraction in the hexagonal, 1,375-seat Theater in the Wild in April 1998. Based on the Disney animated film, *The Jungle Book* (which was in turn based on Rud-yard Kipling's *The Jungle Book*), the show used highly mobile costumed characters, known as "Humanimals," as well as innovative puppetry to allow the characters to step right off the pages of the book and into this fun, lively, 30-minute stage show. It closed in April 1999.

23. d.) "Coming together"
Say "Jambo" (hello) to a Cast Mem-ber when you enter the East African village of Harambe. Its name means "coming together" in Swahili.

24. b.) The drinking straw
Marvin C. Stone patented the first

waxed drinking straw on January 3, 1888. Straws, balloons, and cup lids are prohibited at Animal Kingdom to protect its inhabitants from potential choking hazards.

25. b.) A mountain in Tanzania
The *Safaris* attraction takes its name from Mount Kilimanjaro, located in northern Tanzania, near the border with Kenya. At 19,335 feet, it is the highest peak in Africa, and home to a great deal of wildlife.

26. c.) The Adirondack Mountains
Camp Minnie-Mickey is designed to look like an Adirondack fishing camp set in an evergreen forest with a rushing river.

27. a.) Discovery Island
When Animal Kingdom opened in 1998, the central area was known as Safari Village. Like the "hub" in the Magic Kingdom, it led to all of the different lands in the park. In early 2001, the name was changed to Discovery Island.

28. d.) DinoLand U.S.A.
Tarzan Rocks!, which opened in July 1999, is a 30-minute, four-act live stage performance. The high-energy show is filled with a wide array of extreme stunts, aerial acts, and live music from the animated film's soundtrack.

29. a.) A town in Kenya
The village of Harambe is based on the ancient, and quite real, Kenyan island town of Lamu. Disney "legend" tells us the park's Harambe, like the real Lamu, was once a hub for the gold and ivory trade but is now a tourist mecca. The Imagineers worked hard to tell the story of the growth and change this small village has experienced over the centuries. They created narrow, winding streets, imported native artifacts, and even created cracks in the sidewalks to make the town look weathered by time. To get the authentic thatched roofs they wanted for Harambe Village Marketplace and the rest of Africa, Disney brought over 13 Zulu craftsmen from Kwa-Zulu-Natal.

30. b.) Logs
You'll notice a sign in the queue area for *Kali River Rapids* referring to recent illegal logging activity. If you listen carefully at the rafting com-

Did You Know?

MORE THAN 61,000 COSTUME ITEMS ARE REQUIRED TO DRESS THE ANIMAL KINGDOM'S CAST MEMBERS.

Did You Know?

TO CONVINCE DISNEY EXECUTIVES THAT THE EXPERIENCE OF SHARING THE SAME SPACE WITH EXOTIC ANIMALS WAS ENOUGH TO ENTERTAIN GUESTS AT AN ANIMAL-THEMED PARK, THE IMAGINEERS BROUGHT A 400-POUND BENGAL TIGER INTO AN EXECUTIVE MEETING AND HAD HIM WALK AROUND THE CONFERENCE TABLE.

pany office, you can also hear the field radio warn you away from a fire at an illegal logging site. It's all part of the attraction's pro-conservation message.

31. d.) Sue
Sue (or Dino-Sue) is not a real fossil, but a 40-foot long, 13-foot tall exact replica of the largest Tyrannosaurus Rex ever found. She was discovered

in 1990 in the Black Hills of South Dakota and named after renowned dinosaur hunter Sue Hendrickson.

32. c.) *Maharajah Jungle Trek*
In Asia's *Maharajah Jungle Trek*, you can walk through the "ruins" of India and see tigers, fruit bats, Asian birds, and more. This self-guided tour opened in 1999.

33. b.) Little Red

About halfway through your safari, you are notified that poachers have taken an elephant mother and child - Big Red and Little Red. Thus begins a chase to track down the poachers and save the two elephants.

34. a.) Olden Gate Bridge

As you enter DinoLand U.S.A., you pass under the Olden Gate Bridge, which is actually made up of the skeleton of a 40 foot tall Brachiosaurus, one of the largest creatures ever to walk the planet. (Immediately after you cross the Olden Gate Bridge, take a look at the bulletin board. It's full of humorous postings from Disney Imagineers!)

35. a.) Wilson Matua

"Dr. K. Kulunda" is the "director" of the "joint effort by the citizens of Harambe and international conservation groups" in the *Pangani Forest Exploration Trail*. "Dr. Seeker" can be found in another of the park's attractions... Can you name it?

36. b.) *Flights of Wonder*

Opened in February 1999, *Flights of Wonder* is a live show performed at the Caravan Stage in the Asia section. The 20-minute show takes place in an open-air, 700-seat theater and lets you watch a fabulous variety of rare and exotic birds display their amazing natural behaviors.

37. c.) 5

The park's logo features (from left to right): a lion, an elephant, a dragon, a triceratops dinosaur, and a bongo (a species of African antelope).

38. d.) Tetak Logging Co.

Look for the "graffiti" in the *Kali River Rapids* queue line s well as the attraction itself defaming the logging company and protesting the destruction of the rainforests!

39. b.) Primeval Whirl

Located in the heart of DinoLand U.S.A., *Primeval Whirl* is themed to match the carnival-like atmosphere of Chester and Hester's Dino-Rama, and offers a wild roller-coaster ride. The zany ride takes you in a "time machine" that can spin 360 degrees along one of two tracks and drops you into the open jaws of a giant dinosaur fossil before it's over. Brightly colored asteroids and dinosaurs, as well as the "dinosaur jaws," make this one fun for all ages.

40. c.) 325

The exterior construction of the 145-foot tall Tree of Life took a crew of thousands over a year and a half. The tree's 325 animals were meticulously carved by 20 artists, led by Chief Sculptor Zsolt Hormay. They included three Native Americans, as well as sculptors from as far away as France and Ireland. Because the cement they were sculpting hardened as they worked, the artists had only six to ten hours to create each intricate image.

41. a.) Carnotaurus
According to Disney, when the Imagineers began working on *DINOSAUR*, they had to pick out certain dinosaurs to inhabit the attraction. Their first dilemma came in making the choice of which dinosaur to cast as the "star" of the show. As in any great movie, they wanted a "hero" and a "villain." They picked the plant-eating Iguanodon to be the hero and the Carnotaurus (whose name means "meat bull") with its savage teeth and huge horns as the menacing creature. The Imagineers liked the idea of choosing the latter as the villain because it is not as familiar

to guests as the T-Rex.

42. b.) Asia
Although the land had been open to guests for several weeks, Asia's "official" opening day was March 18, 1999, almost one year after the park's opening day.

43. c.) Discovery River
Encircling the Safari Village is the Discovery River, the former home to a short-lived boat ride, known as the *Discovery River Taxis*.

44. b.) Cretaceous
Guests on *DINOSAUR* climb aboard their Time Rovers and take a bumpy trip back 65 million years to the Cretaceous period in search of an Iguanodon.

45. a.) Giraffe

Although there are literally hundreds of different species of animals residing in Disney's Animal Kingdom, Zari and Miles, a pair of reticulated giraffes, were the park's first residents. Zari, a female, was born at the Metro Washington Park Zoo in Portland, Oregon. Miles was (at the time), a two-year-old male from the St. Louis Zoological Park. Zari can now be found on the Animal Kingdom Lodge's savanna.

46. d.) Diesel

The train that transports guests to Rafiki's Planet Watch is powered by a 60-ton British-built diesel locomotive.

47. b.) Wild Animal Kingdom

Originally called the Wild Animal Kingdom, the park was to be separated into three separate lands themed around live animals, extinct animals, and mythical animals. Disney removed the "Wild" from the name in part to avoid a potential conflict with Mutual of Omaha's "Wild Kingdom" TV show.

48. c.) Chester and Hester's Dino-Rama!

Added in November of 2001, this tiny "land" is designed to look like a tacky, "tourist trap" carnival run by a local couple, Chester and Hester. Here, guests can play midway games for prizes and ride the *Triceratops Spin* and *Primeval Whirl*.

Did You Know?

THE ROCKS IN THE LION AREA OF *KILIMANJARO SAFARIS* ARE CLIMATE-CONTROLLED. THEY ARE HEATED IN THE WINTER AND COOLED IN THE SUMMER TO ENCOURAGE THE LIONS TO LIE IN GOOD VIEWING AREAS!

CHAPTER SIX

BEYOND THE PARKS

WDW RESORTS, WATER PARKS, DOWNTOWN DISNEY & THE MONORAIL

1. Pleasure Island takes its name from:
- a.) An island from the story of Pinocchio
- b.) Merriweather Pleasure
- c.) This was the original name for Discovery Island before it was changed
- d.) It is a takeoff on the name "Treasure Island"

2. Disney's Fort Wilderness Resort and Campground has about how many campsites?
- a.) 150
- b.) 300
- c.) 780
- d.) 1,120

3. Who was the original voice of the monorail? (You know, the "Please stand clear of the doors" guy?)
- a.) Thurl Ravenscroft
- b.) Paul Frees
- c.) Jack Wagner
- d.) Corey Burton

4. Which of the following hotels was not open to guests on Opening Day, 1971?
- a.) Disney's Fort Wilderness Resort and Campground
- b.) Disney's Grand Floridian Resort & Spa
- c.) Disney's Wilderness Lodge
- d.) All of the above

Did You Know?

AT THE HOME RUN HOTEL IN DISNEY'S
ALL-STAR SPORTS RESORT, IT WOULD TAKE
OVER 20 MILLION CANS OF COCA-COLA TO FILL
ONE OF THE GIGANTIC COKE CUPS.
THAT'S EQUAL TO ALL OF THE WATER IN
TYPHOON LAGOON'S WAVE POOL! IT WOULD
TAKE JUST TEN OF THOSE LARGE COKE CUPS
TO FILL SPACESHIP EARTH AT EPCOT.

5. What is the current name of the restaurant once known as "Flagler's"?
   a.) Citrico's
   b.) Bongos Cuban Cafe
   c.) Wolfgang Puck's Cafe
   d.) Victoria & Albert's

6. How many rooms are there in Disney's Pop Century Resort?
   a.) 2,112
   b.) 3,971
   c.) 1,971
   d.) 5,760

7. The monorail travels through the center of which of these hotels?
   a.) Disney's Polynesian Resort
   b.) Disney's Contemporary Resort
   c.) Disney's Grand Floridian Resort
   d.) Walt Disney World Swan Resort

8. Who hosts the CyberSpace Mountain attraction in DisneyQuest?
   a.) Mr. Wizard
   b.) Mr. Rogers
   c.) Bill Nye, the Science Guy
   d.) Figment

9. At the All-Star Sports Resort, the palm trees are shaped to look like what?
   a.) Golf clubs
   b.) Football goal posts
   c.) Basketball players at tip-off
   d.) A surfer riding a wave

10. What is the name of the body of water between Disney's Board-Walk and Beach Club Resorts?
   a.) Bay Lake
   b.) Seven Seas Lagoon
   c.) Echo Lake
   d.) Crescent Lake

11. There is a strange animal in the mosaic mural in the fourth-floor lobby of Disney's Contemporary Resort. What is it?
   a.) A two-headed cow
   b.) A five-legged goat
   c.) A two-headed bird
   d.) A four-legged man

12. The Cabana Bar and Grill is located in which Resort?
   a.) Disney's Polynesian Resort
   b.) Disney's Contemporary Resort
   c.) Walt Disney World Dolphin
   d.) Disney's Beach Club Resort

13. Which of the following areas is not part of Downtown Disney?
   a.) Disney's BoardWalk
   b.) Disney's West Side
   c.) Disney Village Marketplace
   d.) Pleasure Island

14. "Chef Mickey's," located in Disney's Contemporary Resort, was originally the name of a restaurant located where?
   a.) It has always been there
   b.) Disney-MGM Studios
   c.) Disney Village Marketplace
   d.) The Magic Kingdom

15. What is "Fantasia Gardens"?
   a.) A garden in the back of the UK pavilion
   b.) A miniature golf course
   c.) A restaurant
   d.) A pool at the All-Star Movies resort

16. December 14, 2003 marked the opening of which Disney Resort?
   a.) Disney's Pop Century Resort
   b.) Disney's Wilderness Lodge
   c.) Disney's Port Orleans Resort—French Quarter
   d.) Disney's Coronado Springs Resort

17. Two of WDW's old monorails were refurbished and put into service elsewhere. Where?
   a.) Las Vegas
   b.) Tokyo Disneyland
   c.) Disneyland Paris
   d.) Marceline, Missouri

Did You Know?

IF YOU COUNT ALL THE DALMATIANS IN THE *101 DALMATIANS* SECTION OF DISNEY'S ALL-STAR MOVIES RESORT, INCLUDING ALL OF THE PUPPIES AND THE LARGE PONGO AND PERDITA, YOU GET EXACTLY 101.

18. From which of these resorts can you NOT see the *Electrical Water Pageant*?
   a.) Disney's Polynesian Resort
   b.) Disney's Contemporary Resort
   c.) Disney's Grand Floridian Resort & Spa
   d.) Disney's BoardWalk Inn

19. How many All-Star Resorts are there at WDW?
   a.) 1
   b.) 2
   c.) 3
   d.) 4

20. On which body of water is Downtown Disney located?
   a.) Buena Vista Lagoon
   b.) Bay Lake
   c.) Seven Seas Lagoon
   d.) Pleasure Island Bay

21. What was used to create the patterns of the draperies in the guest rooms of the BoardWalk Inn?
   a.) Antique postcards
   b.) Old movies
   c.) Original drapes from Atlantic City hotels
   d.) Ride tickets from old Atlantic City boardwalk attractions

22. How many tennis courts are there at WDW?
   a.) 11
   b.) 25
   c.) 31
   d.) 71

23. If you wanted to spend a night in every guest room, in every hotel that is currently open on WDW property, how long would it take you?
   a.) More than 5 years
   b.) More than 11 months
   c.) More than 33 years
   d.) More than 68 years

24. The maximum capacity of a monorail train is:
   a.) 145 people
   b.) 229 people
   c.) 364 people
   d.) 417 people

25. What is the name of the body of water running from the hotel lobby to the pool at Disney's Wilderness Lodge?

a.) Typhoon Lagoon
b.) Roaring Rapids
c.) Slippin' Falls
d.) Wilderness Rapids

26. Which of these resorts was NOT originally planned for Walt Disney World?
a.) The Asian
b.) The Persian
c.) The Venetian
d.) The European

27. In what year did Disney's Grand Floridian Resort & Spa open?
a.) 1988
b.) 1983
c.) 1971
d.) 1999

28. The Fort Wilderness Resort and Campground is located on how many acres?
a.) 100
b.) 47
c.) 750
d.) 970

29. What toy company opened its own merchandise location at Downtown Disney Marketplace in 1997?
a.) Mattel
b.) LEGO
c.) Beanie Baby
d.) Hasbro

Did You Know?

50,000 SPRINKLER HEADS AND 2,000 MILES OF IRRIGATION PIPE ARE NEEDED TO WATER WDW'S MORE THAN 3,500 ACRES OF LANDSCAPING.

30. The largest sand-bottom pool in the world is found at which of the WDW resorts?
a.) Disney's Caribbean Beach Resort
b.) Disney's Polynesian Resort
c.) Disney's Beach Club
d.) Disney's Grand Floridian Resort & Spa

31. How many different monorail trains currently operate at Walt Disney World?
a.) 6
b.) 10
c.) 12
d.) 20

32. The ESPN Club is located near what resort?
a.) Disney's Coronado Springs Resort
b.) Disney's Contemporary Resort
c.) Disney's All-Star Sports Resort
d.) Disney's BoardWalk Inn

33. Which is NOT a theme used at the All-Star Sports Resort?
  a.) Football
  b.) Soccer
  c.) Baseball
  d.) Basketball

34. The musical notes behind the registration desk at Disney's Port Orleans Resort—French Quarter spell out the first verse of what song?
  a.) "Zip-A-Dee-Doo-Dah"
  b.) "America the Beautiful"
  c.) "it's a small world"
  d.) "When the Saints Go Marching In"

35. At what restaurant can you make reservations to dine at the "Chef's Table" in the kitchen?
  a.) Citrico's
  b.) 1900 Park Fare
  c.) Victoria & Albert's
  d.) Mama Melrose's Ristorante Italiano

36. What happened to one of WDW's original monorail trains after it was replaced by the Mark VI series?
  a.) It was sold on eBay
  b.) It was accidentally dropped from a crane and destroyed
  c.) It was sent to Walt Disney's home town in Missouri
  d.) When Walt Disney was cryogenically frozen after his death, he was put inside the train, which was later buried behind the Magic Kingdom

37. The "Tempo Bay Resort Hotel" was the working title for what Disney Resort?
  a.) Disney's Contemporary Resort
  b.) Disney's Polynesian Village Resort
  c.) Disney's Coronado Springs Resort
  d.) Disney's Grand Floridian Beach Resort & Spa

38. How many slides are there at Blizzard Beach?
  a.) 4
  b.) 11
  c.) 21
  d.) 29

Did You Know?

SUMMIT PLUMMET IN BLIZZARD BEACH IS TWICE AS HIGH AS HUMUNGA KOWABUNGA, TYPHOON LAGOON'S BIGGEST WATER SLIDE.

39. The California Grill replaced what dinner show at Disney's Contemporary Resort?
a.) *Mesa Grande Lounge Theater*
b.) *The Tip Top Supper Club Show*
c.) *Gulf Coast Room Dinner Theater*
d.) *Broadway at the Top*

40. What can you find in the lobby of the Polynesian's Great Ceremonial House?
a.) A waterfall
b.) Mickey and Minnie statues
c.) A monorail station
d.) A pool

41. How many different monorail routes are there?
a.) 1
b.) 2
c.) 3
d.) 4

42. What song do the musical notes on the front desk at Disney's All-Star Music Resort spell out?
a.) "When the Saints Go Marching In"
b.) "When You Wish Upon a Star"
c.) "Zip-A-Dee-Doo-Dah"
d.) "The Mickey Mouse Club Theme Song"

43. Of the resorts on Seven Seas Lagoon, which is closest to the Magic Kingdom?
a.) Disney's Contemporary Resort
b.) Disney's Wilderness Lodge
c.) Disney's Polynesian Resort
d.) Disney's Fort Wilderness Resort and Campground

44. What do the musical notes on top of the beverage stand in Disney's All-Star Music Resort's Intermission Food Court spell?
a.) "Heigh-Ho"
b.) "Be Our Guest"
c.) "Hakuna Matata"
d.) "I Just Can't Wait to be King"

45. What hotel can be seen from Tomorrowland in the Magic Kingdom?
a.) Disney's Polynesian Resort
b.) Disney's Grand Floridian Resort & Spa
c.) Disney's Wilderness Lodge
d.) Disney's Contemporary Resort

46. How many Zones are there in DisneyQuest?
- a.) 2
- b.) 3
- c.) 4
- d.) 5

47. What is unique about Mannequins Dance Palace?
- a.) It is located on a beach in Pleasure Island
- b.) It has a revolving dance floor
- c.) It contains Audio-Animatronics figures
- d.) It does not serve alcohol

48. At what Disney resort can you find a pool with a *Fantasia* theme?
- a.) Disney's All-Star Movies Resort
- b.) Walt Disney World Swan
- c.) Disney's Caribbean Beach Resort
- d.) Disney's Grand Floridian Resort & Spa

49. What is "Big Bertha," found at Disney's Grand Floridian Resort & Spa?
- a.) The game room
- b.) A 45-foot yacht
- c.) Victoria & Albert's 36-ounce steak
- d.) An old fairgrounds organ

50. How many hotels have stops on the monorail route?
- a.) 1
- b.) 2
- c.) 3
- d.) 4

51. Which Major League baseball team holds its Training Camps at Walt Disney World's Wide World of Sports Complex?
- a.) Anaheim Angels
- b.) New York Mets
- c.) Atlanta Braves
- d.) Florida Marlins

52. What is the name of the piano at the Adventurer's Club in Pleasure Island?
- a.) Indy
- b.) Fingers
- c.) Big Nick
- d.) The Harmonizer

Did You Know?

THE 11 CLAY TENNIS COURTS IN DISNEY'S WIDE WORLD OF SPORTS ARE AUTOMATICALLY MOISTENED WHEN THEY GET TOO DRY THANKS TO A BUILT IN SENSOR SYSTEM.

53. Before Disney's Pop Century Resort opened, what was the largest resort on WDW property?
a.) Disney's Grand Floridian Resort & Spa
b.) Disney's Wilderness Lodge
c.) Disney's Animal Kingdom Lodge
d.) Disney's Caribbean Beach Resort

54. In what year were the Mark VI Monorails put into service in Walt Disney World?
a.) 1971
b.) 1989
c.) 1999
d.) 2001

55. What is the name of the geyser at Disney's Wilderness Lodge?
a.) Fire Rock Geyser
b.) Hidden Springs Geyser
c.) Iron Spike Geyser
d.) Roaring Forks Geyser

56. The Disney Vacation Club Resort that opened in 2004 is called:
a.) Disney's Venetian Resort
b.) Disney's Old Key West Resort
c.) Disney's Pop Century Resort
d.) Disney's Saratoga Springs Resort

57. What is the former Empress Lilly riverboat now known as?
a.) Fulton's Crab House
b.) Portobello Yacht Club
c.) Empress Lilly's Cafe
d.) The Adventurers Club

58. How many passengers travel on the monorails every year at WDW?
a.) 10 million
b.) 25 million
c.) 50 million
d.) 75 million

59. What is unique about Victoria & Albert's Restaurant in Disney's Grand Floridian Resort & Spa?
a.) It is a vegetarian restaurant
b.) There are only four dining tables in the restaurant
c.) It contains a private room with Walt Disney's personal dining table and chairs
d.) All of the waiters are named Albert and all of the waitresses are named Victoria

60. Disney's Dixie Landings Resort is now known as:
a.) Disney's Port Orleans Resort-Riverside
b.) Disney's Coronado Springs Resort
c.) Disney's Port Orleans Resort-French Quarter
d.) Disney's Old Key West Resort

61. What Disney character is on the "Pleasure Island Tonight!" sign located at the entrance to the island?

a.) Pinocchio
b.) Belle
c.) Jessica Rabbit
d.) Scrooge McDuck

62. WDW's largest ballroom can be found in which resort?
a.) Disney's Contemporary Resort
b.) Disney's BoardWalk Inn
c.) Disney's Saratoga Springs Resort
d.) Disney's Coronado Springs Resort

63. A monorail train carrying guests travels at a maximum speed of about:
a.) 25 mph
b.) 40 mph
c.) 55 mph
d.) 60 mph

64. The Pleasure Island nightclub 8TRAX replaced what other nightclub?
a.) Cage
b.) The XZFR Rockin' Rollerdome
c.) The Wildhorse Saloon
d.) Mannequins

65. Which of the following is the name of one of the ferryboats that take guests from the Transportation and Ticket Center to the Magic Kingdom?
a.) Magic Kingdom 1
b.) Golden Dream
c.) Kingdom Queen
d.) Richard F. Irvine

66. Can you name the Chinese junk (boat) that once docked at Disney's Polynesian Resort?
a.) Buena Vista
b.) East Wind
c.) Chinese Charter
d.) Polynesian Dream

67. What famous New York architect designed Disney's Beach and Yacht Club Resorts?
a.) Robert A. M. Stern
b.) Michael Graves
c.) Jeffrey Beers
d.) Frank Gehry

68. How large is the World Of Disney shop at Downtown Disney Marketplace?

Did You Know?

IF A FOOTBALL PLAYER WANTED TO WEAR ONE OF THE LARGE HELMETS FOUND IN THE TOUCHDOWN HOTEL AREA OF DISNEY'S ALL-STAR SPORTS RESORT, HE WOULD HAVE TO BE OVER 200 FEET TALL - THAT'S TALLER THAN THE TOWER OF TERROR.

a.) 10,000 square feet
b.) 30,000 square feet
c.) 50,000 square feet
d.) 75,000 square feet

69. The original name of Disney's Old Key West Resort was:
a.) The Disney Inn
b.) Disney's Vacation Club Resort
c.) Disney's Club Lake Villas
d.) The Disney Institute

70. What was the third hotel to open in Walt Disney World after Disney's Contemporary and Polynesian Resorts?
a.) Disney's Fort Wilderness Resort and Campground
b.) Disney's Golf Resort Hotel
c.) Disney's Grand Floridian Beach Resort
d.) Disney's Caribbean Beach Resort

The Answers
TO CHAPTER SIX

1. b.) Merriweather Pleasure
Merriweather Adam Pleasure is a fictitious adventurer who originally owned the island before disappearing in 1941. According to Disney legend, the island fell into ruin in the following years, and a hurricane severely damaged the existing buildings. Many years later, Imagineers cleared out the overgrown jungle and rebuilt the island, using the original owner's philosophy and passion for great fun and good entertainment to turn the old buildings into innovative nightclubs, shops, and restaurants.

2. c.) 780
Want to bring your own place to stay when you visit WDW? That's fine!

Just head on over to Disney's Fort Wilderness Resort and Campground, where there are 784 private RV and tent campsites surrounded by beautiful wilderness. The campground has two swimming pools, a beach, horseback riding, and more. It is located near the Magic Kingdom.

3. c.) Jack Wagner
"Por favor mantenganse alejado de las puertas." The early monorail spiels (including the parts in Spanish) were done by Jack "The Voice of Disney" Wagner (no, not the actor from TV's "General Hospital" soap opera). During your journey on the "Highway in the Sky," Jack

Wagner describes what you can see out your windows and offers information about the parks and resorts, special events, and safety information. During his more than 20 years with Disney, he also voiced many attractions including the *WEDway People Mover*, the pre-ride warnings in *Space Mountain*, and the introduction to *Mickey's Very Merry Christmas Parade*. In fact, many of his recordings were made in his Southern California home, where he had a recording studio that was connected to a voiceover booth in Anaheim. This way, whenever Disney needed an announcement, Jack could just sit at his microphone and the recording would be directly linked from his home to Studio D in Disneyland. Jack is also the voice of another monorail that you probably have heard: the one in the Orlando International Airport.

4. d.) All of the above

When WDW opened on October 1, 1971, the only two resorts that were operational were the Contemporary and Polynesian Village Resorts. Although it is often considered one of the "original three" resorts that opened with the Magic Kingdom, Disney's Fort Wilderness Resort and Campground actually didn't open until November 19, 1971. Disney's Grand Floridian Resort & Spa opened in August 1988 as WDW's fifth resort hotel. Disney's Wilderness Lodge opened on May 28, 1994.

5. a.) Citrico's

Yet another fabulous dining experience at WDW's flagship Grand Floridian resort, Citrico's replaced Flagler's in November 1997. The restaurant features the cuisine of both Florida and the Mediterranean, prepared in a show kitchen.

Tip: Book Priority Seating way in advance, and try to get a seat by the window to watch the fireworks in the Magic Kingdom. Or for an even more spectacular experience, book the "Chef's Domain." You can be seated in a private dining area and have the Chef personally create a special dining experience with wine pairings for you and up to 11 of your best friends — if you're willing to spend at least $650.00, the mandatory minimum purchase.

6. d.) 5,760

When complete, Disney's Pop Century Resort will have 5,760 rooms spread across 20 buildings. It was constructed in two phases, with the first phase opening on December 14, 2003. Phase 1, the "Pop Century Classic Years," has 2,880 rooms and features the decades of the 1950s through the 1990s. Phase 2, the "Pop Century Legendary Years," will also have 2,880 rooms, and will focus on the 1900s through the 1940s. The two parts of the resort are separated by Hourglass Lake and joined by the Generation Gap Bridge. The resort is located in the northeast quadrant of

Osceola Parkway and Victory Way, just south of Disney's Caribbean Beach Resort and north of Disney's Wide World of Sports Complex — and not too far from Disney's Animal Kingdom. When completed, this Pop Century Resort will bring the total number of guest rooms at WDW resorts to nearly 30,000.

7. b.) Disney's Contemporary Resort
The Contemporary was created as a modern backdrop to the Magic Kingdom's Tomorrowland. The 1,000-plus room resort is unique for many reasons, the most obvious of which is that the monorail to the MK runs right through the center of the 15-story, A-frame hotel's fourth-floor Grand Canyon Concourse.

8. c.) Bill Nye, the Science Guy
CyberSpace Mountain, located in DisneyQuest, allows you to design your own virtual reality roller coaster, then ride the coaster you just created! Your host, TV's Bill Nye, the Science Guy, guides you through the building portion, in which you design your custom coaster using a touch-screen monitor. Start by picking your environment (space, ice world, etc.), then select the track pieces that you want to ride on. Add as many loops, twists, and even jumps as you like! Then pick your speed and hop in the simulator, 'cause you're gonna ride the coaster you just created using virtual reality and motion simulation!

9. c.) Basketball players at tip-off
One of the value properties, Disney's All-Star Sports Resort, uses larger-

than-life icons, music, landscaping, and lighting to create sports scenes, among them palm trees arranged to look like a basketball team at tip-off and a pool in the shape of a baseball infield. It is located near the two other All-Star value-priced resorts, Music and Movies, on a 62-acre site near Disney's Animal Kingdom theme park.

10. d.) Crescent Lake

Crescent Lake provides beautiful views to guests of Disney's Board-Walk Inn, the WDW Swan, the WDW Dolphin, and Disney's Yacht and Beach Club Resorts. Although there is a beach on the lake, swimming is not allowed, but there are a variety of water activities. Guests can rent sailboats, pontoon boats, "water mice" (small two-person speedboats), and even arrange a two-hour fishing excursion.

11. b.) A five-legged goat

Known as the "Grand Canyon Concourse," the fourth floor of Disney's Contemporary Resort includes a 90-foot high mural created by Disney artist, Mary Blair in 1971. The Southwestern-themed mosaic contains 1,800 one-square-foot tiles and took 18 months to construct. The mural includes a five-legged goat (although some say it's a cow) on the monorail side, allegedly to illustrate humanity's imperfections.

12. c.) Walt Disney World Dolphin

The Cabana Bar and Grill is located by the pool at the WDW Dolphin Resort and features salads, snacks, burgers, and sandwiches.

13. a.) Disney's BoardWalk

Disney's BoardWalk takes guests back to 1940s Atlantic City and Coney Island. Located in the Epcot resorts area alongside Crescent Lake, it features wonderful clubs, restaurants, shopping, and entertainment.

14. c.) Disney Village Marketplace

In July 1990, the Village Restaurant, located in the Disney Village Marketplace (now known as Downtown Disney Marketplace), was renamed "Chef Mickey's Village Restaurant." The restaurant closed on September 30, 1995, and was replaced by the Rainforest Cafe. In 1996, Chef Mickey's buffet, featuring character meals with Mickey and his pals, opened on the Grand Canyon Concourse in Disney's Contemporary Resort.

Did You Know?

THE INSPIRATION FOR WDW'S MONORAIL IS THE WORLD'S LONGEST-RUNNING MONORAIL IN THE GERMAN CITY OF WUPPERTHAL, WHICH BEGAN RUNNING ITS "SUSPENDED" SYSTEM IN 1901. WALT DISNEY SAW AN UPDATED VERSION WHILE TRAVELING IN GERMANY IN THE 1950S, INSPIRING HIM TO HAVE A SYSTEM BUILT FOR DISNEYLAND, WHICH DEBUTED IN 1959.

15. b.) A miniature golf course
Located behind the Dolphin Resort on Epcot Resorts Boulevard, Fantasia Gardens Miniature Golf features 36 holes of fun in two courses, Fantasia Gardens ("The Hippo-est Golf Around") and Fantasia Fairways ("A Miniature Golfing Adventure"). WDW opened the two courses in 1996.

16. a.) Disney's Pop Century Resort
On December 14, 2003, Disney's Pop Century Resort, the fourth WDW Value property, opened near Disney's Animal Kingdom. The Resort takes a nostalgic trip through American pop culture, featuring larger than life icons representing each decade of the 20th century. To decorate it, Disney Imagineers spent more than a year scouring antique shops, yard sales, and eBay looking for treasures from days gone by. Lobby walls are covered with shadowboxes displaying tons of artifacts that are sure to bring back fond memories. Icons such as a giant Rubix Cube anchor the 1980s; a Mickey Mouse telephone and a Big Wheel can be found in the 1970s section; Duncan Yo-Yos and Flower Power in the 1960s section, and jukeboxes and giant 45-rpm records in the 1950s section. (Do kids today even know what a record looks like?) The Cast Members' golf carts are designed to look like '57 Chevy's, complete with tail fins.

17. a.) Las Vegas
Located between the MGM Grand and Bally's Resorts, the dual-beam monorail system opened in Las Vegas in 1995. The original track was just 0.7 miles long, had two stations (one at each end), and used two refurbished Mark IV trains. The old Mark IV cars have since been replaced.

18. d.) Disney's BoardWalk Inn

The *Electrical Water Pageant* has been floating along the waters of Bay Lake and the Seven Seas Lagoon since October 26th, 1971. This popular nighttime attraction contains two strings of seven barges to make up a 1000-foot long water parade. Each float carries a 25-foot-tall screen of lights featuring sea creatures and a salute to America, all accompanied by Disney and classical music, played through the barges' powerful sound system. The parade, created by Imagineer Bob Jani, provided the original inspiration for the Magic Kingdom's *Main Street Electrical Parade*, and can be seen from the following resorts on the Seven Seas Lagoon and Bay Lake at these approximate times:

Polynesian – 9:00 p.m.
Grand Floridian – 9:15 p.m.
Wilderness Lodge – 9:35 p.m.
Fort Wilderness – 9:45 p.m.
Contemporary – 10:05 p.m.
Magic Kingdom – 10:20 p.m. (only during extended Magic Kingdom park hours)

19. c.) 3

The fun, themed All-Star (Movies, Sports, Music) Resorts are value-priced and offer casual "food-court" style dining, multiple pools, arcades, playgrounds, and free transportation to all parts of WDW. WDW's newest value resort, Disney's Pop Century, is not an All-Star Resort.

20. a.) Buena Vista Lagoon

Downtown Disney was at one time called Lake Buena Vista Village, and maps of the shopping and dining district referred to Lake Buena Vista as the "Buena Vista Lagoon."

21. a.) Antique postcards

A collection of antique postcards found at an Atlantic City bookstore was used to create the patterns of the draperies in the BoardWalk Inn's guest rooms. In fact, during construction, a carpenter noticed a postcard dating back to 1933 written by a young man to his girlfriend. Oddly enough, the man and woman from the postcard are the carpenter's aunt and uncle! It's a small world after all.

22. b.) 25

Tennis, anyone? WDW has 25 tennis courts scattered among its properties. The Contemporary Resort is home to Disney's Racquet Club, featuring six clay (Hydrogrid) courts. Other court locations include Disney's Grand Floridian (two Har-tru Clay courts), Fort Wilderness (two hard courts), Yacht and Beach Clubs (one hard Plexiplave court), Old Key West (three hard courts), and BoardWalk (2 hard Plexiplave courts). All are lighted for night play, and tennis lessons are available at the Contemporary and Grand Floridian. You can also play on one of the 11 lighted, world-class clay courts at Disney's Wide World of Sports Complex.

The center court stadium there has permanent seating for 1,100 and was host to the men's Clay Court Championships from 1997 to 2000.

23. d.) More than 68 years
With more than 25,086 rooms in 23 resorts, you better pack a BIG bag if you want to spend a night in each one. (I hope you got a good package deal!)

24. c.) 364 people
The maximum capacity of a six-car Mark VI monorail is 364, with a normal capacity of around 316.

25. b.) Roaring Rapids
If you enter the hotel lobby of Disney's Wilderness Lodge, you will notice a small, bubbling geyser. If you follow the path of the water, you will see that it travels under a small bridge and turns into a pebble-bottomed stream outside, eventually crashing over a landscaped waterfall that empties into the pool. This water trail is known as "Roaring Rapids." However, things aren't always as they seem at WDW. Even though the spring in the lobby appears to travel all the way down to the pool, it doesn't. There are actually three separate water systems. The first feeds the geyser and empties into Bay Lake; the second begins at the spring and ends at the walkway near the pool's edge; and the third handles the actual pool water.

26. d.) The European
The Asian, the Persian, and the Venetian were to be opened within a few years of Disney's Contemporary and Polynesian Resorts, which opened with the Magic Kingdom in 1971. The Asian and Venetian Resorts were to be located on the Seven Seas Lagoon, with the Asian sitting between Disney's Polynesian Resort and the Magic Kingdom, and the Venetian between Disney's Contemporary Resort and the Transportation and Ticket Center. The Persian would have been on Bay Lake, northeast of Disney's Contemporary Resort.

27. a.) 1988
WDW's flagship property, Disney's Grand Floridian Resort & Spa, opened on June 28, 1988, as the "Grand Floridian Beach Resort." The third Magic Kingdom (MK) monorail resort, it is located on the shores of the Seven Seas Lagoon between Disney's Polynesian Resort and the MK. Themed as a late 19th century Florida resort, the Grand Floridian's exterior was inspired by the Hotel del Coronado in San Diego. The resort is home to a marina and a lovely white sand beach (the site of 1995's professional beach volleyball "King of the Beach" tournament). Each of its more than 800 rooms includes distinctive Victorian décor, complete with ceiling fan. The hotel also features several dining options, with none better (probably in all of

WDW) than Victoria & Albert's.

28. c.) 750
The Fort Wilderness Resort and Campground is tucked away on a 750-acre cypress and pine forest between the Magic Kingdom and Epcot. It includes 784 RV and tent campsites and 408 Wilderness Homes and Cabins.

29. b.) LEGO
The Denmark-based toy company's shop can still be found in Downtown Disney, right next to the World of Disney shop. This 4,400 square foot store opened on November 6, 1997, and is modeled after the original LEGO store at the Mall of America in Bloomington, Minnesota. The store boasts a 3,000 square foot outdoor LEGO playland, which includes some amazing LEGO sculptures. The 30-foot sea serpent in the Lake is made up of over 1,000,000 pieces and even shoots water from its nostrils! *Tip:* Be sure to find the sleeping LEGO man on the bench and take a picture. (Can you hear him snoring?)

30. c.) Disney's Beach Club
"Stormalong Bay" is the name of the 750,000-gallon pool shared by Disney's Yacht and Beach Club Resorts. It is the largest sand-bottom pool in the world and its three acres of waterfalls and whirlpools also include a lazy river and a water slide through an abandoned shipwreck. It's like a mini-water park in itself!

31. c.) 12
When WDW opened in 1971, there were five Mark IV monorails in operation. The fleet reached a total of 12 trains in 1977. Colored stripes identify each of the 12 monorails to the pilots and traffic controllers. The monorails currently in operation are the Blue, Red, Black, Gold, Silver, Pink, Coral, Orange, Green, Lime, Purple, and Yellow trains.

32. d.) Disney's BoardWalk Inn
The ESPN Club, which opened in 1996, is the 13,000-square-foot, interactive sports entertainment facility located at Disney's Board-Walk — which is itself anchored by Disney's BoardWalk Inn and Villas. The world-famous club boasts an interactive entertainment center (including 90 TV monitors and big-screen displays), TV and radio broadcast facilities, an arcade of interactive sporting games, and a full-service restaurant. Often, guests can witness live interviews with popular sports figures or catch live demonstrations of golf or billiards. Even the restrooms have TVs in them so you won't miss a second of the action! The club is divided into three main areas: Sports Central (the main dining area, themed to look like a sports arena), The Sidelines (lined with 40 monitors, a bar, and interactive video

games), and The Yard (designed to look like a city playground, it features interactive sports games and a merchandise shop).

33. b.) Soccer

One of Disney's value resorts, Disney's All-Star Sports opened in May 1994, and is made up of five guest room buildings themed to different sports: football, tennis, baseball, basketball, and surfing. Along the top of each building are cutouts of spectator heads, as if a crowd were watching the games below. The dual, three-story "Touchdown!" buildings have giant football helmets, with large Xs and Os lined up on a football field in the courtyard. "The Home Run Hotel" pays tribute to baseball, with giant baseball bats and a Coke cup that could hold more than 20 million 12-ounce cans of Coke. The "Hoops Hotel" theme features basketball nets, whistles, a 45-foot-tall megaphone, and pennants along the roof. "Center Court" has a tennis theme, with referee chairs, 5-foot diameter tennis balls, tennis ball cans, and a 51-foot-tall racquet that is actually large enough to cover an entire tennis court! Finally, "Surf's Up!" features gigantic surfboards and 38-foot shark fins. If there were a shark attached to the two fins, it would have to be 300-feet long! All guests check in at "Stadium Hall," themed to resemble a basketball gymnasium with caged lighting and red lockers.

34. d.) "When the Saints Go Marching In"

The notes on the musical staff behind the registration desk at Disney's Port Orleans Resort-French Quarter represent the first verse of that classic tune.

35. c.) Victoria & Albert's

For the most elegant dining experience you can have during your stay at WDW, Victoria & Albert's, located in the Grand Floridian, has no equal. It is an intimate, elegant retreat for world-class dining, complemented by an award-winning wine list. It has been awarded the prestigious AAA Five Diamond distinction and earned Zagat's Triple Crown for being number one in food, décor, and service in Orlando. The Chef's Table is located just off the kitchen, and allows up to 10 guests to interact with and observe the chef and his team as they prepare a special menu just for you and your party.

36. a.) It was sold on eBay

Wow! If you're a fan of Walt Disney World (and I think you are), the Holy Grail of Disneyana collectibles would have to be an original monorail train used at the park. (Let's ignore the problem of where to keep the train once you get it home.) Anyway, believe it or not, a monorail car was once put up for auction and sold on eBay. On May 27, 2002, "Monorail Red" was put on the auction block by Disney Auctions, which often sells theme park, movie, and animation memorabilia on eBay. As part of WDW's year-long "100 Years of Magic" Celebration commemorating the 100th anniversary of Walt Disney's birth, the single pilot car or "nose," which had logged a total of 943,976 miles (the equivalent of 38 trips around the circumference of the Earth) was up for grabs. When the auction concluded on June 6, 2002, the winning bidder was Chip Young of Georgia. So, how much might it cost to have a real monorail sitting in your backyard? Young paid $20,000 plus shipping expenses. Like I said, Wow! Sadly, most of the other monorail trains were sold as scrap metal to a Tampa metal yard.

37. a.) Disney's Contemporary Resort
The "Tempo Bay Resort Hotel" was the working title for what would eventually become Disney's Contemporary Resort. The use of "Tempo" (short for "Contemporary") was intentional, as the hotel was intended to be a backdrop for Tomorrowland. Although the resort opened as Disney's Contemporary Resort, early postcards picturing it referred to it as the Tempo Bay Resort Hotel.

38. c.) 21
Blizzard Beach, which opened in 1995, is the larger of WDW's two water parks, with 66 acres in total.

In 2001, The Travel Channel named Disney's Blizzard Beach the #3 water park in the United States.

39. d.) Broadway at the Top
The Top of the World (or Top of the World Supper Club) restaurant, located at the top of the Contemporary Resort, featured a dinner show and musical revue highlighting three decades of Broadway hits called "Broadway at the Top." Prior to this show debuting in 1981, the Top of the World featured performances by celebrity entertainers as well as dancing and a cocktail lounge. The Top of the World closed on September 30, 1993, and reopened as the California Grill in May 1995. The Mesa Grande Lounge was the former name of the Top of the World Lounge. The Gulf Coast Room was a separate establishment that closed on May 28, 1988. It and the Top of the World Supper Club were two of the few WDW restaurants that required jackets for men.

40. a.) A waterfall
A large, soothing waterfall graces the lobby of the Polynesian's Great Ceremonial House, which includes the hotel's registration desk, shops, restaurants, and more. The monorail station is right outside the House on the second floor.

41. c.) 3
When WDW opened in 1971, the original monorail loop connected

the Contemporary and Polynesian resorts with the Magic Kingdom and the Ticket and Transportation Center. In 1982, the monorail route was extended to Epcot, including a brief swing through Future World. Today, the system has three routes. They run between the MK and the Transportation and Ticket Center (TTC), between Epcot and the TTC, and among the Magic Kingdom resorts.

42. b.) "When You Wish Upon a Star"

The musical notes that appear across the registration desk in the All-Star Music Resort are the opening of "When You Wish Upon a Star." The music on the curtains in some rooms is an orchestral version of the song.

43. a.) Disney's Contemporary Resort

The 15-story Contemporary opened on October 1, 1971. It is the closest resort to the Magic Kingdom. Guests can reach it by monorail or footpath.

44. b.) "Be Our Guest"

The music on the top of the beverage stand in the All-Star Music Resort's Intermission Food Court is "Be Our Guest" from *Beauty and the Beast.*

45. d.) Disney's Contemporary Resort

The three Magic Kingdom resorts are themed to match the lands in the park from which they are visible. Disney's Contemporary, visible from Tomorrowland, has a futuristic theme. Disney's Grand Floridian, which can be seen from Main Street, U.S.A., reflects its 19th century charm, while Disney's Polynesian is themed to match Adventureland, which lies directly across the Seven Seas Lagoon from it.

46. c.) 4

DisneyQuest is not an arcade, but an "immersive, interactive adventureland" with fun activities for the entire family. Like the Magic Kingdom, this five-story building houses various themed "lands," known here as "zones." Guests enter through Ventureport and can choose to explore any of four themed zones: The Explore Zone contains many of the virtual reality attractions, includ-

Did You Know?

THE 1,671-SEAT SHOWROOM IN DOWNTOWN DISNEY IS THE FIRST FREESTANDING PERMANENT THEATER EVER BUILT FOR CIRQUE DU SOLEIL.

ing *Aladdin's Magic Carpet Ride* and *Pirates of the Caribbean - Battle for Buccaneer Gold.* Score Zone immerses guests in a giant comic book and provides countless hours of classic and modern video games. Create Zone lets you try your creative hand at animation and invention. Replay Zone, a three-floor futuristic area, includes classic rides and *Buzz Lightyear's Astro Blaster.* The fifth floor contains The Cheesecake Factory Express food area, serving salads, sandwiches, burgers, pizza, coffee, and incredible desserts.

47. b.) It has a revolving dance floor

Mannequins Dance Palace is hip, hopping, and often very crowded. This dance club at Downtown Disney's Pleasure Island has been voted the #1 dance club in the United States. You can dance the night away on a revolving floor that spins you to the beat of high-intensity dance and techno music backed by state-of-the-art sound and light systems. If you just want to sit back, relax, and watch the single people hit on each other all night, there are numerous lounge areas and bars as well.

48. a.) Disney's All-Star Movies Resort

Disney's All-Star Movies Resort opened in January 1999. It includes five areas inspired and named after Disney movies: "Fantasia," "Toy Story," "101 Dalmatians," "The Mighty Ducks," and "The Love Bug." This fun resort is truly "larger than life," with a 40-foot-tall Pongo and a 35-foot-tall Perdita in the 101 Dalmatians building; a 35-foot-tall Buzz Lightyear and a 25-foot-tall Woody with Green Army Men on top of the Toy Story building; a "Herbie" VW bug that is five times its normal size atop the Love Bug building, and giant sorcerer's hats, spell books, brooms, and buckets around the Fantasia buildings. There are two pools at the Resort, one themed to Fantasia, the other reminiscent of the Duck Pond hockey rink in *The Mighty Ducks*.

49. d.) An old fairgrounds organ
"Big Bertha" is a 100-year-old band organ from Paris that sits 15 feet above the 1900 Park Fare restaurant. The organ will periodically play during the character meals featuring Mary Poppins, the Mad Hatter, Alice in Wonderland, Pinocchio, and Gepetto.

50. c.) 3
Disney's Contemporary Resort, Disney's Polynesian Resort, and Disney's Grand Floridian Beach Resort & Spa are the only hotels with monorail stops.

51. c.) Atlanta Braves
Major League Baseball's Atlanta Braves hold their spring training at Cracker Jack Stadium in Disney's Wide World of Sports Complex. The park offers all of the amenities of a major league ballpark, but with a feeling of days long gone by.

The Complex is also home to the Orlando Rays, the AA affiliate of the Tampa Bay Devil Rays. Basketball's funny men, the Harlem Globetrotters, work out here as well.

52. b.) Fingers
In the Adventurers Club Library, one can't help but notice the piano that has crashed through the ceiling and taken up permanent residence on the club's main stage. It's even got a name, Fingers.

53. d.) Disney's Caribbean Beach Resort
Disney's Caribbean Beach Resort was once the holder of two distinctions at WDW. It was the first "moderately priced" resort on property and the largest, with 2,112 rooms. It's still plenty big. In fact, it has its own bus system to get from one side of the property to the other!

54. b.) 1989
Walt Disney World opened in 1971 with a fleet of Mark IV monorail trains, built by the Alweg Company from Cologne, Germany. They were replaced by new trains built by Bombardier, the largest mass-transit manufacturer in North America. This new fleet, known as the "Mark VI" monorail, began operating in 1989 and offered a number of benefits. In addition to a 30 percent increase in guest capacity, the new, more reliable trains were taller and allowed for

a mix of seated and standing passengers. They also boasted better suspension for a smoother ride, increased air conditioning capacity, and improved sliding-door systems that made it more convenient to get on and off the trains. (Guests who rode the older cars will remember Cast Members walking by the trains as they were about to depart — they had to slam each door shut manually.) Despite many people's belief, Walt Disney and his Imagineers did not "invent" the monorail. In fact, a steam-powered monorail system operated in California as early as 1878 and an electric car monorail system was used in Long Island, New York in 1892.

55. a.) Fire Rock Geyser

Fire Rock Geyser, with sprays that can reach up to 120 feet in the air, is located near the main pool area at Disney's Wilderness Lodge. It erupts hourly from 7:00 a.m. to 10:00 p.m. Did you know that not long after Disney's Wilderness Lodge opened, Disney began receiving complaints about the geyser from hotel guests? Most of the complaints came for one of two reasons. First, the geyser would erupt throughout the night, waking guests whose rooms were close by. Disney quickly stopped eruptions from 11:00 p.m. to 6:00 a.m. The second complaint came from guests with lake-view rooms close to Fire Rock. The trouble came not from the time of the eruptions, but from the fact that winds would often blow the water onto the guests' balconies and drench them! Quick to react, Disney installed a wind gauge to detect wind speed and adjust the height of the geyser accordingly.

Oh, and as for the other choices, Hidden Springs is a pool, Roaring Forks is a Snack Shop, and the Iron Spike is a game room and lounge area.

56. d.) Disney's Saratoga Springs Resort

Disney's Saratoga Springs Resort and Spa opened in the spring of 2004. Named for Saratoga Springs, New York, a popular summer retreat, the resort is the seventh Disney Vacation Club (DVC) resort to date. When completed, it will also be the largest, with 552 total accommodations including studio, one- and two-bedroom villas, and Grand Villa units housed in 12 separate buildings. The new resort is located on the former site of the Disney Institute. It covers 16 acres and overlooks Lake Buena Vista near Downtown Disney.

57. a.) Fulton's Crab House

The restaurant is actually a large paddleboat, permanently docked on the shore of Lake Buena Vista in Downtown Disney.

58. c.) 50 million

The WDW Monorail System is the most heavily traveled passenger monorail system in the world. It carries an average of about 150,000 passengers every day, with a maximum capacity of 200,000 passengers daily. Each year, the monorails transport more than 50 million people. Since WDW opened in 1971, they have carried over 1 billion passengers.

59. d.) All of the waiters are named Albert and all of the waitresses are named Victoria

The crown jewel of dining options in Disney's Grand Floridian Resort & Spa is Victoria & Albert's. This small, intimate restaurant has just 18 tables in the dining room and is the ultimate dining experience at WDW. It is the only restaurant in Central Florida to earn the prestigious AAA Five Diamond Award. One of the

Did You Know?

THE CHEF'S TABLE AT VICTORIA & ALBERT'S RESTAURANT, WHICH OFFERS A PRIVATE DINING EXPERIENCE FOR UP TO 10, MUST BE RESERVED A MINIMUM OF SIX MONTHS IN ADVANCE.

restaurant's unique features is that all of the servers wear name tags that say either "Victoria" or "Albert" (after England's Queen Victoria and her husband, Prince Albert).

60. a.) Disney's Port Orleans Resort-Riverside

Disney's Dixie Landings Resort opened in a series of phases, beginning on February 2, 1992, with Alligator Bayou, followed by the Magnolia Bend plantations. Dixie Landings was located next to its "sister" resort, Port Orleans, which was themed to New Orleans' French Quarter. While Port Orleans was meant to represent the main city of New Orleans, Dixie Landings was themed to the more rural bayous and featured large front gates, live oaks, and Spanish moss, reminiscent of the old South. On March 1, 2001, Dixie Landings was renamed Disney's Port Orleans Resort-Riverside, merging it with the original Port Orleans, which is now called Disney's Port Orleans Resort-French Quarter. It is rumored, though never confirmed by Disney, that the original Dixie Landings was renamed and "updated" somewhat to remove any concern about the "plantation" setting and its association with slavery in the old South. This is evidenced by the renaming of the Colonel's Cotton Mill food court, which is now called The Riverside Mill. As part of the merger of the two properties, Port Orleans' Bonfammile's restaurant closed, leaving Boatwright's Dining Hall at the former Dixie Landings as the only full-service restaurant.

61. c.) Jessica Rabbit

Jessica Rabbit was the groundbreaking animated star of the Disney film, *Who Framed Roger Rabbit?* She can be seen striking her sexy pose on the giant neon sign at the entrance to Pleasure Island.

62. d.) Disney's Coronado Springs Resort

Disney's Coronado Springs Resort has the largest ballroom in the entire

Did You Know?

DISNEY'S GLASS-ENCLOSED, VICTORIAN-STYLE WEDDINGS PAVILION IS BUILT ON A PRIVATE ISLAND ON THE SEVEN SEAS LAGOON, NOT FAR FROM DISNEY'S GRAND FLORIDIAN RESORT & SPA. IT HAS HOSTED MORE THAN 4,000 WEDDINGS SINCE IT OPENED IN 1995.

southeastern United States, 60,214 square feet. It is also the largest convention center at WDW, and the third largest in the region. The resort, which opened in 1997, currently has 95,000 square feet of meeting space (including the ballroom), and is equipped with wireless Internet access. A new 86,000-square-foot exhibit hall opening in spring 2005, will bring the total to 181,000 square feet of meeting space.

63. b.) 40 mph
Although the monorails can do 50 to 55 mph, their top speed with guests aboard is about 40 mph.

64. a.) Cage
Cage opened April 7, 1990, replacing Videopolis East, an under-21 "new wave" and "alternative" club that was one of Pleasure Island's original nightspots. Cage featured music videos (which were shown on 170 monitors). It closed and was replaced by the 70s/80s-themed club, 8TRAX, in December 1993.

65. d.) Richard F. Irvine
To celebrate WDW's 30th anniversary, the three ferryboats that cross the Seven Seas Lagoon were renamed after individuals important in the creation of Walt Disney World: Richard F. Irvine, Admiral Joe Fowler, and General Joe Potter. The Magic Kingdom I (with green panels) was renamed the Admiral Joe Fowler.

The Magic Kingdom II (red panels) was renamed the Richard F. Irvine. The Kingdom Queen (blue panels) was renamed the General Joe Potter. Unlike the other two ferries, the General Joe Potter, which used to be chartered for weddings and corporate events, has two smoke stacks and offers seating only on the lower deck. When it was refurbished to be used in regular ferry service (you can no longer charter it), its two wet bars were removed. The Potter is also lighter than the other two boats, 180 tons empty versus 190 tons.

66. b.) East Wind
The "East Wind" was a Chinese junk available for charter from the shores of Disney's Polynesian Resort. The boat featured a galley and wet bar, and the charter included a captain, chef, server, bartender, and cocktail waitress. After being retired from service, it was sold to Joe Namath, former quarterback for the New York Jets.

67. a.) Robert A. M. Stern
New York architect Robert A. M. Stern, who also served on The Walt Disney Company Board of Directors from 1992 to 2003, has designed many buildings for The Walt Disney Company. Stern's BoardWalk at WDW suggests an American seaside village from the early 20th century. There is an ice cream parlor, a piano bar, a 1930s' dance hall, a vintage

scale-model roller coaster, and an authentic 1920s' miniature carousel. The Yacht Club, just across the lake from the BoardWalk, is modeled after America's turn of the (20th) century Atlantic coast resorts, while the Beach Club reflects 19th century American resort architecture. Stern was one of the master planners for Celebration, Disney's permanent community near WDW. He also designed the Casting Center, an employee training area on Route I-4 near Orlando. Since 1998, Stern has served as dean for the Yale School of Architecture.

68. c.) 50,000 square feet

Are you looking for the ultimate Disney store? Say 50,000 square feet filled with everything from toys to jewelry, art, magnets, and more? No problem. You'll find the **World Of Disney** in the heart of Downtown Disney. Each of the 12 rooms in this — the world's largest — Disney merchandise shop is themed in true Disney fashion. In these rooms you'll find everything from gourmet cooking items, to clothing, videos, and toys — not to mention hidden Mickeys just waiting for you to find them. Consider it "Disneyana Nirvana" (and bring your credit card!). Oh, and don't worry about carrying all that stuff you bought home on the plane — they'll box it and ship it for you!

69. b.) Disney's Vacation Club Resort

Disney's Vacation Club Resort opened in late December 1991 and was renamed the Old Key West Resort in January 1996. The resort has 761 rooms in 531 homes. It features a waterfront boardwalk and buildings decorated in pastel hues. It was built as the flagship resort of the Disney Vacation Club (DVC) and is still a DVC property.

70. a.) Disney's Fort Wilderness Resort and Campground

In November 1971, just one month after the Magic Kingdom opened, Disney's Fort Wilderness Resort and Campground opened near Disney's Contemporary Resort. Disney's Golf Resort Hotel opened in 1973. The Grand Floridian Beach Resort (later renamed Disney's Grand Floridian Resort & Spa) opened in 1988, while Disney's Animal Kingdom Lodge opened in 2001.

Index

This Index is designed to help you locate all the fun facts in this book. Look for subjects by name (for example, "Audio-Animatronics figures," "Space Mountain," "WDW statistics"). For quicker lookup and shorter entries, we have abbreviated some names. For example, we generally drop the words "Disney's" and "Resort" from resort names and also drop the "The" from attraction names and abbeviate some of the longer ones. For example, "The Hall of Presidents" is indexed as "Hall of Presidents" and "The Twilight Zone Tower of Terror" is indexed as "Tower of Terror." We list information related to Walt Disney World® Resort as a whole under "WDW."

Since WDW is enormous and the trivia questions include former attractions, restaunts, and so on, as well as current ones, we identify subjects with the following abbreviations:

AK – Disney's Animal Kingdom   FW – Fort Wilderness
DD – Downtown Disney   MK – Magic Kingdom
DM – Disney-MGM Studios   P   – Pleasure Island
E   – Epcot   R   – Resort
WP – WDW Water Park

For example, "Fingers (P)" lets you know you'll find Fingers somewhere in Pleasure Island.

Of course, you won't find every Walt Disney World attraction, resort, shop, or eaterie in this Index. As we said in the Introduction, while this book contains hundreds of trivia questions, WDW has thousands of nooks and crannies and it is constantly changing. No one book will ever cover it all. But that's good news for trivia lovers: there'll always be something new to look forward to. Enjoy!